THE ROAD
TO SAFWAN

THE ROAD TO SAFWAN

THE 1ST SQUADRON, 4TH CAVALRY IN THE 1991 PERSIAN GULF WAR

Stephen A. Bourque

John W. Burdan III

University of North Texas Press

Denton, Texas

10 9 8 7 6 5 4 3 2 1

Permissions:
University of North Texas Press
P.O. Box 311336
Denton, TX 76203-1336

The paper used in this book meets the minimum requirements of the
American National Standard for Permanence of Paper for Printed
Library Materials, z39.48.1984. Binding materials have been chosen
for durability.

Library of Congress Cataloging-in-Publication Data

Bourque, Stephen A. (Stephen Alan), 1950–
    The road to Safwan : the 1st Squadron, 4th Cavalry in the 1991
    Persian Gulf War / Stephen A. Bourque, John Burdan.
        p. cm.
    Includes bibliographical references and index.
    ISBN 978-1-57441-232-1 (cloth : alk. paper)
        1. Persian Gulf War, 1991—Regimental histories—United States.
    2. United States. Army. Cavalry, 4th. Squadron, 1st. I. Burdan,
    John, 1955– . II. Title. III. Title: 1st Squadron, 4th Cavalry in the
    1991 Persian Gulf War.
    DS79.724.U6B683 2007
    956.7044'342—dc22

                                                                2007022336

To the men of the 1st Squadron, 4th Cavalry
who served during
Operations DESERT SHIELD and DESERT STORM.

Your service to our nation is not forgotten.

Contents

List of Illustrations

Figures

Maps

List of Photographs

Introduction

n the early morning hours of March 1, 1991, Lieutenant Colonel (LTC) Robert Wilson and his 1st Squadron, 4th Cavalry arrived at a small airstrip outside the Iraqi village of Safwan. A temporary cease-fire following Operation Desert Storm had been in effect for almost twenty-four hours and his division commander, Major General Thomas G. Rhame, had told Wilson to secure the runway forward of the American battle lines, for the upcoming negotiations between Iraqi officials and American General H. Norman Schwarzkopf, the commander of the allied coalition. Unfortunately, a large Iraqi force occupied the directed conference site. Wilson, in his M3 Bradley Cavalry Fighting Vehicle, drove onto the airfield, dismounted, and approached the senior Iraqi officer at the site. He told the colonel that the airfield at Safwan was now under the control of the United States Army and he must move his men and equipment immediately. Obviously disturbed by the American's words and unaware that there even were negotiations scheduled between the two forces, the Iraqi officer left to speak to his commander. As he departed, four Iraqi tanks moved in front of Wilson's vehicle and lowered their gun tubes.[1]

The 1st Squadron, 4th Cavalry's encounter on that small airfield in southern Iraq was one of hundreds of similar dramas that played out that winter during the 1991 Persian Gulf War. To the generation of Americans who came of age during that conflict, it was a whirlwind of television images of sand, airpower, and precision technology. Countless articles, television shows, and documentaries obscured the context and content of Operation Desert Storm by burying it in a haze of smart bombs, Tomahawk missiles, jet aircraft, and long lines of armored vehicles. Hours watching CNN left many with a perception that the war was somehow sterile and technical and had little probability of spilling friendly blood in the process. The allied coalition's military performance in this conflict was hailed at the time as a *crusade*, an amazing demonstration of American armed power, and, in the words of the United States Army's book published soon after the war, a *Certain Victory*.[2] Returning American troops, in contrast to the Vietnam-era soldiers, were treated as heroes and honored in parades across the United States.

However, by 2006, that image of American omnipotence was beginning to recede in the minds of most thoughtful citizens. Post-Desert Storm uprisings in the Shi'a south and Kurdish north, as well as a botched intervention in Somalia in 1993, tarnished the United States military image in the region. Political victory in Iraq eluded the presidential administrations of George H. W. Bush and William J. Clinton as Saddam Hussein continued to challenge the United States in spite of selective bombing, military deployments, and economic sanctions. Finally, after the attack on New York's World Trade Center in September 2001, President George W. Bush connected the Iraqi dictator to his declared "War on Terror" and decided to end Hussein's defiance. American and British soldiers again attacked Iraq in March 2003, and in only a few short weeks defeated the incompetent Iraqi Army, a shadow of the force that had existed in 1990. However, political victory remained elusive as conventional military success degenerated into an insurgency and appeared, by 2006, to be degenerating into a civil war. By that fall, with casualty numbers rising, Americans appeared to have lost their stomach for military adventure in Iraq.

In some ways, those who marched off to war against Iraq in 1991, in the shadow of the Vietnam era, had a better appreciation of the problems they would face once the battle was joined. Unlike the confidence of the generals and politicians of 2003, the outcome of the impending war against Iraq in 1991 was anything but certain. Commissioned and noncommissioned officers, many veterans of the war in Indochina, knew not to take this enemy lightly. Their studies at the army's extensive service school system had sensitized them to the penalty of underestimating the enemy. Battles such as Kasserine Pass, Task Force Smith, and the Tet offensive were case studies of American setbacks that tempered their pride in their equipment and fellow soldiers. Vietnam veterans, now commanding brigades, divisions, and corps, knew that no amount of technological superiority could prevent defeat if they were arrogant and unprepared for the competence and determination of their opponents.

Forgotten in the years following Operation Desert Storm was the fact that the Iraqi Army in 1991 was a force to be respected. An eight-year struggle with Iran supported at various levels by American and allied military advisors had resulted, at least on paper, in a veteran army. Final large-scale operations on the al-Faw peninsula and other parts of the border displayed a degree of teamwork and sophistication that indicated the Iraqi military was a competent force. Its liberal use of missiles and chemical weapons against the Iranians and their own Kurdish citizens hinted at a willingness to fight at a level of violence unfamiliar to most western soldiers. If nothing else, its size gave leaders of the professional U.S. Army serious concerns.

The goal of this book, therefore, is to return to that era and recapture the fear, concern, and competence of the soldiers of one small U.S. combat unit, the approximately 800 troopers of the full-strength 1st Squadron, 4th Cavalry; the cavalry squadron for the famous Big Red One. This book seeks to remind readers what the 1991 Gulf War was like for those who participated at the squadron and battalion levels. As in the case of other units, this cavalry squadron experienced four distinct phases during this conflict: preparation, security, battle, and postwar operations. While each phase was unique, together they refute the image that this campaign was simply a matter of technological superiority. The framework for this unit's success began with sound political and military objectives, facilitated by the United States Army's excellent equipment, by competent and confident soldiers, and by its commanders who were proficient in the art of war. Also, there can be no question that the comparative tactical incompetence of the Iraqi Army contributed to this squadron's success. Finally, at least in the case of the 1st Squadron, 4th Cavalry, they succeeded also because they were fortunate.

This manuscript began as a labor of love by the squadron's operations officer, or S3, John Burdan. Before his retirement in 1997, he began to collect squadron documents and conduct interviews with former members who found themselves stationed in the vicinity of Fort Leavenworth, Kansas. While working on this manuscript, he discovered that an old friend and former assistant operations officer in division headquarters, Stephen Bourque, was completing a manuscript about the United States VII Corps during the war.[3] Reflecting a joint effort, this book gives a perspective of war from the battalion level within the context of the entire conflict.

Of course, we could never have written this book without the help of a wide variety of people who went out of their way to give us support. At California State University (CSU), Northridge, Dr. Charles Macune, Dr. Tom Maddux, and Susan Mueller provided a wonderful working environment. In addition to running the office, Kelly Winkleblack transformed the interview tapes into manageable typed transcripts. CSU graduate student Jennifer Jones read and edited an early version of this manuscript.

This nation is fortunate to have so many dedicated and competent historians working for the government, many of whom contributed to our efforts over the years. At the top of this list must be Timothy Nenninger at the National Archives in College Park, Maryland, who continues to be the first source for advice for any American military historian and who assisted us in a variety of ways. At the United States Army Center of Military History, Jeff Clarke and Brigadier General John Brown, together with their staff provided a wide range of help with references and documents. Sherry Doudy did the original work on many of the maps and is perhaps the finest cartographer in the business today. Bill Epley was instrumental in locating important documents, which made our work much more accurate. Frank Shirer was extremely gracious in supporting our work in the center's superb library. David Keough at the Military History Institute in Carlisle, Pennsylvania, consistently provided solid research support and advice. Donald Hakenson and his staff at the Center for Research of Unit Records in Springfield, Virginia, helped to locate many of the squadron's journal logs, the ultimate in primary sources. Terry Van Meter and Shannon Schwaller of the U.S. Cavalry Museum at Fort Riley, Kansas, served in locating documents and provided a wealth of information on squadron and divisional history. Dale Steinhauer at the Combined Arms Center history office at Fort Leavenworth, Kansas, commented on the entire manuscript and provided important assistance with the VII Corps Archives. Operation Desert Storm veteran and award-winning author Peter Kindsvatter from the U.S. Army Ordnance Center gave an early copy of this manuscript a thorough review, thereby saving the authors from unnecessary mistakes of substance and context. At the Command and General Staff College's Department of Military History, Dr. James Willbanks, a noted soldier, scholar of the Vietnam era, and department chair, provided the inspiration, support, and encouragement to bring this manuscript to conclusion. Bourque's colleagues in the department were a constant source of sound advice and contributed immeasurably to this narrative.

Outside of the government, others were essential to our success. John Votaw at the 1st Division Museum in Wheaton, Illinois, provided a generous grant that permitted the transcription of the large number of interviews with squadron members and kept this process alive when it looked like it would run out of steam. At the University of Cincinnati, George Hofmann, one of the armor community's premier historians, reviewed portions of the manuscript and provided many important suggestions. General Donn A. Starry, one of our army's most distinguished retired officers, historians, and an expert on cavalry operations, kindly reviewed our initial draft and provided sound criticism and encouragement. Richard Swain, a noted expert on the 1991 Persian Gulf War and former Third Army historian, reviewed an early draft and provided many insightful comments and criticisms. At the University of North Texas Press, our editor, Ron Chrisman, continued to encourage our efforts in spite of our delays and excuses, and Karen DeVinney helped make sense out of this complicated story. Without Ron's support, this manuscript would never have seen the light of day.

Of course, without the active participation of many former members of the squadron and the 1st Infantry Division, this book would never have been written. Those who graciously consented to interviews are listed in the bibliography. Active support during the writing process came from Mike Bills, Doug Morrison, Ken Pope, VJ Tedesco, Bob Wilson, and Bill Wimbish. Without their critiques and comments, it would not have been possible to make sense out of all that transpired that winter.

Finally, our sincere thanks go to our wives, Bridget Burdan and Debra Anderson. In addition to surrendering many happy hours of quality time as their husbands headed off to their offices, they read and commented on this manuscript. Their love and support are a big part of our lives.

Of course, history is not simply a collection of facts but an interpretation of events. Based on the evidence accumulated to date, this is ours. For every event described in detail, dozens are ignored. For every person the reader meets in this story, ten or twenty are not introduced. We apologize in advance to those brave members of the squadron not identified in the text. However, this is your story, and we hope it reflects your experience during that event so recent, yet so long ago.

1   The Quarter Horse to 1990

The military organization that arrived on the Iraqi airfield that winter day was the heir to over 135 years of American military tradition. Battle streamers on the squadron's colors attested to participation in wars around the world. While the nature of these conflicts ranged from insurgency operations against lightly armed foes to combat against sophisticated armored units, the single unifying theme throughout its history was that the squadron fought as a mounted force.

While military purists might argue that this mounted heritage may somehow be traced to knights on medieval European battlefields, American cavalry units developed in response to a specific need: the rapid movement of troops to protect settlers as they migrated to the West. Their Native American foe, whether in the swamps of Florida, the mid-continent plains or the desert Southwest, moved with a speed and cunning that regular infantry simply could not match. Far different from the European hussars and lancers, it was dragoon-style cavalry that policed the West and fought in the American Civil War.[1] By 1942 at the beginning of World War II, the American cavalry had turned in its horses for a variety of light armored cars and jeeps. Its primary role was now reconnaissance, or finding the enemy, and providing security or early warning to the main body. Because cavalry commanders were prone to act independently, senior officers often gave them a third type of mission: economy of force. Reinforced with the means of heavy combat such as tanks and artillery, cavalry commanders fought mobile battles to the front, flanks, or rear of the main force. During the Vietnam era, cavalrymen accepted an additional mode of mobility, the helicopter, which extended the mounted troops' range and effectiveness. However, while the means had changed, the end remained the same: act as the eyes, ears, and reaction force for the division or corps commander. As leaders of the post-Vietnam era were fond of saying: "Cavalry is about mobility, not about equipment. It is a state of mind."[2]

The 1st Squadron, 4th Cavalry, nicknamed "Quarter Horse," like other military units still on the army's rolls, has a long and notable history and traces its lineage back to Company A, 1st Cavalry formed in March 1855 on Governor's Island, New York. It campaigned against the Comanche and Cheyenne Indians in the late 1850s and attempted to maintain order in "bleeding Kansas" as slavery and anti-slavery proponents clashed over the territory's statehood.[3] Early in the Civil War, the War Department reorganized the army's mounted regiments. Since the 1st Cavalry was the fourth oldest of these units, it was designated the 4th Cavalry. As of July 1862, the regiment had twelve companies and a little over 1,100 assigned soldiers.[4]

During the Civil War, the 4th Cavalry fought primarily in the western theater. Its campaigns include Stones River, Tullahoma, Chickamauga, and Atlanta Campaigns against Confederate cavalry led by Generals Nathan Bedford Forrest, John Hunt Morgan, and Joseph Wheeler. It ended the war pursuing John B. Hood's decimated army after the decisive Battle of Franklin. Its last engagement was against Forrest's mounted forces on December 18, 1864, when the 4th Cavalry overran an artillery battery on the West Harpath River, in central Tennessee.[5] Following the Civil War, Washington ordered the regiment to Texas, where it reestablished national authority from San Antonio to the Rio Grande. Under Colonel Ranald Slidell Mackenzie, easily the most dashing commander in the regiment's history, it fought Kickapoo and Comanche Indians in central Texas and across the border in Mexico.[6]

More organizational changes took place in 1883 as the War Department redesignated all cavalry companies as "troops" and all mounted battalions as "squadrons." These units carried the now familiar red and white guidon into battle.[7] With the outbreak of the Spanish American War, the War Department sent the 4th Cavalry to the Philippines, where it arrived too late to fight the Spanish, but found itself involved in the Philippine Insurrection for the next several years. It did not participate in World War I.[8]

When war broke out in Europe in 1939, the 4th Cavalry was still riding horses and practicing charges with sabers, .45 caliber pistols, and 1903 Springfield Rifles. After several reorganizations in response to the changing nature of war in Europe, the future 1-4 Cavalry became the 4th Cavalry Reconnaissance Squadron (Mechanized), of the 4th Cavalry Group (Mechanized). It was now a vehicle-mounted reconnaissance unit that employed fire and maneuver as well as infiltration tactics to gather the information senior commanders needed. Combat was supposed to be performed only when the unit was required to defend itself.[9]

A small detachment of the 4th Cavalry actually stormed ashore in Europe before the amphibious assault on Normandy. At 0430, two hours before the main landings on June 6, 1944, 132 troopers invaded two small parcels of land four miles offshore from Utah Beach, called the St. Marcouf Islands. Within sight of Utah Beach, they were potential outposts supporting the German defenses on the mainland. Other 4th Cavalry units arrived on Utah Beach on D-Day and linked up with the 82d Airborne Division, which had parachuted into France the night before the invasion.[10] Assigned to Major General (MG) J. Lawton Collins's VII Corps, the 4th Cavalry Group fought across Europe. Collins reinforced the 4th Cavalry Group with a battalion each of light tanks, motorized artillery, tank destroyers, infantry, and engineers. By the middle of December, the cavalry was screening the VII Corps's eastern flank as it headed towards the rail junction at Düren, on the edge of Germany's Roer River.[11] When the Germans counterattacked in the Ardennes, the 4th Cavalry helped to hold the Bulge's northern shoulder.[12] With the defeat of the Nazi offensive in January 1945, the Allies resumed their advance into Germany and the 4th Cavalry Group's last World War II battle took place in the

Harz Mountains northwest of Leipzig on April 11.[13]

In 1952, following a short constabulary tour in Austria and Germany, the army inactivated the group except for a small headquarters company. It returned to active service again in February 1957 as 1st Reconnaissance Squadron, 4th United States Cavalry assigned to the 1st Infantry Division at Fort Riley, Kansas. After several years of routine training activity, it found itself preparing for war in Indochina. The squadron deployed with the Big Red One in October 1965. Its three ground troops (A, B, C) used M113 armored personnel carriers and M48A3 tanks, while its air troop (D) used a mixture of command and control and helicopter gun ships. It was the army's first armored unit to arrive in Vietnam.[14]

From October 1965 to April 1970, the squadron, usually assigned by troops to the three individual brigades of the division, operated in the III Corps area north of Saigon. As in the case of World War II, the complete story of the squadron's Vietnam experience is beyond the scope of this book. However, there is no question that a soldier's assignment to this unit ensured he would be in the thick of battle for most of his tour. In February 1970, the squadron performed its last mission, screening the redeployment of the division from Vietnam, and its colors returned to Fort Riley on April 5.[15]

Like other units, the squadron recovered from the Vietnam conflict and adapted itself to the realities of warfare in the last quarter of the century. The lethality of the 1973 Arab-Israeli War motivated American officers to overhaul the army's approach to education, equipment, and training. The unit's activities, often called operational tempo, increased as the squadron routinely deployed to Europe (for REFORGER or Return of Forces to Europe exercises) and to California's Mohave Desert for exercises at the National Training Center.

One of the problems of the Vietnam-era army was the rapid turnover of unit leaders. In the postwar years the army stabilized these assignments and by the early 1980s battalion and squadron commanders could expect to remain with their units for a two-year assignment. In the spring of 1990 Lieutenant Colonel (LTC) Richard A. Cowell was finishing his term as commander. With experience in ground and aviation units, he had been an ideal choice to lead the unit. Building on his years of troop duty, including command of the squadron's D Troop and a tour in Vietnam, Cowell had led the squadron on training exercises from Germany to the National Training Center. Like many leaders, he preferred field training and disliked the administrative work that came with command. He enjoyed history and sought to encourage his officers and men to educate themselves in order to gain a historical perspective. As a part of that effort in 1990, Cowell had created a place of remembrance, a grove of trees planted outside the squadron headquarters, to honor those regimental troopers who had won the Congressional Medal of Honor. Presidents had awarded this most prestigious award to twenty-six 4th Cavalry members, two twice. The dedication ceremony, a moving event for all involved, included the families of two soldiers, Sergeant Donald R. Long (Troop C, 1-4 Cavalry) and Lieutenant Russell A. Stedman (Troop B, 3-4 Cavalry), who had been awarded the medal posthumously for their heroism during the Vietnam conflict.

Cowell's most challenging and thankless duty was supervising the change in the squadron's organization in 1989. In spite of warnings from World War II and Vietnam-era cavalrymen, the army pulled all the tanks from divisional cavalry squadrons to use in other combat organizations. This new divisional cavalry organization was no longer assigned directly to the division commander but to a new organization: the Aviation (sometimes referred to as the 4th) Brigade. To make matters worse for Cowell, one of his two ground troops was now permanently stationed in Germany as part of the 1st Infantry Division's forward deployed brigade. This arrangement left him with only the Headquarters Troop, one small ground troop (B Troop), and two small air cavalry troops (C and D Troops). Because of its lack of firepower, standard division practice was to attach a tank company from the 2nd Brigade for all training exercises and contingency plans. Nevertheless, commanding the squadron represented the fulfillment of his hopes and dreams, which had begun on his commissioning day so long ago.[16]

On June 22, 1990, the moment Cowell had always dreaded finally arrived: it was time to surrender his command to a new leader. Standing in front of squadron headquarters for the last

time, he looked out at his almost four hundred officers and
men. He knew he was leaving the unit in good shape with a
first-class group of commanders and noncommissioned officers. Posted in front of Headquarters and Headquarters Troop
(HHT) was Captain (CPT) Douglas Morrison. Morrison, a graduate of West Point, was one of his most experienced officers,
having served as a tank company commander in 2-34 Armor
and as his operations officer (S3) since 1988. He had recently assumed command of HHT from Major John Burdan, who in turn
took his place on the staff as S3. An intense professional, Morrison was the right man to lead that complex collection of maintenance and support soldiers.[17]

Formed up on HHT's left was B Troop. When Cowell had
first arrived in the cavalry as a young lieutenant, the cavalry
troop was a powerful organization with nine tanks, fifteen
scout vehicles, three 106-mm mortar carriers, and three infantry
squads. The new troop was an untested organization with only
nineteen M3 Bradley Cavalry Fighting Vehicles and three mortar carriers. The commander, Captain (CPT) Michael Bills, was
another seasoned officer with a depth of experience. Beginning
his career as a helicopter mechanic in 1976, he returned to college in 1979 and graduated from George Mason University in
1984 with a degree in sociology and a commission from ROTC.
He had served as the squadron personnel officer for almost two
years and since May commanded B Troop.[18]

Cowell glanced next at the air cavalry troops. The old organization he had commanded was one powerful unit of helicopters with over 170 soldiers and twenty-five aircraft organized into scout, aero-weapons, and aero-rifle platoons. The one
large unit was now reorganized into two identical troops, C and
D, led by Captains James Tovsen and Roy Peters respectively.
Each commander led only thirty-five troopers flying six OH-
58C Kiowa scout helicopters and four old AH-1F Cobra attack
helicopters. Both units were fresh from a rotation at the National Training Center, learning how to fight and fly in a desert
environment.

Once the troops were in position, his staff moved to the
front of the organization. Major (MAJ) William Wimbish, an
aviation officer and a graduate of Columbus College and the

Command and General Staff College class of 1989, ran his head-quarters as the executive officer (XO). The XO has the thankless job of paying attention to the details of making the unit function. With over a year in the job, Wimbish was one of the most experienced executive officers in the 1st Infantry Division. Major John Burdan was the new operations officer or S3. A graduate of West Point, his year as commander of HHT had given him an intimate knowledge of the workings of the squadron headquarters. Captain Shelby Seelinger, the intelligence officer (S2), Captain Kenneth Stokes, the personnel officer (S1), and Captain Steven Harmon the logistics officer (S4), were the other principle staff officers. Unusual in an armored unit, Harmon was an engineer officer who had worked with the squadron on previous exercises. In an era of personnel turbulence, when it was unusual for officers to remain in the same battalion for more than a year, Cowell's greatest achievement may have been keeping so many of his strong leaders together for so long. Now it was time for him to pass the squadron colors to the new commander, Lieutenant Colonel (LTC) Robert Wilson.

Commissioned in 1972, the incoming commander had gone to Vietnam right after flight school. Injured in a helicopter crash shortly after his arrival, he was evacuated first to Japan, then to Walter Reed Army Hospital in Washington, DC. After his recovery, he served in a series of command and staff assignments in Europe, Hawaii, and the United States. Like Cowell, Wilson suspected that his selection for squadron command represented the high point of his military career, an achievement that most officers only dreamed of. He realized that with the Soviet Union in retreat and the American military on the edge of force reductions, this was probably one of the best commands available. He also knew that he had inherited a seasoned unit with a proud history.

For the last time, Cowell took the squadron's colors from his Command Sergeant Major (CSM) John Soucy. Thanking his senior noncommissioned officer for all he had done, he passed the colors to the division commander. Major General (MG) Thomas G. Rhame was a no-nonsense infantryman from Louisiana with a southern drawl and love of colorful phrases that hid a deep intellect. His ability to grasp the essence of a

problem and an intolerance of unprofessional behavior was
greatly respected by his officers. A natural leader, he appreciated what Cowell had accomplished over the previous two
years. Taking the colors, he handed them to Wilson and
charged him to maintain the squadron's readiness and tradition
of excellence.

2   Preparation

s LTC Robert Wilson stood on the parade ground that June day, he anticipated that most of his training focus would remain consistent with the unit's traditional doctrine and war plans. This meant deploying to Germany, taking possession of the trucks and tracked vehicles stored in large warehouses near Kaiserslautern, road-marching to an assembly area, and joining the other American units in defeating an attack by the Warsaw Pact. For over twenty-five years this reinforcement mission had been the Big Red One's first priority and there was no reason for Wilson to expect any fundamental changes in his task as a unit commander until the American government removed troops from Europe. Several weeks after assuming command, he joined other division staff officers and commanders on a trip to Germany to inspect the equipment they would acquire if they ever had to execute such a mission. Of course, such a prospect was becoming more remote as the Iron Curtain was coming down and Germany was beginning the long road to reunification.

While walking through the warehouses near Kaiserslautern during the first week of August, he learned that Iraqi troops had crossed the border into Kuwait. Within days of the Iraqi invasion, American forces were on their way to the Persian Gulf. The first unit to go was the U.S. Army's strategic ground force, the XVIII Airborne Corps, drawing "a line in the sand" to let the Iraqi government know that if it intended to continue into Saudi Arabia it would have a serious fight on its hands.[1]

Upon Wilson's return from Germany, the division gave him a new training focus. MG Rhame, anticipating the orders to go to Southwest Asia and join the forces there in what the govern-

15

ment was now calling Operation Desert Shield, directed his staff and commanders to assume a potential deployment. While the essential deployment aspects of Wilson's tasks would not change, the Iraqi invasion now modified many of their details and gave him and his officers a renewed sense of purpose. Many cavalry troopers envisioned themselves flying to Saudi Arabia to reinforce the units from the XVIII Corps. Since Rhame had no solid instructions, he and other officers were simply prudent in anticipating a combat role for the command.

Squadron leaders now began paying attention to administrative details that they often glossed over. For starters, they took steps to improve combat vehicle and helicopter crew stability, leaving soldiers in their positions longer so they could improve their proficiency. Troopers[2] inventoried unit equipment and ensured that their hand receipts, indicating property they had responsibility for, were up to date. They updated their load plans, documents that acted as a packing guide for each piece of equipment to prepare vehicles and soldiers for overseas deployment. In addition, leaders began making tough decisions regarding their soldiers and began removing those whom they could not count on from positions of responsibility and even from the army.[3]

The pre-deployment training in which the 1-4 Cavalry participated was based on a rather routine cycle of activities common in the 1980s. The parent unit, in the cavalry's case the division's 4th (Aviation) Brigade, planned and evaluated these exercises. These included soldier training, crew and platoon weapons firing events, maneuver exercises from squad through platoon level, and staff training sessions. The squadron also participated in externally sponsored or evaluated events, such as rotations to the National Training Center and a demanding series of simulated combat experiences, to include a rotation with the Fort Leavenworth-controlled Battle Command Training Program, which trained the squadron, brigade, and division staffs. The squadron had several of these events scheduled before the Iraqi invasion, and the prospect of deployment to a war zone heightened the soldiers' sense of purpose.

In August, as units from the XVIII Corps continued deploying from bases across the United States to Southwest Asia, the

Quarter Horse headed for Fort Riley's range complexes. Building on the army's published standards, Wilson organized his gunnery training into three distinct elements. First, the ground scout crews fired their weapons systems in a series of progressive events called gunnery *tables*. The M3 Cavalry Fighting Vehicle, nicknamed the Bradley, was a modification of the M2 Infantry Fighting Vehicle designed in the 1970s. Equipped with a 25-mm Bushmaster chain gun, a 7.63-mm machine gun, and a TOW antitank missile launcher, it was a potent weapon system.

Not simply shooting exercises, these events sought to develop proficiency in crew duties such as acquiring and engaging targets, using all of a vehicle's weapons and fire control systems, and selecting the correct ammunition for the target. These firing tables progressed from relatively simple exercises, such as engaging one stationary target with one weapon, to complex qualification events using all the weapons systems of the combat vehicle and requiring its crew to function as a seamless whole. Qualification tables usually required the crew to destroy multiple stationary and moving targets while on the move. Ranges ran day and night, using all weapons in both offensive and defensive scenarios. These were demanding tests and failure to qualify during a gunnery period was a serious situation that resulted, as a minimum, in the crew receiving additional training and another opportunity to pass. It could also have consequences for promotion and advancement for the vehicle commander and even the platoon or troop commander.

While the ground troops fought their battles on the range complex, the helicopter crews participated in the second element of Wilson's training program: aviation gunnery. Each aviation table required at least two aircraft, an OH-58C Kiowa scout helicopter and one or more AH-1 Cobra Attack helicopters organized into a scout weapons team, or SWT. The aeroscout coordinated with ground troops in the area, located the enemy force, and alerted the attack helicopters to their presence. They then guided the attack aircraft to a firing location and helped it identify and acquire the enemy force. Armed with up to eight TOW antitank missiles, a 20-mm cannon, and "pods" that contained as many as seventy-six 2.75-inch rockets, the AH-1 after twenty-five years of service was still a potent weapons system. Once the Cobra crew was ready, the aeroscout ordered it to execute its attack, while simultaneously it began searching for more targets and evaluated the effect of the Cobra's weapons on the enemy.

Since there were no air gunnery tables that fit the squadron's requirements, Colonel (COL) James Mowery, the 4th Brigade commander, gave Wilson permission to modify existing scenarios to suit his own needs. Chief Warrant Officer 3 (CW3) Craig Winters, the squadron's standardization officer, and First Lieutenant (1LT) John Manning, the flight operations officer, were chiefly responsible for developing the innovative program that paid dividends.[4]

As the aviation crews worked on their target acquisition and battle hand-off techniques, they had to fight another battle with equipment maintenance problems. Two specific issues plagued the aviators: keeping the 20-mm guns functioning properly and keeping the Cobras flying. The guns seemed to jam because of problems with the mechanism that fed the shells into the breech. The aircraft had many maintenance problems, the result of old aircraft flying too many hours and not enough replacement parts. At one point, these maintenance problems so affected the Cobras that the attack crews were forced to train with only one serviceable aircraft. However, the squadron persevered, added a few more days to the gunnery-training program in September, and improved on the teamwork between scout and attack helicopter crews. In addition, they began working with the ground troops on coordinating their actions, especially in the hand-off of targets between air and ground weapons systems. In terms of vision and speed, the view of the battlefield is fundamentally different from the ground and the air. Substantial training and practice are needed to overcome the inherent perception difficulties in order to ensure the smooth hand-off of responsibility for a target from the air to ground, or ground to the air. Proficiency gained in all of these complex tasks led to effective scout weapons teams in the Arabian Desert.[5]

The final element of the gunnery period was the platoon battle run. Wilson wanted to integrate his aviators into this event, because that is how they would operate once in the field. Since the army's manuals did not address a combined ground cavalry platoon and scout-weapons team live-fire exercise, the squadron developed its own. Under the scenario developed by MAJ Burdan and his staff, each of B Troop's three platoons moved down a live-fire course under CPT Mike Bills's control. In addition to the six M3 Cavalry Fighting Vehicles ("Bradleys"), for the first time a scout-weapons team participated in the event. The battle run was the first opportunity Bills had both to command his ground troop and to work with the squadron's aviators.[6]

The summer gunnery period was also Wilson's first opportunity to command the squadron in the field and the threat of war gave him a singleness of purpose. During the final qualification period, he moved the entire command from garrison at Fort Riley to the main gunnery complex and kept them there for almost three weeks. The squadron staff had its first opportunity to sort out its logistics and command and control structure. While not training, they all lived in the same barracks complex, allowing them to mingle and get to know each other, something not usually done between ground troops and aviators. These common experiences helped to mold Wilson's command into a cohesive unit.

Gunnery set the stage for a larger field training exercise, called Gauntlet, directed by the 1st Infantry Division headquarters. While the battle runs trained platoons and troops, Gauntlet challenged the squadron commander to put it all together. Wilson had the opportunity not only to maneuver his squadron, but also do so against a live, thinking enemy in battle. Taking place in October 1990, the exercise's primary purpose was to help COL Lon E. (Burt) Maggart's 1st Brigade Combat Team prepare for its November deployment to the National Training Center in Fort Irwin, California. The division's staff controlled, evaluated, and managed the exercise, while the squadron provided the opposing force, usually called OPFOR. The cavalry's role was to replicate an enemy motorized regiment and challenge the brigade in a series of simulated offensive and defensive battles. Wilson's combat capability more than doubled as the division assigned him two tank companies, a mechanized infantry company, an antitank company and an engineer company to use in the aggressor role. In a more exotic vein, he also had long-range surveillance teams to use behind the brigade's lines and a military intelligence company with electronic jamming and interception capability.

In these mock engagements on Fort Riley's small training area, Wilson had his first chance to practice commanding his squadron in the field. Given a new squadron commander, ground troop commander, operations officer, and the expanded size of the force he commanded, the battles went very well from his perspective. At the end of each engagement, Wilson and his leaders sat through an evaluator-led critique, or after-action review. They considered the comments, adjusted their tactics and command techniques, and prepared for the next round of maneuver. In five out of six iterations, the squadron was successful and more than held its own against Maggart's brigade. Only in the last battle, when the brigade "destroyed" the squadron's scouts, was the cavalry outmaneuvered.

More important than winning mock engagements was the value of the training. It was the first time Wilson's entire squadron had had the opportunity to work together and with other elements of the division. The leaders practiced their logistics and maintenance procedures, operated the squadron's tactical operations center (called the TOC), rehearsed the air troop's flight operations plans, and performed a host of details that a unit simply cannot simulate in garrison. Wilson and Burdan practiced their jobs from the same vehicles they would use in combat, while MAJ Wimbish controlled operations from the TOC. The leaders became more comfortable with one another and worked out the procedures they would need in a few months in Saudi Arabia.

Simultaneously with increasing the pace of training, Wilson had to begin changing the organization of his squadron. These changes included adding another cavalry troop, reorganizing aviation assets into a special unit, incorporating tanks into the two ground troops, and exchanging old equipment for new. As part of a general build-up of forces in Germany in the post-Vietnam era, a brigade of the 1st Infantry Division, called the 1st Infantry Division-Forward, had deployed to Europe in the 1970s. Located in Göppingen in southern Germany, this unit was designed to act as the advance force for the remainder of the division. The army detached the squadron's A Troop from the Fort Riley contingent and sent it along with the brigade. By 1990, however, the collapse of the Iron Curtain and the ending of the Cold War made the forward-deployed brigade superfluous, and the army had begun to withdraw it from Germany and reassigned A Troop to Wilson's command. This reassignment was essentially a paper transaction however, and the squadron had to build the actual unit from scratch.[7]

Wilson tapped CPT Kenneth W. Pope Jr. to take command of his new A Troop, which he did in a short ceremony at the squadron parade field on November 19. A 1985 graduate of Appalachian State University's ROTC program, Pope had been serving as the unit's S3 (Air), the usual staff position for a commander in waiting. With his new troop authorized 128 soldiers, he was initially able to find about forty-five from a variety of sources, including B Troop and the Fort Riley Noncommissioned Officers Academy. Most of his other sergeants came from across the United States, primarily from light cavalry units. Most of these had no experience on the M3 Bradley, a fact that compounded training problems later in the Persian Gulf. His initial mortar squad came as a unit from within the squadron. Therefore, Pope's focus between November and the squadron's move to Saudi Arabia in late December was torn between preparation for unit deployment and the creation of an entirely new organization, melding new soldiers and equipment into a cohesive team.[8] To help CPT Pope train his new command, Wilson contacted the chief of the Armor Cavalry Tactics Division at Fort Knox, the home of armored operations, and arranged for a training team to come to Fort Riley at the end of December.

Another change concerned the organization of the squadron's aviation units. Most senior-level leaders, such as MG Rhame, COL Mowery, and LTC Wilson, had received their initial combat experience in Vietnam. In the old D Troop organization, the aviation commander, a major, controlled both the tactical employment of helicopter platoons and their maintenance. When the army changed the squadron's organization to two ground and two air troops in the 1980s, it placed both the flight operations and aviation maintenance elements in the

headquarters troop, and the aircrews into the air troops commanded by captains. Neither the ground nor the air commanders were satisfied with this organization. Therefore, in mid-Sep-
tember, Wilson and Mowery adjusted what was, in their minds,
an inefficient structure. As a minimum, there appeared to be a
lack of cooperation between ground and air leaders. Certainly,
the aviation maintenance problems were an indication that the
brigade needed to make some changes. So, they resurrected a
semblance of the old organization in an attempt both to solve
the problems they were aware of and to centralize the control of
their aviation systems. They gave CPT Peter G. Smith command of E Troop (Provisional) and appointed Master Sergeant
(MSG) Robert H. Gdula his first sergeant. They then transferred
to them all aviation-specific maintenance soldiers and equipment. Of course, since the army had not approved this change,
this adjustment created a completely new array of administrative problems as senior supply and personnel officers failed to
recognize the new unit as legitimate.[9] Finally, Wilson made CPT
Christopher Philbrick the new squadron flight operations officer, responsible for the coordination and execution of all the air
troop missions. Based upon those responsibilities, Philbrick became known as the "commander of air troops."

In addition to training and reorganizing the squadron, Wilson and his leaders had to supervise the integration of a wide
array of new and improved equipment. One of the lessons cavalrymen learned during World War II was that they could not
always rely on simple reconnaissance and observation to discover information about the enemy. They often had to fight to
gather the kind of information needed by senior commanders.
In most instances, light vehicles were not sufficient and senior
leaders had augmented the cavalry with tanks. Postwar cavalry
leaders took these lessons to heart and assigned light or
medium tanks to the cavalry. Time dulls such memories and by
1990, the army had pulled all of the tanks away from the divisional cavalry in a decision most armor officers deplored. Removing tanks from the cavalry squadron was not doctrinally
based, but in response to the limited number of soldiers available to man the new Division 86 force structure. While it seemed
logical at the Pentagon, armor officers constantly sought ways

to reintroduce this firepower back into the squadrons.[10]

Finally on November 8, after four months of rumors and anticipation, Secretary of Defense Richard Cheney ordered the 1st Infantry Division to deploy as part of the European-based VII Corps. Most of the division would be on the way right after Christmas. During this period, from early August until late December, LTC Wilson trained, reorganized, and re-equipped his command for its new missions. Rather than an assembly area southwest of Frankfurt, Germany, the cavalry was heading to the Persian Gulf.[11]

On November 22, LTC Terry Bullington, the 1st Infantry Division G3 or operations officer, gave Wilson an opportunity he could not refuse. The Department of the Army notified him that the Big Red One was going to turn in most of its old M1 tanks and pick up new M1A1s, in Saudi Arabia. In the process, Bullington discovered that he would acquire nine more of these modern systems than he had planned. He offered them to the Quarter Horse if Wilson could produce a sound doctrinal basis for organization and employment. While eager to increase his firepower, Wilson understood that accompanying his new Abrams tanks would be a long list of other requirements and headaches.[12] Fortunately, he knew that the Armor School at Fort Knox, Kentucky, was working on a new organization (called a Modified Table of Organization and Equipment or MTOE) that put nine tanks in each ground troop. Since his previous assignment was as chief of cavalry at Fort Knox, he had his old organization send Bullington the organizational details and the G3 now had the information he needed to complete the transaction in Saudi Arabia. While this test organization called for twice as many tanks as the squadron was getting, it provided planners the guidelines they needed to requisition soldiers and supporting equipment. With this document in hand, squadron leaders and Fort Riley's force modernization staff began working out the details of this unanticipated gift. Wilson assigned six tanks to CPT Bills and his experienced B Troop, and three to CPT Pope's new A Troop.

In addition to picking up the tanks in Saudi Arabia, the squadron faced four important problems. First, it required soldiers to operate and maintain the tanks. Second, it needed equipment to maintain them including additional toolboxes, special tools, and test equipment. Third, it required army authorization to requisition repair parts to keep the vehicles running. Finally, the squadron now needed additional equipment for the soldiers who crewed and maintained the tanks. This included machine guns, radios, crew helmets, binoculars, tents, cots, and so forth. From a paperwork perspective, the Department of the Army ignored many of their bureaucratic procedures, and based on the draft organizational document from the Armor School, gave the squadron authority to order the equipment needed. All of the crews and equipment would have to arrive from a variety of locations and develop into a semblance of a fighting team before the squadron, and especially the still-organizing A Troop, could go to battle. Wilson and Rhame agreed that under no circumstances would Pope's command fight if Wilson did not believe it was combat-ready.

The M1A1 main battle tank was a complex item of equipment that required two separate groups of soldiers. Most pressing was the need for nine trained tank crews. The squadron received several experienced sergeants from Europe and a group of young soldiers direct from tank-crew training at Fort Knox. Initially, all of these replacements went to CPT Morrison's Headquarters Troop. He provided them initial training and individual equipment. For crew training, he sent them to a post training facility called the Unit Conduct of Fire Trainer. [13]

The squadron also needed trained mechanics to maintain the tank's sophisticated gunnery and automotive components. These positions required a high degree of formal and informal training at both individual and section levels. With only a month to go until deployment, these troopers had to be located, moved to Fort Riley if not already there, and organized into a cohesive tank maintenance section. Fortunately, other tank battalions on post could spare the few mechanics that the squadron needed. Of course, they arrived in the cavalry without equipment, which had to be requisitioned or obtained by cross-leveling within the division.

One major complication was that the tanks the division was to receive were not at Fort Riley but in the process of being transferred from the warehouses in Germany to Saudi Arabia.

The M1A1, with its 120-mm main gun, was not even on post, as the division's tank battalions all used the older M1 with a 105-mm gun. Support from the Armor School continued as Fort Knox sent a new equipment training team with a company (fourteen) of M1A1s to Fort Riley. Before the squadron deployed, most of the tank crews were familiar with the operation of the new equipment they would take into battle.[14]

In addition to tanks, the squadron incorporated other new equipment into its inventory. For example, one morning CPT Morrison, the headquarters troop commander, walked into Wilson's office and showed him an advertisement for the Magellan Global Positioning System or GPS. Essentially, this small box allowed a unit to travel cross-country, using satellite information, without needing a compass, truly an advanced concept for ground soldiers at the time. Such devices were not yet on any of the standard army authorization documents, but both leaders knew about the technology and understood its promise. They prepared a request and sent it on to division headquarters and they received a shipment in time for deployment.[15]

Other new equipment arrived just before departure. The division's leaders exchanged their World War I-era .45 caliber, M1911A2 pistols for the new 9-mm Beretta. This change, in a era of little free time, required the user to attend a class on how to fire and maintain this much lighter weapon. Then the new owners had to go to the firing range to qualify. The unit received and issued wrist compasses, Motorola walkie-talkies, and quiet Honda generators for mobile power in the desert. In addition, M939A2 five-ton trucks, M998 High-Mobility Multipurpose Wheeled Vehicles (HMMWV), affectionately called the "Humvee," and the ten-ton heavy trucks arrived in the squadron to replace older equipment.[16]

One aspect of the division's long-standing mission of going to war in Europe was that the equipment was camouflaged in shades of green, dark brown, and black. The new orders required repainting so that vehicles would blend in with the desert environment. In addition, the paint provided a simple resistance to chemical weapons effects. Within four weeks, division soldiers and Fort Riley's logistics operation had repainted the Big Red One's entire complement of 6,800 vehicles, using

Teflon-based paint, in the desert camouflage color the army required. Of course, aggressive leaders throughout the division wanted their units painted first. Morrison, who was certainly aggressive, rolled his HHT down to one of the paint facilities ahead of schedule in hope of infiltrating ahead of another unit. After a few phone calls between the division project officer and the division staff, Morrison returned to his motor pool to wait his turn. The division commander gave Wilson a call and reminded him of his deployment priorities. The squadron received their new coat of paint in time for deployment.[17]

3   Deployment

O n November 27, retired General William E. DePuy spoke to the 1st Infantry Division's officers. DePuy's career had begun as a lieutenant in the 90th Infantry Division during World War II's Normandy Campaign. He went on to command the 1st Infantry Division in Vietnam, and concluded his career as the first Commanding General of the U.S. Army's Training and Doctrine Command. As one of the primary innovators in the army's reform movement of the 1970s and 1980s, his words were sobering to the officers, few of whom were veterans of other conflicts. Reminding them that in World War II, "my division lost 40 percent of its platoon leaders each week for seven weeks." DePuy asked the division's leaders: "Why fight the battle the way the enemy wants?" He then answered his own question by advising them instead to "fight the battle on our terms." Emphasizing "synchronization is important," he urged them to "try to fight the battle as smart as you can and use all of the tools that are available."[1] It was a fitting send-off and the last time all of the division's officers would reassemble for many months.

Traveling to Saudi Arabia, or deployment as the army called it, was the squadron's next step in its journey that culminated along the Euphrates several months later. This 6,500-mile trip took place in several phases. First, the squadron moved equipment to the port of Beaumont, Texas, for shipment. Then the soldiers departed Fort Riley and flew to Saudi Arabia, where they unloaded their Bradley Fighting Vehicles, trucks, and aircraft from the ships and received the new tanks and other equipment that was waiting for them. Finally, when ready to fight, the troopers each traveled to the desert of northern Saudi Arabia to a region marked on the division's maps as TAA (Tactical Assembly Area) Roosevelt.

After the vehicles were painted at the various facilities at Fort Riley or in Junction City, each unit returned them to its motor pool to prepare them for shipment by sea transport. For each commander, an early priority was loading wartime or "service" ammunition into each tank,[2] Bradley, and mortar carrier. Unlike the routine deployments in the past, this was not a simple administrative move but to a war zone where crews might have to fight soon after their arrival. Next, soldiers ensured that all of the required tools, radios, cables, and repair parts were cleaned, packed up, and correctly stowed with the weapon system. Any items considered hazardous had to be given special packing consideration. Of course, as soon as a crew thought they had packed their vehicle with everything they needed, some other item would show up and they would have to revise the load plan and fit it in somewhere. Crews also painted a standard identification number and an inverted "V" on all vehicles, part of a coalition-wide standard marking system. Once a cavalry troop was ready, it requested certification and a trained unit inspector then checked each vehicle for proper loading, hazardous materials placards, and unauthorized items such as pornography and alcohol that the army strictly prohibited in Saudi Arabia. Once approved, the inspector attached a metal seal, and the equipment was ready for loading onto a rail car.[3]

Soon trains arrived at the rail loading dock at Fort Riley's Camp Funston. While this loading process was complicated and potentially dangerous, there were plenty of experienced troopers to move it along. SFC Allen C. Piper, the newly arrived Headquarters Troop maintenance sergeant, and SSG William A. Ball ran the squadron's railhead operation. Since Piper had just arrived at Fort Riley, Ball found himself directing several rail teams and acting as the principal director of the effort. Each of these teams consisted of a noncommissioned officer and three soldiers whom the division had trained and certified to do the job safely. Their first task was to locate all of the required equipment including vehicle tie-down cables, large wooden blocks, and vehicle shackles; usually there were four of these hook-like appendages on each vehicle. Unfortunately, they were also detachable and, over the course of several years, they often disappeared. Without them the truck or Bradley could not be properly secured on the train. Even though the squadron had ordered extra shackles, Ball, his teams, and vehicle crews spent many hours searching for these precious items of equipment. In addition, there was the normal friction that accompanies these operations, such as unserviceable rail cars and vehicles leaking oil. However, after several long days and sleepless nights, the troopers had secured the squadron's ground equipment on the train and it was on the way to Beaumont, Texas. Leaving on December 5, the train with the squadron's equipment arrived at the port a few days later. There, another group of division soldiers loaded the vehicles on to the ships.[4]

In a way that would cause great concern among its leaders, the squadron's equipment lost its unit integrity in the loading process. Vessel loadmasters brought equipment on board ships based on the space available without considering that the unit might need to organize quickly upon arrival. As a result, rather than a cohesive organization sent to sea and ready to fight on the other end, the Quarter Horse's fighting power was broken down among the eighteen different vessels that carried the Big Red One to the Persian Gulf. Of course, by the time the trains arrived in Beaumont it was fairly obvious that there was no need for the command to be configured as if in an amphibious landing, since Operation Desert Shield had apparently deterred any Iraqi attack. Since carrying capacity and speed of deployment were now more important than combat capability, the loadmasters did the best they could to fit all the odd-sized vehicles into the fewest ships possible. That rationale was lost, however, on the officers watching their units' growing disorganization.[5]

In addition to shipping ground vehicles and equipment, the division had to transport its aircraft and special support equipment. Soon after Thanksgiving, CPT Christopher Philbrick, Warrant Officer (WO) Gary D. Notestine and a team of aviators and aviation mechanics flew to Ellington Field near Houston, Texas, to serve as the squadron's advanced party for the helicopter deployment. On December 4, the division's 4th (Aviation)

Brigade began its journey to Texas, with the squadron's aircraft departing three days later. By December 9, all the aircraft were at Ellington being prepared for ocean shipment. Once all the maintenance issues were resolved on each aircraft, and the blades were taped to prevent wear and tear in the desert, the aircraft were moved to the port. There, with the blades folded, they were wrapped in plastic to protect them from the elements, heated until the plastic shrank close to the metal (shrink-wrap they called it) and loaded on the ships. Philbrick and his team then boarded buses and returned to Fort Riley.[6]

People are not machines and their deployment was more complicated. All of the squadron's troopers, except for a small rear detachment, were going to Saudi Arabia. Only the rear detachment, consisting of eight soldiers who had some kind of medical condition, remained behind. A few, such as the operations sergeant major, SGM Kenneth A. Shields, had already planned to leave the army and had an approved retirement date. The Department of Defense changed these plans as each service issued an order called "stop-loss" that essentially prevented anyone from departing. Wilson's task was to ensure that each trooper's financial and family affairs were in order and that each had the clothing and other personal equipment he needed. Then it would be time to load him on the appropriate airplane. From the time of President Bush and Secretary Cheney's announcement on November 8, until the squadron was in the air, its leaders had to respond to an amazing array of personal problems.[7]

Of course, from the beginning it was important to respond to the concerns of the soldiers' families. Almost as soon as Bush and Cheney were off the air, families started telephoning the squadron. The calls that CPT Morrison received were typical: "What about my son?" one mother demanded to know. "What is going to happen?" Another grandmother called to express concern that her grandson was going to be all right. Even the wife of his First Sergeant (1SGT), Richard L. Colangelo, dropped by the unit in tears. Since nobody knew much, other than that they were heading to the Arabian Peninsula, there was little information that leaders could share, except that their loved one was departing with the unit.[8]

The squadron leaders' wives began a family support group within the framework of the formal chain of command to handle many of the problems that arose since "Dad can't come home." For example, the Headquarters Troop's maintenance platoon had a chain of concern headed by SSG William Ball's wife Crystal. Bridget Burdan did the same for the S3 Section's families. The troop commanders' and first sergeants' wives headed each unit's chain and coordinated with Wilson's wife Lynn. On a larger scale, this group worked with the division's support group headed by Mrs. Lin Rhame, the commanding general's wife, and handled more and more of the personal aspects of the deployment.[9]

Each soldier passed through a series of stations called "preparation for overseas movement" or POM. At one station, sergeants checked and rechecked uniforms and individual field equipment, called TA-50 in army jargon. The list of required items seemed endless; each soldier had four uniforms with all patches and name tags sewn on, two pairs of boots, eight pairs of socks, six pairs of under shorts, two field jackets, his web gear to carry his pack, two canteens, a sleeping bag, shelter half, chemical protective over-garments, protective mask, helmet, and so on and so forth. All of this personal equipment was supposed to fit into two duffel bags and a rucksack. This list did not include the other items wanted or needed by the trooper including extra socks, wool caps, extra gloves, batteries for tape players, radios, and cassette players, and books. These items were either stashed away in the shipping vans and vehicles that were heading for the port, or were mailed by the soldier to his unit address in Saudi Arabia.[10]

Continuing their POM, troopers went to numerous additional stations, manned by staff specialists, and designed to protect the individual's health and welfare. Military lawyers ensured that wills and insurance were up to date and prepared powers of attorney to take care of any legal problems that might arise while they were gone. Finance clerks checked troopers' records and verified that their paychecks were deposited directly into bank accounts that their wives would have access to. Each trooper made arrangements to take care of his automobile and, if needed, store it in a guarded lot on post. Those who were unmarried (or married to another service member who was also deploying) and lived in the nearby towns of Junction City or Manhattan, moved out of their apartments and put their personal items in storage on post. Sergeants directed those in the barracks to pack up their gear and move it to storage areas in the unit supply and arms rooms. Finally, each trooper visited the dispensary where he received the required shots. Ultimately, each commander validated his troop's individual administrative readiness for deployment to LTC Wilson.

Of course, all of this activity took place in the middle of the holiday season. On Saturday, November 17, the squadron's officers and senior noncommissioned officers held a formal party, or "dining out." Arrayed in blue uniforms, troopers accompanied their well-dressed wives to the Ramada Inn in nearby Manhattan. With departure around the corner and so much to do, many leaders simply could not see the need to take time away from the tasks they needed to accomplish and begged for permission to skip the party, but Wilson insisted that all attend. Many leaders arrived at the reception still grumbling about being torn away from the motor pool or some other task. Once there, however, they all had a chance to relax, reflect on the squadron's long history, and spend some quality time with their wives and friends. For the first time since the deployment preparation began, the wives had a chance to gather and talk about what was going on and their plans for how they would manage with the men away. It gave a real boost to the development of the family support groups.

A few days later, the squadron celebrated Thanksgiving. Traditionally, Thanksgiving dinner is an important event and a day in which the unit's leaders don their formal uniforms and help serve the meal to those soldiers who live in the barracks and others who care to join them in the dining facility, the formal name for the old "mess hall." The cavalry's officers continued this practice and everyone, from the lowest private to the squadron commander, had a chance to socialize away from the work environment and foster that bond that is so important among fighting men.

In early December the squadron's troopers filed into Fort Riley's Normandy Theater and listened to MAJ Don Osterberg, the chief of the division's G3 plans section, describe the land to which they would soon travel. Osterberg, along with the division commander and other key officers, had recently returned from a reconnaissance to Southwest Asia, and his slides displayed the absolute desolation found in northern Saudi Arabia. Rather than the expected sand dunes and palm trees, he showed them rocks, hills, dry riverbeds, and little vegetation, and surprised them with his discussion of the weather by warning the troopers to bring gloves and long underwear.[11]

With the equipment gone, leaders spent a great deal of effort revising the tactical standard operation procedures. The TACSOP, as it is known in military jargon, provides the basic outline of how to operate in the field. This document provided a framework for routines: radio procedures, how to set up a command post, how to conduct a road march, and how to request and execute a medical evacuation operation. The S3-Air, CPT Scott M. Sauer, took the lead in refining, publishing, and distributing this essential document.

In the middle of all of this hustle and bustle, troopers continued to wrestle with all kinds of personal issues. One of the more interesting incidents concerned CPT Vincent J. (VJ) Tedesco. Tedesco was attending the Armor Officers' Advanced Course at Fort Knox, with orders to the squadron, when the Iraqi Army invaded Kuwait. Having just returned from an assignment with the 11th Armored Cavalry Regiment in Germany, he and his wife, Lianne, an army nurse, looked forward to having their first joint assignment together after almost five years of marriage. However, just as Lianne was about to leave for the United States, her unit, the 97th General Hospital in Germany, the army issued its stop-loss order. Now she had to remain in Europe at work until the end of the war, and they would not see each other before VJ headed for Saudi Arabia. After many phone calls, the Armor School allowed him to graduate a few days early from Fort Knox and delay his arrival to the squadron in order to fly back to Germany for a short leave and a few precious days with his wife. Then it was back in the air and travel to Fort Riley.[12] Hidden behind the visible preparations and departure activities were many similar incidents, as families struggled with the emotional and financial problems of deploying to a combat zone. Unlike the era of World War II, Korea, and Vietnam, most Americans of the early 1990s had little memory of the effect of going to war on young families.

Troopers continued arriving daily right up to the beginning of the ground war in February. CPT Pope received his first platoon leader, 2LT James C. Copenhaver, from the Armor Officers' Basic Course in November. Of course, he had received his training in armor rather than cavalry, so Pope sent him over to Bills's B Troop for a cavalry orientation. Less than a year after graduating from college, this young man, like many others in the theater, would be leading other young soldiers into combat.

In another instance, SFC Donald J. Wehage arrived on post without an assignment. Just as he was getting settled, someone in the personnel system wanted to send him to Fort Benning for training and then have him join the division in Saudi Arabia. He walked into the A Troop headquarters and asked 1SGT Jack Taylor if he could join the troop, which would allow him to stay at Fort Riley and spend a few more days with his family. As short of leaders as A Troop was, Taylor was able to convince the personnel staff to let Wehage join his troop and cancel the trip to Georgia. [13]

Another important late arrival was CSM Robert M. (Mike) Cobb. The previous senior enlisted soldier, CSM John Soucy, had left the squadron in September assigned to the 24th Infantry Division's 2nd Squadron, 4th Cavalry, joining it en route to Operation Desert Shield in Saudi Arabia. Cobb, a twenty-year veteran and native of Kentucky, was an experienced noncommissioned officer, having held the same position in a battalion in Europe. He lost no time in taking the reins as the squadron's senior noncommissioned officer and quickly developed a strong rapport with LTC Wilson and the rest of the unit's leaders.

The division's advanced party, called Danger Forward, began deploying on December 12. The main body of the Big Red One would commence its travel over the Christmas holidays. MAJ Wimbish, his driver SPC Christopher M. Harper, CW2 Gerald M. Kovach the squadron maintenance technician, and SFC Larry E. Hughes, the S4's senior noncommissioned officer, boarded a C5A Galaxy at Forbes Field in Topeka on December

15. Their task was to conduct the initial reconnaissance of the squadron's assembly area and to arrange for the arrival and reception of the main body in Saudi Arabia. They crammed their personal gear and supplies into the executive officer's HMMWV and tied it down inside the aircraft. Flying through Torrejon, Spain, where they had some maintenance problems, they arrived in Dhahran, Saudi Arabia, on December 17.[14]

The squadron cased its colors, signifying its formal departure from the United States, in a ceremony on December 18. This was another milestone in preparation for departure for war and was reminiscent of a similar affair in October 1965 when the division had headed for Vietnam. Conducted on the parade ground just outside the squadron headquarters on a cold and blustery day, it was attended by families and friends of the troopers, as well as local businessmen and dignitaries who wanted to show their support for the cavalrymen.

The preparation for traveling to a strange part of the world and combat included more than just shipping equipment and training units. There was also a need to prepare new troopers mentally for combat. Senior leaders usually accomplished this by counseling and advising their younger troopers. For example, SGM Ken Shields gathered the S3 Section soldiers together in mid-December and talked with them about doing their jobs, of being afraid in combat, and of his desire to bring them all home. The young, eighteen- to twenty-five-year-old soldiers were riveted in place by what he had to say. For the first time war was no longer just a prospect and training a game; it was real and the young looked to the veterans for advice and to bring them through it all. Similar scenes took place across the division that week.

As Christmas approached, MG Rhame encouraged unit commanders to grant as much leave as possible for the soldiers, as long as it did not interfere with the deployment. Everyone wanted a few quiet days with family before departure. Wilson authorized a three-day holiday for the squadron and many soldiers spent their Christmas in the local area. Some made quick trips back home to say their final goodbyes.[15] Families went through the motions of trying to make the Christmas celebration as normal as possible, but it was not normal. A few days after the holiday, Wimbish's wife Delores slipped CPT Morrison a package to take to her husband who had left with the advance party. It was his Christmas present from her and their two children.[16]

The Burdans hosted a gathering of the squadron's operations section. This gave Bridget a chance to talk to those wives remaining behind so that the S3 chain of concern would be firmly in place before the squadron's departure. MAJ Burdan took that chance to say "thanks" for the hard work that everyone had put into the deployment effort to this point. Of course, not everyone in command was able to enjoy Christmas. CPT Morrison and 1SGT Colangelo spent Christmas Eve getting about forty troopers loaded into buses with their bags for an early departure to Saudi Arabia. It was an unexpected departure responding to an available aircraft arriving at Forbes Field.

Just after Christmas, A Troop began its scout platoon leader training. LTC Wilson arranged to have an abbreviated version of the Armor School's Scout Platoon Leaders' Course taught at Fort Riley and the Fort Knox instructors gave up much of their Christmas break in Kentucky to pull it off. To accommodate this badly needed training opportunity, A Troop would not depart as scheduled, but would take a later flight with the aviation troops. Those with experience, such as SFC William Molitor, A Troop's 1st Platoon Sergeant, saw it as a great opportunity to work with the other members of the unit for the first time.[17]

A heavy snowstorm delayed the squadron's scheduled departure for twenty-four hours. The next day, December 29, was cold and clear at Fort Riley when the Quarter Horse's main body began its deployment to Saudi Arabia. The first elements to go were CPT Bills's B Troop and the remainder of CPT Morrison's Headquarters Troop, accompanied by Wilson, the squadron's colors, and his staff. The remainder of the unit was scheduled to depart on January 10, with CPT Chris Philbrick in charge of the remaining soldiers.

Most families came to the unit barracks where the deploying soldiers were assembling to say goodbye. The nagging personal problems continued right up to departure. While everyone was forming up, SSG William Ball's mother called the office with an urgent request that he call home. Ball had to wait in line for almost an hour to return the call at the phone booth, waiting while others said a few last words with loved ones on the few phones available to call off-post. Finally, he got through to his mom, and now faced a dilemma as she told him that his grandmother had died and that they wanted him to come home. Torn between his family and his soldiers, the motor sergeant decided to stay with his troops, although 1SGT Colangelo offered to send him home for the funeral and let him catch up later. Ball believed his duty was to his soldiers and he did not want to let them down at the most important moment in their career.[18]

The soldiers boarded buses and rode over to the aircraft hangers at Fort Riley's airfield. There they waited in a reception area manned by volunteers from the Red Cross, Veterans of Foreign Wars, and members of the "Old Troopers," such as retired LTG Richard Seitz and community leaders. Seitz was a prominent member of the retired military community and had led a bayonet charge during the Battle of the Bulge in 1945 and went on to serve in Korea and Vietnam. He had stories to entertain and motivate the young troopers. While they waited until being ordered to the departure airfield, some troopers passed the time talking to families and girlfriends who came to wait with their loved ones. Others just collapsed in a corner, trying to get a little sleep. Just before he left headquarters, Morrison learned that he had promotion orders for one of his soldiers. There, in the cold hangar with bags packed high and soldiers tired of hurrying up to wait, Headquarters Troop had an impromptu promotion for one of their own.[19]

Next stop was Forbes Field in Topeka, Kansas, about an hour east of Fort Riley. It was a quiet bus ride. In the dark most troopers were lost in their thoughts or just tired, now caught up in something far larger than any of them could control. Then, it was off the buses and into the reception area for another muster and finally a briefing and the last check by customs agents and the drug dogs. Just before they boarded the aircraft, a snowstorm delayed the departure and everyone, again, found a place to relax. Then they got clearance to fly and the tired, somewhat dazed soldiers formed up again. MAJ Burdan found himself remembering his father's stories about departing from Forbes Field in 1952 during the Korea War, when he had been a navigator on a B-29 bomber. Somehow, he felt very close to his dad that snowy night.

Although both COL Mowery and LTC Wilson were on the aircraft, CPT Morrison had the duties of flight commander. For one last time, he called off their names: "Bassett, Beasley, Cobb, Collins, Davis, Dozier, Dixon" and on and on as almost four hundred soldiers climbed into the Boeing 747. Doug looked over his shoulder and saw his wife, Catherine, who had made the journey from Fort Riley. She watched him call these names for the last time. How many would come back? Holding back his emotions, he waved, climbed on board and closed the door with everything on board. One of the pilots thought the air-craft was a little heavy, about 2,000 pounds overweight, and was not sure it would be able to take off. However, in the cold early morning hours of December 29 the squadron was in the air and on its way.[20]

4   The Port

Headquarters and Bravo Troops celebrated New Year's at 33,000 feet over Shannon Airport, Ireland, and landed at Brussels where the aircraft refueled and took on a new flight crew. Some of the soldiers had developed a strong attachment to the flight attendants during the journey, and spent time waiting on the tarmac saying goodbye. Soon the new pilots arrived; both were Air Force veterans who had flown combat missions over North and South Vietnam, and joined the group in the discussion. They seemed to take their role in this war personally and commented that they hoped the soldiers' "hands would not be tied the way theirs were in Vietnam." They were obviously pleased that the country was behind the deployment and supporting its troops.[1]

The flight into Saudi Arabia took the squadron from Brussels, southeast across France to Cairo. Then it traveled south, down the Egyptian coastline for about 300 miles, turning east over the Red Sea. Dawn broke as they crossed over the water and glimpsed, for the first time, what the Arabian Desert looked like. The land was huge and empty, with wadis, mesas, and plains colored in various shades of purple, browns, and grays. The terrain looked like someone had emptied an ocean bottom of water and plants and left it standing. It was awesome and sobering to realize that the soldiers would soon be in the middle of it.

Before touching down at King Fahd International Airport at 1200 hours local (or Charlie) time CPT Morrison, in his role as flight commander, spent some time talking to the crew. He discovered they were all volunteers; for flying into Saudi Arabia, the airlines wanted *only* volunteers. The reason for this policy became obvious as the pilot gave the troops an intelligence briefing over the intercom while they were on the way in:

> OK . . . if something happens in the area and Dhahran and King Fahd Airport are under attack, we will divert to Jiddah or wherever we can, like Bahrain. If we are on final approach, we'll do the best we can, land, off-load the airplane as quick as we can and get back into the air.[2]

As the aircraft came to a halt, Morrison, who was up front and paying attention to everything around him, watched as the flight attendants kept everyone in their seats and kicked open the door. One of the ground crew pushed in a huge cardboard box. The Headquarters Troop commander looked inside and discovered, to his consternation, that it contained chemical-biological protective masks, one for each member of the flight crew. A pretty stewardess looked him in the eye and assured him that they were all trained on how to use the masks and what actions to take in the event of an attack on the aircraft on the runway.[3]

The somewhat shocked officers and men disembarked and moved under Air Force direction off the runway to wait for buses. MAJ Bill Wimbish and CPT Steve Harmon, who had traveled on an earlier flight, arrived in the executive officer's HMMWV. They were a welcome sight, being familiar faces in a very uncertain environment. After an exchange of greetings and small talk, Wimbish outlined what was ahead for the squadron. Over the next two weeks the troopers would assemble at the port of Dhahran, unload the equipment they had sent by ship, and receive new tanks and M3 Bradley Cavalry Fighting Vehicles. They would then move in stages out to an assembly area called TAA Roosevelt. The XO had already visited this inhospitable patch of desert south of the Kuwaiti border that was going to be the squadron's home for the remainder of Desert Shield.

Since the buses to take the troops to the port had not yet arrived, the squadron took the opportunity to uncase the colors on the airfield. It was a traditional ceremony that gave notice to all that the 1st Squadron, 4th United States Cavalry was in South-

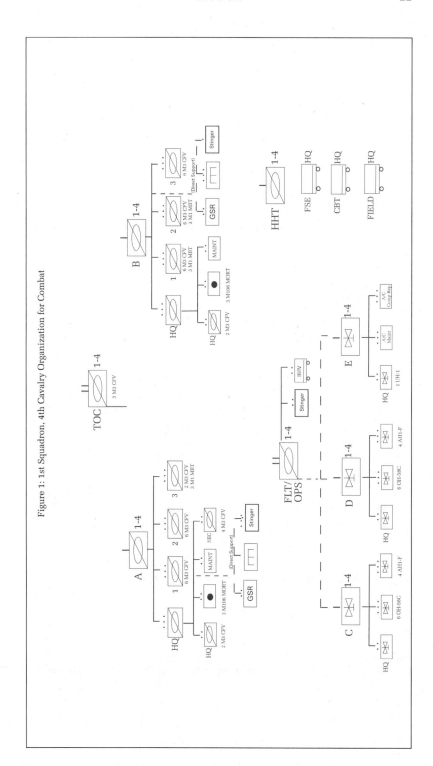

Figure 1: 1st Squadron, 4th Cavalry Organization for Combat

west Asia and ready for business. With the troops lined up as if they were on the parade ground back at Fort Riley, the honor guard, led by CSM Michael Cobb, brought the squadron's flags forward. LTC Wilson and his sergeant major moved to the front of the formation and directed the flag bearers to lower their bulky staffs. Together they removed the flags from their canvas cases and unrolled the fabric. As the yellow squadron flag, with its fifty-one colored battle streamers, opened and caught the gentle breeze, the soldiers knew they were now involved in something much larger than themselves. Turning to his anxious soldiers, Wilson spoke about the tasks confronting them and his determination to bring them all back home.

After a short briefing by MAJ Wimbish, the troopers filed onto ten buses for their twenty-five-mile trip to the port. The squadron, along with many units from the army's European-based VII Corps, was housed in the Khobar housing area. Located just south of the port of Ad Dammam, Khobar Towers, as it was known by the troops, was a large housing area built by the Saudi government as a way to lure Bedouins from the desert into the cities. The buildings had hot and cold running water, showers and baths, air conditioners, heat, and electricity. However, there were a number of cultural and social problems that made these modern buildings unacceptable for the Bedouins. For example, each apartment had only one door, which meant that men and women had to use the same entrance, a serious cultural transgression. Therefore, most of the apartments were empty when the Americans arrived.

Military policemen provided security for the complex that the army had ringed with barbed wire, concrete obstacles, and guard posts. Heavily armed guards monitored the facility's entrance behind a series of barriers designed to slow traffic. Once inside, the soldiers headed for the eight apartments assigned to the squadron and quickly fell asleep. Each apartment had a living room, reception area, kitchen, three bedrooms, and two bathrooms. The rooms varied in size and, in general, five to ten men occupied an unfurnished room, with as many as twenty-five per apartment. Soldiers and their sleeping bags and gear filled every square foot of free space in living rooms, dining rooms, and even the balconies. With only two bathrooms in each apartment, toilet stoppages were frequent and engineers scrambled to figure out how to keep the overtaxed sewage system operating in the face of this unanticipated demand.

Not all of the squadron's members remained at Khobar Towers, as Wilson had to keep troopers at the port to assist in off-loading vehicles.[4] In addition, LTC Wilson elected to house most of his leaders there to ensure he could find them when a ship arrived. All of his soldiers lived in one of the large dockside warehouses leased by the American government. The corps's logistics staff had arranged for showers, latrines, washbasins, a small post exchange, mail room, and a check-cashing facility on the pier. Each trooper signed for a cot, and loaded down with duffel bags and backpack, made a home in about eighteen square feet of open space. The entire floor of the warehouse was covered with cots and just enough space between them to store the bags. There was no privacy and women soldiers from other units slept right next to the men. An army-operated bus service ran between the port and the Khobar complex, and the division assigned the squadron several commercial light trucks (usually Jeep Cherokees) for local transportation.

The remainder of the squadron, led by CPT Chris Philbrick, left Fort Riley on January 10, and flew out of Topeka in very much the same sequence as the earlier flight. As with the squadron's initial deployment, there were worried wives and kids seeing their husbands and fathers off. There were some emotional moments between the soldiers and their families. Chief Warrant Officer 3 (CW3) Kirk Waymire enjoyed his Christmas break with his family where he spent some special time with his father-in-law, who had fought in the Pacific during World War II. When he got to the staging area at Fort Riley that morning, he realized that he did not have a current will. The clerks at the legal station in the hangar quickly prepared one and handed it back to him. Obviously, he could not take it with him so he returned to where the families were and gave it to his wife Mary. When she asked what was in the package he responded without thinking, "my will." Within a few moments everyone was crying.[5]

After the early morning bus ride through the Kansas hills, the troopers boarded an American Airlines L-1011 aircraft at

Forbes Field and, in a snowstorm, headed to Boston and then to Rome. Everybody was tired but had trouble sleeping in the cramped aircraft. SFC William Molitor thought he would solve the problem, for a short while, by stretching out in the aisle while they were on the ground in Italy. In a few moments he was sound asleep. The next thing he knew, the aircraft was shaking and he thought it was moving down the runway. In reality, they had been in the air for half an hour!

Next stop was King Fahd airfield, arriving around 2100 hours on January 11. Captains Bills and Morrison met the flight on the runway. After a long bus ride, they ended up in the tent city (also called Seaside) that was being formed down at the port. As they pitched their tents, the sky became dark and threatening. Somewhat surprised to be in this situation in the Middle East, some soldiers dug small trenches around their tents, just as they would during a training exercise in Germany. Those who did not found their living quarters flooded the following morning. Sometimes even those precautions did not matter, as CPT Pope learned when his trench gave way and four inches of water drenched the floor of his tent. It rained for the next five days and some tents had four to five inches of water inside.[6]

The squadron continued to receive new troopers after it arrived in Saudi Arabia. In most cases they came either from the reserves (both the Army Reserve and the Army National Guard) or from non-deploying units in the United States. Six mechanics joined Headquarters Troop: three from one of the army's service schools, one from the National Guard, one from the Individual Ready Reserve, and one regular army sergeant. In A Troop, among other arrivals, 2LT Copenhaver received a corporal from the National Guard to serve as his Bradley gunner. Three full tank crews arrived in B Troop. CPT Bills arranged to keep these together throughout the campaign. These arrivals brought the squadron almost up to full-strength and, with the arrival of air crews from Fort Drum, the C and D Troops now had more than enough crew members for their aircraft. The only exception to this wealth was the newly formed A Troop. It was still short of Bradley crewmen and CPT Pope had not met any of his tank crews. Until a few weeks before it attacked into Iraq, the troop would continue to struggle with personnel shortages. Most importantly, Pope would receive thirty new Bradley crewmen only ten days before the ground war began.[7]

The squadron's vehicles and equipment began arriving in the port on January 8. Over the next three weeks, trucks, tracked vehicles, and aircraft continued to trickle in on eight different ships. Once the unit heard it had vehicles on board, it had to unload them from the ship, inspect them, and give them the maintenance attention tanks and armored personnel carriers always require. In addition, the crews had to locate the vehicle's equipment, such as radios and weapons, which were shipped in separate containers called milvans, a nickname for "military vans." While this was going on, Wilson received word that he was to turn in his old Cavalry Fighting Vehicles for newer M3A2 models. The old M3s were later distributed to units within the division and used to provide additional convoy and command post security. At the same time, he was receiving the new M1A1 Tanks. The result was a busy couple of weeks that saw troopers and their leaders running in a variety of directions.

The vehicles came off the boats in fairly good shape, with only a few dents and many dead batteries. Crews and mechanics rushed to the docks to inspect and reassemble their equipment and begin moving it to staging areas where they prepared for the trip to the desert. There was no single way to unload the cargo that arrived at port because of the many types of ships used in the deployment, and soldiers had to learn a few new tricks each time a ship arrived. This variety was caused because the navy had only eight fast sealift ships, which carried only thirteen percent of all American military ocean cargo sent to Southwest Asia. There were also ninety-six ships in the Ready Reserve Fleet, many between twenty and forty years old and some had not been to sea or tested in over thirteen years. Needing yet more shipping, the Department of Defense chartered 213 ships of various sizes and nationalities to carry equipment and supplies to Saudi Arabia. The best of these were the "Ro-Ro" (roll-on-roll-off) ships, which allowed combat vehicles to be driven on and off the ship. Most vessels, however, required cranes to lift vehicles and cargo off the deck and onto the pier below, a much slower and more precarious process.[8]

Once a ship arrived in port, the VII Corps's port assistance task forces supervised the discharge of cargo with unloading teams based on the specific type of vessel and the kind of equipment that it was carrying. Several ships arrived each day, and the length of time a vessel remained in port for off-loading depended on a number of factors: its size, method of unloading (drive-off or cranes) and the type of equipment it carried (containers, tanks, pallets, etc.). On a normal day, the teams removed between 300 and 1,000 items of unit equipment from the ships, but the exact tonnage varied considerably.[9]

If the vessel was a Ro-Ro type, the driving team unchained each vehicle and drove it out of the hold and onto the pier. On other ships, one team unhooked vehicles inside the ship, while another team lifted them by crane vertically off the ship and onto the dockside. Once on land, logistics inspectors checked shipping documents and maintenance teams from the 593d Area Support Group made safety checks, and fueled and organized them by company. At the port of Ad Dammam, the team of unit drivers then drove the vehicles to a local staging area.[10]

As mentioned earlier, while the squadron unloaded its M3 Cavalry Fighting Vehicles (or CFVs), it received word that they would turn them in for the new M3A2. With a 25-mm Bushmaster cannon, a TOW2 antitank missile, improved fire-control systems, a 7.62-mm coaxial machine gun, and improvements in armor protection, power management, and fuel stowage, the M3A2 was greatly superior to the Iraqi BMP and all of the other enemy personnel carriers.[11]

Exchanging these vehicles was a three-step process: removal of all the squadron-owned equipment (radios, guns, etc.) from the old CFVs, reinstallation of it on the new, and training on the improved aspects of the M3A2. In the confusion of the period, turning in the old vehicles was a bit of a problem. Changes were happening so fast that it was difficult to find someone in the port area to sign for them. The squadron initially parked the old ones near the new equipment training area; however, other units began removing parts and equipment for use on their own vehicles. This process, called cannibalization, was generally frowned on and Wilson had to post a guard to keep it from happening until the appropriate support command representatives arrived to secure the vehicles.

On January 9, the squadron began inventorying and signing for their new M3A2s, with MAJ Wimbish supervising the process of ensuring proper installation of radios and installation kits. The crewmen also received their training session on differences between the old and new models. Many of the unit's Bradleys were truly brand new, with only four to six kilometers on their odometers. The 22nd Support Command's maintenance units provided the specialized support the squadron needed to mount their old equipment, including installing cables and radio antennas and mounts. This exchange and turn-in process is always frustrating, but it was obvious that each crew was excited as it took possession of its new war chariot. One could also see the special attentiveness each trooper displayed as the new equipment training team instructed him on his new weapon system.[12]

That same day the division headquarters gave Wilson final approval to sign for twelve M1A1 tanks. He sent six to B Troop immediately and three to A Troop once they arrived in Saudi Arabia. The three remaining tanks, identified for MG Rhame's command group, were soon transferred to the division's Headquarters Company. These tanks came from the warehouses near Kaiserslautern, Germany, that Wilson had walked through when the Iraqi Army invaded Kuwait six months earlier. The army shipped them to Ad Dammam where a 600-person material fielding team conducted essential maintenance checks and applied a variety of modifications to each tank, including additional armor, improved optical sights, more efficient fire extinguishers, and all of the manuals and tools they were required to have. Each tank crew then inspected the vehicle and installed radios, machine guns, and other items. Then, the crews loaded ammunition on each tank and prepared to move it to the desert.[13]

Of course, the transition for Quarter Horse was not as smooth as it could have been, especially in regards to manning the tanks. Added to the diversion of supervising the preparation of the commanding general's three tanks, Wilson struggled to find enough experienced soldiers to crew his own vehicles. The 2nd Brigade provided some experienced sergeants to command tanks, while Wilson met with other tank battalion commanders to work deals to exchange privates for more experienced specialists. Finally, a few crews arrived from the United States and joined the squadron. While B Troop, which already had a cadre of leaders, was able to get its tanks manned and ready relatively quickly, the newly formed A Troop would not be ready for almost a month.[14]

As a new organization, CPT Pope's command also struggled to find basic issue items that the other soldiers and crews were able to bring from the United States. These shortages included armored crew helmets (called CVCs for Cover, Vehicle Crewmember) that contained headsets and microphones for communications, protective masks, machine guns for all vehicles, night vision goggles and radios. The 4th Brigade Commander, COL Mowery, went to great lengths to ensure the troopers would be ready when the battle began. MG Rhame and BG William G. Carter III, the Assistant Division Commander-Maneuver, also visited the troop regularly to ensure that all that was humanly possible was being done to properly outfit the unit.[15]

Meanwhile, the two aviation troops waited in the rain at the tent city for their helicopters to arrive by ship. When they finally arrived around January 15, the crews jumped into action. They helped move them off the ship and into an aviation holding area. They removed the protective plastic from each aircraft and began the long checklist of steps that were required before they could fly. Each helicopter received modifications to its electronics and navigation equipment. Of course, "friction," an ever-present participant in military operations, reared its ugly head when crew chiefs discovered that much of the required avionics and radio equipment had already been shipped out to the desert assembly area. Chief Warrant Officers Kirk Waymire and Craig Winters borrowed radios from another unit and flew the squadron's old UH-1 out to TAA Roosevelt to bring back everything they needed. The air troops lost a couple of days of preparation time while these aviators flew out, found the squadron's assembly area, located the aviation troops' milvans, cut the locks, found the equipment, and returned.[16]

The war began shortly after midnight January 16 with coalition air attacks and retaliation by Iraqi Scud missiles. Around midnight, in anticipation of these counterstrikes, which would possibly contain chemical munitions, the division commander ordered all soldiers to go to a higher level of chemical protection, called MOPP (for Mission Oriented Protective Posture) and start taking the PB (pyridostigmine bromide) pills to assist in case of a chemical attack. The aviators felt rather helpless as they waited to move away from the port area. Few of them knew what was going on and rumors circulated in an ever-increasing tempo. MAJ Wimbish remembered listening to the radio stations as they made several erroneous reports of attacks on King Fahd airfield and the port area. The soldiers all took the announcement in different ways. Some became very quiet and turned to their Bibles for support, while others, caught up in the excitement, did not give much thought to the consequences of the attack. Some were visibly scared and it took the efforts of their chain of command to calm them down. Wilson, not willing to accept the uncertainty and confusion, ordered the aviation troops to be ready to move to the tactical assembly area as soon as possible.[17]

At 0400 hours, the air raid sirens at Ad Dammam Port sounded, warning of a possible Scud attack, and the soldiers went to full chemical protective gear for about thirty minutes, and then took off their masks but stayed essentially ready until 0700 hours. Most lay on their cots listening to the radio or playing their Game Boys, little electronic pocket games that were popular among troops. In some cases, there was a mad scramble for the chemical protective gear as the soldiers had to pull it out of their duffel bags.[18] After the last Scud attack, LTC Wilson had had enough. To some of his officers he exclaimed: "You know, this is stupid! I'm not going to hang around here. I'm going out to join our guys in the middle of the desert. He then looked at his executive officer and said, "OK Bill, you've got it." Wilson then headed out to TAA Roosevelt where he escaped the port and took command of the squadron in the field.[19]

That morning there was no hot breakfast, since the contract civilian servers had not been allowed into the port area. The soldiers broke open their MREs (Meals, Ready-to-eat) and until the chow situation could be restored, this healthy but bland food was the order of the day. Those troopers still in port would not remain there much longer, however, as they would soon be on the way to join the remainder of the squadron in Tactical Assembly Area Roosevelt.

5   Operations in the TAA

The squadron's new home was a tactical assembly area 270 miles northwest of the port just north of the Tapline Road and east of the Wadi Al Batin. There, LTG Frederick M. Franks, Jr.'s, entire VII Corps assembled for its upcoming offensive against Iraq. With 142,000 soldiers organized into five heavy divisions and an armored cavalry regiment, it was the largest mechanized unit ever assembled by the U.S. Army. The corps assembled in a large assembly area called Juno.

Within TAA Roosevelt, the division's portion of TAA Juno, each of its subordinate brigades and separate units occupied its own assembly area. The 1st Squadron, 4th Cavalry, named its area Camp Mackenzie, in honor of its dynamic leader of the 1870s. While at Camp Mackenzie, LTC Wilson had three main tasks to accomplish: move the entire unit to the TAA, train it for its upcoming mission in desert warfare, and defend its portion of the assembly area in case of an Iraqi attack. While these were three distinct activities, they took place simultaneously and continued until just before the beginning of the ground offensive in February.

Moving the entire squadron from the port area to the assembly area was the first task. It entailed conducting a reconnaissance of the sector, deploying an advance party to prepare it, moving the main body consisting of most of the squadron's equipment and soldiers, and finally, bringing A Troop's recently trained and assembled crews to the desert in time for the campaign. Wilson, SPC Harvey Kenworthy his driver, MAJ Burdan, COL Mowery, and some of his staff conducted a leader's reconnaissance of the assembly area on January 3 and 4. Armed with

51

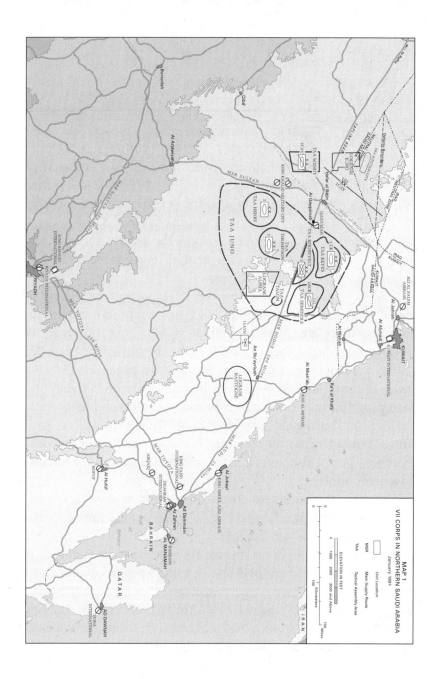

only a few rounds of 9 mm ammunition each and using a large-scale (1:250,000) map that showed few details and their new GPS instrument, they headed into the unfamiliar landscape. For the first seventy or so miles they drove north along the coastal highway, a good four-lane road, then they turned northwest on the Tapline Road. This road, consisting of only two lanes with shoulders of soft sand, was packed with bumper-to-bumper military and civilian traffic moving in both directions. Local civilian drivers barreled down the sides of the highway with no thought of safety, often playing a game of "chicken" with vehicles in the opposing lane. The hulks of wrecked automobiles and trucks littered the sides of the highway, indicating that these games often ended in tragedy. In one incident on December 30, an Aramco tanker truck hit an American troop bus that had stopped behind a Saudi truck. Fortunately, none of the thirty casualties, all soldiers assigned to the 128th Combat Support Hospital, were seriously injured. A few days later, another truck accident sent two more soldiers to the hospital. Although there were no injuries in the squadron, these incidents continued throughout the deployment, adding another element of risk to an already dangerous mission.[1]

That night the leaders arrived at the 1st Infantry Division's tactical command post in the assembly area. It looked pretty bleak, as a group of M577 Command Post Vehicles sat alone in the middle of a hastily constructed sand berm. Inside, duty officers monitored the VII Corps communications nets and reported the continually changing status of the division. Communication back to the port was difficult and restricted to one tactical satellite telephone. The division staff gave the recon party a quick overview of how the assembly area operated and what terrain the remainder of the division would occupy.[2] Arriving too late to share in the dinner, they looked for the Aviation Brigade's temporary headquarters. They found Majors Mark Landrith and Dan Pike from the 1st Battalion, 1st Aviation housed in a small tent belonging to the squadron left behind by MAJ Wimbish on his previous trip to the area. There they set up their cots and bunked for the evening. The next morning Wilson, Mowery, and Burdan were up early and examined the aviation assembly area. Given the uncertain situation, COL Mowery thought it best to consolidate all of his helicopters to get the best use of his maintenance assets, especially his supporting AVIM (aviation intermediate maintenance) company, and to simplify support to and from the division. Of course, Wilson was not happy about this since it meant that his aviators would be living away from the ground troops in the squadron assembly area.

Later in the morning, Wilson and Burdan drove to the squadron's future location twenty kilometers away. Although they had all seen pictures of the northern desert, they were surprised at how flat and featureless the terrain was. As operations officer, Burdan was responsible for combat plans and was concerned by the lack of any kind of key terrain on which to anchor the defense of the assembly area. It was obvious they would have to prepare dug-in fighting positions if they were to have any kind of cover and concealment in the assembly area.

The return trip to port was every bit as difficult as the trip out. The roads were crowded and the lines at the refueling point on Tapline Road were long. Later that night, after discussing the situation with his staff, Wilson decided to send Burdan back to the desert with an advance party to establish Camp Mackenzie. The commander and MAJ Wimbish would remain in the Ad Dammam area to attend to their first priority: getting everything off the ships and the soldiers issued with their new tanks and Bradleys. Wilson directed Burdan to organize the assembly area as one large perimeter, with the squadron's command post in the center. As more platoons and crews arrived, they would continue to expand this circle until it resembled a large wagon wheel. This "circle the wagons" defense was the best in an uncertain situation when all-around defense, especially against raids or small unit attacks, was important.

Early on January 6, the S3 led his convoy of fifteen vehicles from the port. Lieutenants Thomas Karns and Blaise Liess, both platoon leaders, controlled the B Troop contingent while CPT John (Jack) Maloney, the HHT executive officer, supervised the headquarters soldiers. Not wishing to be at the mercy of an unfamiliar distribution system, they brought along three 2,500-gallon HEMTT (Heavy Expanded Mobility Tactical Truck) fuel trucks. This was a good move since they later discovered the official "gas station" on Tapline Road was backed up with a two-hour wait. Bypassing this over-loaded fuel point, they drove a few miles farther up the road, pulled over to the side, refueled their own vehicles and broke open their first of many cases of MREs. Burdan and his party were on their way again in about an hour, and by 1830 were approaching Camp Mackenzie in TAA Roosevelt.

Pulling off the Tapline Road in the dark, about ten kilometers south of the projected assembly area, they used their new GPS to find the exact spot for the squadron's new home. The troopers were excited, tired, and scared as they moved closer to their potential enemy. Once in the center of the designated area, they "circled the wagons" in good old cavalry style. CPT Maloney took charge of posting guards and established a standard security rotation for the night. Some people slept on cots they had brought from Fort Riley, while most simply collapsed in the back of their trucks.

Of course, this "camp" was nothing more than a few acres of flat, wet, barren sand. The image that has emerged of a tidy, push-button war does no justice to the problems soldiers encountered in the desert that winter where relatively simple tasks, such as setting up living quarters, were major challenges. The advance party had supplies for only a few days and had to get this area ready for the entire unit. The squadron's tents, along with a great deal of other essential equipment, were still in Milvans somewhere in the division's assembly area, at port waiting to be brought forward, or still on ships in the Arabian Sea. Compounding these issues was the sheer size of the division's tactical assembly area. Having spent most of their professional lives on relatively small maneuver areas at Fort Riley and in Germany, appreciating the scale of the assembly area required some adjustment by the troopers. The Big Red One alone occupied about 1,500 square kilometers of desert. Travel to and from the division's headquarters, cross-country or on very old and dusty trails, took close to an hour. When darkness came, there were no lights, and the moon and stars took on a significance not appreciated in the industrial world.

Because of a limited number of routes to the desert and limited transportation assets, vehicle movement from the port was closely controlled by Army Central Command's (ARCENT's) 22nd Support Command. For example, there were only 1,300 HETS (Heavy Equipment Transporters) in the entire theater, including tractors from several coalition partners, to carry all of the coalition's tanks and smaller tracked vehicles. The result was a backlog of combat power in port assembly areas waiting to move out to the desert.[3] The support command's movement control center gave Wimbish permission to move some wheeled vehicles as well as a handful of HETs to carry some of the squadron's tracked vehicles to the desert. MAJ Wimbish led the squadron main body out from the port early in the morning on January 8. The troops themselves traveled on leased Saudi Arabian busses that were designed for use inside urban areas. For army leaders used to uniformity and precision, this convoy had something of a "gypsy" air as army and commercial HETs intermingled with the five red and white civilian buses. The local national drivers were obviously not too happy carrying American soldiers toward the Iraqi border and were fearful that a war would break out soon. 1LT Matthew Vanderfeltz, the support platoon leader, greeted this convoy outside the assembly area shortly after 1800 hours that same day.

Wilson now had about twenty-five percent of his squadron in the assembly area and more soldiers and equipment were arriving every day. His leaders spent the next few days organizing the essential elements of survival in a primitive environment. Mail began to trickle in, but until the end of the war, it would never arrive as quickly as it should have. The squadron borrowed two large general purpose (GP-Medium as they were called) tents from the Aviation Brigade and additional tents from the Division Support Command general supply section, to get most of the soldiers under cover. Those without cover continued to sleep in their vehicles. Water was also a problem as there was initially only one 500-gallon water trailer (called a water buffalo) and a large assortment of five-gallon storage containers, to serve all of the cooking and sanitation needs of more than 200 soldiers. With the resupply point a two-hour round trip away, water had to be carefully managed.

Troopers traveling about the vast TAA sometimes got lost. On one occasion a vehicle containing the medical platoon leader, 2LT Nathan T. Butler, squadron surgeon MAJ Roger Hanson, personnel officer CPT Theodore K. (Ken) Stokes, Jr., and the squadron mail clerk went out to visit the division support command several kilometers away. They did not return that night. The next morning, having spent the night with another unit, they returned to the TOC complaining about their GPS. Of course, the device was fine. However, the division learned that there were periods of time when the satellite coverage was not sufficient to provide accurate GPS readings.[4]

It was becoming obvious to all that war was right around the corner. The first indication of danger came in the early evening of January 9. A little before 2100 hours a huge fireball lit up the pitch-black sky. Something had exploded about six kilometers south of the squadron's headquarters. Without being told, soldiers grabbed their protective masks and put on their chemical protective over-garments. Those soldiers assigned detection responsibilities broke open their kits and began to sample the air. Soon it was confirmed that that the air was clear and the troops were able to relax. MAJ Wimbish was on Tapline Road when the explosion took place and he and his driver, SPC Christopher Harper, put on their protective masks. Once they got their bearings and determined that they were not under any kind of continuous attack, they headed in the direction of the fireball. They were first on the scene, and found aircraft wreckage all over the area. Soon Air Force security police arrived and secured the wreckage. For whatever reason, a low-flying F-16 Fighting Falcon had hit the ground at high speed. It was an early reminder that, to quote Dorothy's famous line from the *Wizard of Oz*, which was appropriate for soldiers from Fort Riley, "we're not in Kansas anymore."[5]

Simultaneously with the build-up of combat power, the squadron began preparing for war. Given the activity across its border, it was reasonable to expect that the Iraqi Army might launch a preemptive attack on Saudi Arabia and the VII Corps's growing combat power. On January 10 the 1st Infantry Division ordered the squadron, still missing most of its Bradleys and tanks, to go to a war footing and begin operating the tactical operations center twenty-four hours a day. Along with the rest of the corps, the squadron conducted a "stand-to" each morning.

This was a drill that got the entire unit out of bed, manning its equipment, and on the perimeter ready to fight each day before dawn. All of this was a sure sign that they were getting closer to war.[6]

On the eleventh, Wimbish moved the recently arrived S2 and S3 M577 Command Post Vehicles from the port, allowing the TOC to move out of its tent and into its normal battle configuration. Even though the squadron now had its command post up and running, communications between Camp Mackenzie and the port, where A and B Troop and much of the squadron remained, were not very good, making it difficult to monitor the movement of vehicles and equipment to the TAA.

Anticipating an Iraqi attack on January 13, the VII Corps commander ordered the 1st Infantry Division to be prepared to occupy a blocking position just north of TAA Roosevelt with the mission of protecting the corps logistics base (Logbase Alpha). Early the next morning, B Troop's M3A2 Cavalry Fighting Vehicles finally began to arrive in the assembly area by HET. The staff duty log reported that four were in the assembly area and five others were "in the desert somewhere." By 1345 hours, the troop officers had found eight, and were off searching for the other. Later that day, division headquarters directed the cavalry, with only under-strength B Troop, to be prepared for combat in the event of an Iraqi attack.[7]

That night, the division alerted all its elements in TAA Roosevelt, most of which had few combat units available, that the enemy was going to attack. Each command was to be ready to move out on a moment's notice. Of great concern to the squadron's leaders were the eighty TOW missiles, 9,000 rounds of 20 mm ammunition, and locked milvans loaded with crew-served weapons, night vision equipment, binoculars, chemical detection kits, and other valuable equipment that would have to be left behind if they were forced to move on short notice. Division headquarters provided no guidance as to what to do with the ammunition and equipment. So MAJ Burdan, the senior officer in the area, directed CPT Jack Maloney to cut the locks on the MILVANs and issue as much of the ammunition, weapons, and equipment as the soldiers could carry on the vehicles. Because this was an emergency, they handed out the contents of the trailers without any special concern as to the rightful owner. Later, the troop commanders and their noncommissioned officers expended a great deal of effort in reestablishing property accountability. In the meantime, they loaded what they could, and the headquarters and combat support elements prepared to head south into the corps logistics area should the Iraqis attack. Fortunately, there was no attack and the Iraqi Army lost a chance to thwart the American build-up in the VII Corps sector. The next morning, the squadron had to unload all the vehicles, and place the equipment back into storage.[8]

Camp Mackenzie continued to expand and improve with the arrival of vehicles and personnel from the port. Work on the perimeter defenses was continuous and a source of pride for the soldiers. The squadron mess section under SFC William J. Zahniser produced some of the best fighting positions in the squadron area and better than those constructed by the tankers and scouts. Credit for these desert masterpieces went to SPC Daniel E. Butts, one of the cooks, who began with a primitive fighting position dug into the hard Saudi dirt and, when not working in the mess, continued to deepen and enlarge it. He added some overhead cover and created a textbook example of a small-unit fighting position, the kind not often found among supporting troops. Creating fighting positions for the heavy equipment was much more difficult and the squadron managed to borrow a few bulldozers from the division engineer battalion, and used them to prepare dug-in fighting positions for tanks and Bradleys.

Troopers working perimeter security took their jobs seriously and reported anything suspicious. The most common reports were of the ubiquitous white Toyota pickup trucks that seemed to appear out of nowhere, observe the Americans, and then disappear into the desert. Other observations were more comical. On the evening of January 14, a scout reported 60–100 unidentified people heading towards the perimeter. A short time later the same team amended its report to indicate that the attackers were a family of wild camels.[9] In another instance, a squadron soldier noticed a man with a backpack moving towards him from about 100–125 meters away. The soldier called out for his guard commander and then yelled out for what he

thought was a person to stop. The figure kept moving toward
him. He again called out to the figure to stop but again it did not
do so. Frightened, the soldier stood up and took his weapon off
safe and yelled, "It's your ass . . ." and was about to shoot. Suddenly a camel veered off at a 90-degree angle, apparently scared
off by the sudden movement to its front. By the time the senior
noncommissioned officer arrived on the scene, the commander
of the relief and the soldier were both in a foxhole and the young
guard was sweating and shaking, never wanting to be that
scared again in his life.[10] While the attacks by the "killer camels"
were somewhat humorous, it was only a few years earlier that
terrorists had destroyed a Marine compound in Beirut, and the
army's leadership was determined to prevent a reccurrence.[11]

While at the TAA, the squadron began to plan for its part in
the coming offensive. During an early meeting of division commanders, MG Rhame had volunteered the 1st Infantry Division
to lead the VII Corps into Iraq. The Big Red One would break
into the Iraqi defenses and open several paths, or breaches, into
its rear. Then, according to the original plan, the remainder of
the corps would follow in search of the Iraqi Republican Guard.
The division called its part of the corps plan Operation Scorpion Danger and the squadron's role was extensive. First, under the control of the 3rd Brigade, it would assist in tearing
down the large sand berm that followed the Iraqi-Saudi Arabian border. Then, under the operational control of the 1st
Brigade, it would attack the initial Iraqi defenses, and then
screen the left flank of the division's attack. Until mid-January,
the division plan for the coming attack had been kept under
tight control. Now the squadron S3 staff was allowed full access
so that it could begin developing its part of the overall plan.
MAJ Burdan assigned CPT VJ Tedesco, the S3 Air, the responsibility for drafting the squadron operation order.[12]

In the process of preparing for battle, Burdan and his officers learned they had a serious problem: there were very few
maps of the area. The squadron had managed to bring over a
few sets of maps, comprised mainly of 1:250,000-scale, from
Fort Riley. They were difficult to use for small-unit commanders. Now that they were planning for operations, it was essential that every troop and platoon leader have a map set of the

preferred 1:100,000 scale. The intelligence officer, CPT Shelby R. Seelinger, looked everywhere for them, but was unable to find all the map sheets needed to cover the anticipated area of operations. Finally, in desperation, Burdan resorted to drawing grid squares on large sheets of paper that were then trimmed and fitted to the gaps in the map sheets they did have. Somehow the vision of the "high-tech" army lost some of its luster as leaders headed back to their vehicles with their hand-drawn charts, which lacked any terrain relief.[13]

Two hours after midnight on January 17, the 1st Infantry Division's duty officer called all of the units on the division's command frequency. "ARCENT OPLAN 0001 in effect as of 170145C. Hostilities have commenced."[14] The squadron's watch officer woke MAJ Burdan, who dressed and headed for the command post. As he walked through the dark and quiet desert, he could hear the sound of aircraft and see the occasional strobe lights of those returning from their first missions. Like other members of the Big Red One, John Burdan was a little scared at first but was determined not to show it. Strolling through the command post and assembly area, he saw soldiers watching the aircraft streak overhead and the tracers and explosions on the northern horizon. Some were listening to their shortwave radios to glean what news they could of the attack. Burdan sensed relief that something had finally happened and the squadron would not continue to sit in the desert waiting out the Iraqis. Realizing there was not much he could do, the operations officer returned to bed around 0300 hours. At 0500 hours, the Division G3, LTC Terry Bullington, called to inform the squadron that the wartime rules of engagement were in effect. While this change was minor, it placed soldiers on notice that they were now in a hostile fire area and they needed to actively prepare to defend themselves. Later that day, the division placed the squadron, which now had almost all of the HHT and B Troop (less its tanks) at Camp Mackenzie, under 1st Brigade's operational control.[15]

MG Rhame visited the squadron area that day at 0900 hours. He wanted to discuss the possible movement of B Troop west of Hafar Al Batin to provide security for the Division Support Area Junction City. Upon his arrival, he found that CPT

Tedesco was the senior member of the squadron staff at Camp Mackenzie, so he discussed this mission with him and directed that the squadron begin initial planning.[16] LTC Wilson arrived from port later that afternoon and Tedesco briefed him on the general's visit and his planning guidance.

On January 18, CPT Bills and MAJ Burdan drove toward the Wadi Al-Batin to see what routes the squadron would use when it moved to the division's designated attack position due west of TAA Roosevelt. The Wadi Al-Batin is a dry riverbed that ultimately forms Kuwait's western boundary. It is about half a mile wide and ringed by small hills and low ridges. With no trees in the region, it was one of the few landmarks available for desert travelers. It was clear to both officers that this was an avenue of approach into Saudi Arabia that the Iraqis could use in an attack south. Indeed, in 633 AD this feature guided the Muslim armies as they began their conquest of Persia. Until the beginning of the air campaign, General Schwarzkopf had done everything in his power to convince Saddam Hussein that this was exactly the avenue his forces would take when they attempted to liberate Kuwait. This terrain feature was also the boundary line between the VII Corps's tactical assembly area in the east, and its attack zone in the west.[17]

Bills and Burdan knew that the 1st Cavalry Division was operating in that area and that friendly Arab units were stationed along the border with Iraq. A Syrian unit that was repositioning eastward across the corps's front startled them, as the two American officers were not used to the sight of Soviet-made vehicles as friendly forces. For all their military lives, these officers had trained to destroy this kind of equipment; now they were on the same side. Of course, since the Iraqis used many of the same type of Soviet-made tanks, trucks, and personnel carriers, the possibilities of confusion and mistaken identity were real. They returned to the squadron that evening.[18]

That same afternoon a British signal unit arrived in the squadron area and set up approximately one mile to the north. As part of the overall operation, they were providing communications for the British units in the corps area. Quarter Horse's enterprising mess steward, SFC Zahniser, wasted no time in catching a ride over to its assembly area to find out how they were set for rations. He ended up trading some standard, but boring, B-rations and MREs for some British fare. Soldiers of the other troops also took advantage of the opportunity to trade for food and uniform items, providing a useful diversion and the development of some mutual understanding and respect between the two armies.

Iraqi Scud attacks were the prime indicator that the Iraqis were fighting back against the coalition. These inaccurate Soviet–made missiles caused quite a degree of terror during the war since they could be armed with either chemical or high-explosive warheads. Early on January 19 the squadron's sleep was interrupted as SCUDs noisily flew over the camp. Someone called, "Gas, Gas, Gas" over the division command radio net because an M8 chemical alarm alerted in the 1st Engineer Battalion's assembly area. In response, the squadron put on all of its chemical protective clothing and masks. This was very uncomfortable, but served to heighten the squadron's sense of discipline. At 0230 hours, the division ordered units to go back to normal status, as subsequent testing showed no sign of a chemical hazard.[19]

As the squadron prepared for its security mission, the division placed it back under its control and assigned it detachments from support units to provide special capabilities. Often, it took time to bring these soldiers up to the appropriate level of readiness for their part in the unit's mission. For example, the Stinger (an air-defense artillery missile) section that arrived on January 19 had a number of problems. While it did have thirty missiles, it had no maps, flak jackets, or communications equipment.[20] Similar issues took place with the arrival of CPT Gary Rahmeyer's field artillery fire support element, 1LT Jimmie Mitchel's Air Force liaison team, and the combat engineers. Once they joined the squadron, they had to achieve the same level of readiness as the remainder of the unit.

Meanwhile the movement of the remaining squadron elements from the port to Camp Mackenzie continued. The next major group to depart the port consisted of the small but essential aviation troops (C/D/E). On January 19, the wheeled convoy departed in the morning and arrived in TAA Roosevelt around 0700 hours the next day. It immediately headed for an assembly area with the remainder of the Aviation Brigade's aviation units. The aviation troops' assembly area consisted of sand walls, called berms, originally constructed to protect the helicopters from observation and artillery. The engineers had anchored steel tie-downs into the ground for the aircraft to prevent damage in case of high winds. However, as it turned out, the berms were too small to accommodate the aircraft, so they became the aviation troops' temporary home. The squadron's twenty-one aircraft departed on the morning of January 20, and, after making one stop at Assembly Area Bastogne, all arrived at the Aviation Brigade's assembly area around 1530 hours that afternoon.[21]

Now that much of the squadron's combat power was in TAA Roosevelt, its emphasis shifted to training and weapons test firing and zeroing. The troopers took every opportunity to hone their combat skills. Sergeants directed individual soldiers, generally covering both survival skills, such as preparation for a chemical attack, and combat skills, such as firing weapons and determining if the vehicle in front of you was enemy or friendly. Sergeants also supervised collective, or group, training at the crew and section level, since a tank, Bradley, or mortar crew had to function as a team to succeed. 2LT Gerardo Cartegena, the squadron chemical officer, was in high demand as a training advisor as the troops emphasized the possibility of a chemical attack in both their training and wartime planning.

The squadron leaders practiced with the new GPS. In what was an amazing transformation from the World War II era of map and compass, the operator simply entered the location of his destination and followed directions. The GPS was extremely effective and allowed the ground units to maneuver with impunity over the battlefield, without worrying about landmarks and compass headings. There were never enough of these precious devices. In B Troop, for example, there were only six: one each for the commander, executive officer, first sergeant, and each of the three platoon leaders. Even with this shortage, CPT Bills later considered it one of his most important systems.[22]

In the desert near the enemy lines, crews had a chance to fire service ammunition for the first time. Service, or wartime, ammunition has a different feel than training ammunition when fired. Of course, when it hits the target, the results are much more deadly. The VII Corps established a weapons firing complex called Jayhawk Range, and each corps combat unit had a chance to rotate crews through the various firing ranges. Its primary purpose was to test fire and calibrate all vehicle weapons, a process called bore sighting, so that the round hit where the gunner aimed. The squadron took advantage of its gunnery time and sent B Troop's Bradleys to the range from January 21 through 23. It was an important event, as Mike Bills discovered when his troop went to the range. One of his non-commissioned officers had put his 25-mm Bushmaster cannon back together improperly and did not ensure the weapon's barrel was properly seated in the receiver. The first round fired ruined it. On January 22, the squadron sent its UH-1 back to the port to get a new barrel from one of its old M3s and bring it out as a replacement for the damaged barrel.[23]

Shortly after midnight, on January 22, CPT Ken Pope led a convoy of seven M3A2s, three M106 mortar tracks, one M577, and two trucks toward Camp Mackenzie.[24] The troopers were glad to see the port in their rear view mirrors as they headed out to the desert. They arrived at Camp Mackenzie late that afternoon. The air troops also flew out that morning to the firing range and test fired all of their weapons, to include their version of the TOW wire-guided missiles. Fog and dust began to set in shortly after they finished firing late in the afternoon. As they flew back to the Aviation Brigade helicopter assembly area, the visibility continued to drop. Finally, they were unable to proceed, so they set down in the middle of the desert, radioed their location, and waited until the next morning to get back into the air.

The next day, CPT Scott Sauer, the assistant S3, led the last convoy, including nine M1A1s and four M3A2s, from the port to the assembly areas. On the way, a HET carrying tanks rear-ended another one about five miles outside Dhahran. The tanks received no significant damage and the convoy continued on its way.

CPT Pope spent January 24 reorganizing his troop due to a shortage of scouts. He retained 1st and 2nd platoons as scout platoons with the 3rd platoon designated as a "reaction platoon." It would consist of 2LT Palmieri in an M3A2 and his three M1A1 tanks. While A Troop was not quite ready for combat, Wilson finally had most of his command together in the desert and was preparing them for combat as fast as humanly possible.

In one of the last and most dramatic acts of this phase of operations, CSM Michael Cobb, working the system as only a senior noncommissioned officer could, found most of the critical equipment A Troop needed to become fully operational. Taking a representative from the squadron S4, he visited the corps's logistics base. There, pressing the flesh and smooth talking people, he was able to solve many problems. In the truck that followed him back to camp were machine guns for the tanks and M3s, GVS-5 laser designators, flak vests, crew helmets, and nearly all the critical equipment CPT Ken Pope needed to make his forming A Troop combat ready. While it is a tale that may make supply bureaucrats cringe, it is a testimony to the ability of the soldiers that deployed to the Persian Gulf in the winter of 1990-91. Without the dedication and initiative of soldiers such as Mike Cobb, none of the army's technology would have mattered much on the battlefield.

The next day, January 25, A Troop went to the firing range. For A Troop, this was the first time many of the crews had ever shot from a Bradley. Each crew fired approximately fifty rounds from the 25-mm Bushmaster and one TOW antitank missile. CPT Pope used the movement to the range as an opportunity for training as he put the troop through a series of reaction drills. For CPT Pope, this exercise was important because it was the first time his troop had ever maneuvered as a unit.[25] A Troop however, had little time to settle down in the tactical assembly area. Almost immediately, the squadron began moving across the Wadi al Batin and to the Iraqi border.

6 Security Operations

Nothing in MAJ Silvia Marable's career as a logistics officer had prepared her for the situation in which she now found herself. Marable commanded Division Support Area (DSA) Junction City in the 1st Infantry Division's forward assembly area, located in the middle of the Arabian Desert. This barren facility was less than thirty miles from Iraqi units to the north and over seventy-five miles from the closest American combat troops in TAA Roosevelt to the southeast. She was here to supervise the large amount of supplies that the Division Support Command, or DISCOM, was stockpiling in preparation for the anticipated offensive against Iraq. Because of the great distance, she had trouble communicating back to division headquarters and had little understanding of the tactical changes taking place around her. Every day new units from the DISCOM traveled along the network of dusty trails that terminated south of the Iraqi border. With them came the thousands of tons of fuel, ammunition, food, and repair parts that allowed a mechanized division to fight. In addition, units from VII Corps were arriving to set up their own support areas, both in the DSA and in the corps's Logistics Base (Logbase) Echo, located near a cluster of old houses a few miles to the southwest. To defend this vulnerable, expanding logistics complex, Marable had only a platoon of military police.[1]

Generals Franks and Rhame were becoming increasingly concerned about the safety of these logistics areas. Even a small Iraqi raid by a squad of commandos with explosives and machine guns could cause massive damage and inflict the equivalent of a tactical defeat on the American forces. Such a raid could delay the grand offensive scheduled for late February. Since Logbase Echo and the breach area were in the 1st Infantry Division's sector, the corps commander directed Rhame to protect the developing logistics complex. The division commander decided to turn the mission over to LTC Bob Wilson and his 1st Squadron, 4th Cavalry.[2]

On January 20, Wilson officially learned that his unit would be assigned to protect the division and corps logistics areas. His original orders were to move B Troop in two days; however, Rhame put the mission on hold the night before because of concerns at army and corps headquarters. The senior chain of command was worried that American armored vehicles would be seen by Iraqi patrols and compromise the entire theater deception plan by revealing combat units well to the west of the Wadi al Batin. After some clarification of orders, the division instructed Wilson to move B Troop on January 24 and he ordered CPT Mike Bills to begin breaking camp. Meanwhile, the squadron commander and MAJ Burdan began studying the division's logistics overlay to develop a plan for how B Troop would secure that sector. On the night of January 23, the planning pace intensified as the division operations officer, LTC Bullington, augmented his previous instructions with a prescribed route to DSA Junction City.[3] For the next twenty-four days, the squadron would establish a screen line, conduct security operations, and eventually form the basis of a larger ad-hoc task force called Combat Command Carter.

CPT Bills's troop, including his six new tanks, his field artillery forward observers (called a FIST or fire support team), under 1LT Jorge Carbello, and other squadron support elements departed at 0800 on January 24 and became the first VII Corps combat element to cross the Wadi al Batin. It headed west, twenty kilometers north of the town of Hafar al Batin to avoid observation by local civilians who were reportedly in sympathy with the Iraqis. With only their Global Positioning System receivers to guide their movements, these troopers stayed off the Tapline Road and away from the town to remain undetected. They arrived in a region where the only important landmark was the never-ending border berm that separated Iraq from Saudi Arabia.[4]

The troop did not simply road march in column to its new location. Since they were traveling cross-country anyway, it was an excellent chance to practice combat maneuvers and integrate the new tanks into the platoon tactical organization. Traveling in battle formation in the open desert is much more difficult than it sounds. Training areas at Fort Riley and in Germany were small and forced vehicles to cluster together more closely than is tactically sound. It required practice getting used to such wide spaces and Bills used all seventy miles to drill proper movement techniques into the minds of his young platoon leaders and track commanders. Practicing a classic zone reconnaissance, Bills put his troop through a variety of battle formations and action drills as he worked through the problems of small-unit command. These normal difficulties were aggravated by the shortage of maps, with only enough for the commander and his platoon leaders and platoon sergeants.[5]

MAJ Marable, who had been expecting another military police platoon, was quite pleased when the reassuring firepower of tanks and Bradleys laagered outside of her small assembly area late that afternoon. Unfortunately, the logistics officer could tell the troop almost nothing of the friendly or enemy situation. Given the nebulous environment, Bills decided it was best to deploy his troop in a screen, or security line, a few kilometers north of the logistics area while 1SGT David Rooks coordinated with Marable's command sergeant major for fuel and water. From the cavalry soldiers' perspective they were now at war, and would remain on a combat footing for the next thirty days.[6]

The mission "screen" is the lowest level of combat security, providing only protection from enemy observation. Such a mission does not include decisive combat operations against an attacking force. Once B Troop was in position, it quickly became obvious that one troop was just too small to do even that job alone. Early on the afternoon of January 24, Wilson and Rhame discussed their options, and after obtaining the corps commander's approval, planning began to move the remainder of the squadron to DSA Junction City. The air troops would move the next day followed by A Troop (when they were ready) and the remainder of the HHT. Wilson ordered Burdan to relocate to the new sector to control the squadron as it arrived. MAJ Burdan

left for DSA Junction City the next day. Once there, he established a forward command post with B Troop's CP and prepared to receive the rest of the squadron.

Moving the aviation troops was a complicated undertaking.
First, they had to complete the relocation from the 4th Brigade's
airfield to Camp Mackenzie and then they immediately had to
reorganize for the move to Junction City. By 2200 hours on January 24, most of the aviators had arrived at Camp Mackenzie,
although some of the support vehicles would trickle in
throughout the night and into the morning. Early the next
morning, CPT Chris Philbrick led the aviation troops' support
vehicles west toward B Troop. Of course, Philbrick did not have
a map and led the convoy by a little luck and occasional radio
calls to CPT Bills who was on the newly formed screen line.
Somehow, he turned off Tapline Road at the right spot and was
soon driving north, past the corps logistics base. Working on
rather vague orders, the aviators continued north, chose a spot
and "circled the wagons."

The helicopters arrived late on the afternoon of January 25
after some of them had had their own adventure on the way.
One of the helicopter flights had trouble finding the squadron
command post and landed near a collection of army vehicles. It
turned out to be an isolated corps maintenance unit, all in dug-
in positions and manning their weapons and machine guns.
"Man are we glad to see you guys!" exclaimed the maintenance
company commander at the sight of the four Cobras and six
scout aircraft. "We think that we have some Iraqis in vehicles
over there behind those hills. Can you help us out?" Although
he doubted that there was anything this far south of the border,
the aviation commander, CPT Jim Tovsen, directed 2LT Steve
Gruenig to take a scout weapons team and "bound out to see if
you can see anything." Gruenig found nothing. Tovsen told the
maintenance commander to relax and the troop took off to locate the remainder of the squadron.[7] The next day COL Mowery arrived in Junction City and visited the Air Troop Assembly
Area. He remarked that they were in the wrong spot, but they
could stay where they were. Philbrick, however, was quite concerned when he discovered that his group was *north* of the B
Troop line. For several nights the ground scouts reported

"troops moving" and the aviators, concerned that someone might be a little trigger happy, had to call back "it's us!"[8]

As the squadron closed on DSA Junction City, CPT Bills continued to screen the logistics area, a task complicated by the local Bedouins. While the Saudi Arabian government had told the local tribesmen to evacuate the border region, many remained. On January 26, after visiting a coordination point with the 1-7 Cavalry in the east, CPT Bills discovered what appeared to be a Bedouin in a Toyota pickup truck driving slowly around the squadron's assembly area at DSA Junction City. Bills tried to intercept him in his M3 Bradley, but the driver saw him coming and sped northward deeper into the desert. Bills gave chase, reaching speeds of over forty miles per hour in his attempt to catch him. The captain fired a warning burst from his Bushmaster cannon, but the truck, bouncing all over the place in the desert sand, still did not stop. Realizing that he would not be able to catch him and afraid that he was going to give the squadron's location away to someone on the other side, Bills ordered one of his observation posts that lay in the path of the truck to mount up and stop it.

Pulling out of his prepared position, SSG Michael Cowden moved to intercept. Again, the American armored vehicles were unable to catch the truck and it looked as if the Bedouin might get away. Carefully judging the distance Cowden ordered his gunner to fire a warning shot. At thirty-five miles per hour, the gunner carefully lay his crosshairs on the target and fired a shot first to the left of the truck and then to its right. The Bedouin's response was to drive faster. Realizing that the Bedouin had to be stopped, the sergeant gave the order to shoot the truck. His gunner put a round through the rear bumper and into the truck's left tire, causing it to come to a screeching halt. The driver leaped out the vehicle and threw his hands into the air, yelling "No shoot! No shoot!" Cowden then loaded him into his track and returned to the troop, where Bills sent him straight back to the squadron assembly area.[9]

This generated a new dilemma as, for the first time, the squadron had a prisoner. The correct procedure after disarming and checking for documents and equipment is to evacuate the captive to the closest prisoner of war camp. Unfortunately,

Marable had not given any serious consideration as to where to put prisoners when she laid out the DSA. After discussing the situation Majors Burdan and Marable decided the prisoner would be turned directly over to the division MP platoon. The Bedouin was placed in a vacant tent near the military police platoon. The captive told interpreters who worked with the MPs that he was a Saudi whose family, contrary to the orders to leave the area, was still in the desert to the northwest, and had stopped to look at our camp because he was curious. The command post called the Saudi police to help resolve the situation, and they arrived as a Bradley towed the Bedouin's damaged truck into the assembly area. Meanwhile, the Saudis decided that the captive was not a threat and released him. The result was that within two days of the capture, the scattered nomad camps that were in the staging area west of the Wadi al Batin had vanished. Apparently, it was getting too dangerous and the tribesmen decided to take their government's word that they needed to move farther south.

Meanwhile A Troop continued its preparations for combat, and as late as January 24, this was still Wilson's primary concern. Many of its scouts were still new to their weapons systems and in one instance CPT Pope found some of his Bradleys with their guns pointed straight in the air, a serious violation for armored vehicles. His quick investigation indicated that the crews were not quite sure of themselves, and trying to figure out how the system worked. The good news was that his three tank crews were good shots and were ready to go. However, still short of soldiers to man three full platoons, he reorganized the troop into two normal platoons and a reaction platoon with three tanks and three Bradleys. He sent his remaining three M3A2s to the field trains until he had sufficient soldiers to man them. They returned to him about ten days later with partial crews. With this modification, Pope told the squadron commander on January 26 that he was ready. The troop departed TAA Roosevelt for DSA Junction City early the next day, along with the squadron command post and Headquarters Troop. Throughout the movement to the desert, Pope had his crews practice fire commands and basic crew drill.[10]

By late afternoon on the twenty-seventh, the entire squadron was at Junction City. The command post set up near the Division Support Command, and Burdan transferred all of his maps and information from B Troop to his own command post vehicle. After making contact with 1st Squadron, 7th Cavalry (1st Cavalry Division) on its right flank, the squadron began to acclimate to its new desolate surroundings. In addition, it was now well beyond the span of effective division command and control. Communication between the unit and division headquarters still back in TAA Roosevelt was tenuous and sometimes intermittent.[11]

The squadron was now deployed in its combat configuration. The center of squadron command activities was the tactical operations center or TOC. It centered on three M577 Command Post Vehicles belonging to the S2 (Intelligence), S3 (Operations), and the FSE (artillery Fire Support Element) staff sections. It also had vehicles from the Air Force liaison officer (ALO) and the division signal battalion. From within this command post, squadron staff officers, especially Captains VJ Tedesco, Scott Sauer, and Shelby Seelinger, and CPT Dave Wallace (the squadron signal officer who ranged between all the command posts) managed all squadron activities under the supervision of the executive officer, MAJ Bill Wimbish. LTC Wilson and MAJ Burdan usually worked from the command post, but operated from their M3s or HMMWVs when on the move.

The squadron's logistics activities were organized into combat and field trains.[12] CPT Harmon, the S4 (Logistics) officer, ran the combat trains. The S1/S4 M577, also known as the ALOC (Administrative-Logistics Center), was the heart of this organization. It also included Chaplain Lou Parker's HMMWV, medical ambulances, maintenance and recovery vehicles, and ten-ton trucks loaded with fuel (called Supply Class III), and ammunition (called Supply Class V). The job of the combat trains was to follow closely behind the combat elements and provide them emergency logistics support, as well as coordinate more deliberate re-supply and maintenance operations.

The field trains, led by the Headquarters Troop commander CPT Doug Morrison, controlled the large number of supply, maintenance, and other support vehicles that routinely followed mechanized units. Working in the M577 assigned to the squadron's communications section, he coordinated a mess section, the medical platoon, maintenance platoon, maintenance personnel sent from the direct support battalion, and initially at least, the three M3A2 Bradleys that A Troop could not fully crew.

Wilson commanded the fighting elements of the squadron through three subordinate command posts. CPT Bills's B Troop was in position on the screen line and was joined by CPT Pope's A Troop on January 28. Both unit commanders led from their M3A2 Cavalry Fighting Vehicles, accompanied by a fire-support team vehicle (a modified M3 called the FIST-V), while their executive officers coordinated troop activities from M577 Command Post Vehicles. CPT Christopher Philbrick's Flight Operations acted as the third subordinate command post. Normally located in the 4th Brigade assembly area during static operations, it now set up just west of the squadron TOC. Flight Operation's mission was to coordinate the combat activities of CPT Jim Tovson's C Troop, CPT Roy Peter's D Troop, and CPT Peter Smith's supporting E Troop.

As the squadron settled in, Wilson's immediate task was to protect the corps forward logistics depot; he therefore had to assess the threat. He deployed air and ground patrols to locate any units in the area. Again, the image of the seamless war portrayed on television disintegrates when confronted by the evidence of unprotected units scattered around the desert. The scouts discovered a corps equipment maintenance unit about ten kilometers west of the squadron's screen line, and a communications unit, with sensitive equipment, even farther away. With nothing between them and the Iraqi units north of the border, they were quite vulnerable.

In another instance, a VII Corps ordnance company began driving north towards Iraq past the squadron's positions. Its company commander was navigating with a large-scale (1:250,000) map, compass, and the vehicle odometer. He did not have a GPS and was quite relieved when MAJ Burdan drove over in his M3 Bradley. The captain explained to Burdan that they were going to set up a corps ammunition supply point a few kilometers north of the squadron. In other words, this unprotected ammunition unit, without appropriate navigation equipment or security, was heading towards Iraq! Burdan briefed the ordnance officer on the squadron's mission, exchanged radio signs and frequencies, and directed them towards their ultimate location. Based upon encounters such as these, Wilson decided to move his screen line a few kilometers north to protect these and other newcomers.

Wilson, Wimbish, and Burdan soon realized the magnitude of their task of protecting a growing number of logistics units in a sector almost seventy kilometers wide. This was far too wide for a small divisional cavalry squadron to provide surveillance twenty-four hours a day. Despite this problem, the squadron's leaders did their best in executing the screen. Pope's A Troop assumed surveillance duties on the sector's western fifteen kilometers while Bills's B Troop observed the next twenty kilometers. Each ground troop deployed its platoons forward along an imaginary line. Typically, each platoon set up two observation posts, "OPs" in army jargon, consisting of two M3 Bradleys and ten soldiers led by a scout section staff sergeant. The observation posts were between three and four kilometers apart. Located farther to the rear was the platoon leader with the remaining CFVs and tanks. The vehicles were generally in the open and exposed, the terrain allowing little opportunity for cover or concealment.[13]

This deployment of the ground troops left about thirty-five kilometers between B Troop and the 1st Cavalry Division to the east unobserved. Wilson did the best he could to screen this area by sending out a series of ground patrols supplemented by helicopter reconnaissance patrols. Flying during the day was no problem and the scout-weapons teams gained valuable flying experience. However, flying at night was problematic as the dark desert night seldom provided enough ambient light for the pilots to effectively use their AN/AVS-6 Aviation Night Vision Imaging Systems. Flying was so difficult that they were unable to perform their tactical mission, so Wilson asked COL Mowery for support from the Aviation Brigade's AH-64A Apaches and OH-68D Kiowas, both equipped with the most sophisticated night optics available, to cover his sector during hours of darkness. In response to this request, the division placed a company of Apache attack helicopters from 1-1 Aviation Bn under the operational control (OPCON) of the squadron.[14]

In the course of conducting his operations, LTC Wilson discovered his unit was not the only one conducting activities along the border. The executive officer for the VII Corps Long Range Surveillance Unit (LRSU) drove into the squadron command post late on January 27. As its name implies, the LRSU's task is to move into hostile territory forward of the corps and observe the enemy. Its mode of operation was to establish small, hidden, observation posts, consisting of two or three soldiers, and locate and report on the enemy using night vision equipment and other detection devices. LTG Franks directed CPT Donald Clark, the unit commander, to observe this sector at the same time the squadron received its orders to do the same. Of course, this was not coordinated properly as neither the squadron nor the division had any indication they would be in the area. The LRSU company executive officer set up his small command post about twenty yards away from the squadron TOC. Although Wilson's troops were supposed to evacuate these teams in case they ran into problems or were attacked by Iraqi troops, the reconnaissance unit's executive officer would not permit the cavalrymen to know exactly where these teams were, as they reported their intelligence information directly to the VII Corps headquarters. When the corps G2 lost communications with the reconnaissance unit, they called the 1st Infantry Division who then called the squadron command post, which then sent a runner to find the unit commander. This breakdown of communications was frequent enough for the corps commander to extract the LRSU on January 31.[15]

Initially, the screen line was fairly quiet; however, things soon changed. At 0315 hours on February 1, a small convoy of Arab soldiers ran into A Troop's screen line. With no warning, and concerned about reports of Iraqi activity north of the border, the troop responded with caution. Each of the nine small pickup trucks had a .50-caliber machine gun mounted on its bed and was accompanied by a total of fifty-two soldiers. One of the Bradley crew fired a 25-mm HEAT (High Explosive, Antitank) round across the front of the column to get them to stop, creating quite a bit of confusion. The scouts approached and found an English-speaking soldier who was upset at being fired at. They all claimed to be Saudi Arabian soldiers who had an outpost near a collection of huts along the border called As Samah. Allegedly, Iraqi troops had attacked them and their headquarters ordered them to fall back to the American lines, leaving behind radios and personal equipment. Taking no chances, Pope's troopers disarmed them and asked for instructions. Meanwhile, now under guard, the Arab soldiers lay down for the night. The next morning the word came that they were indeed Saudis and that they were to be released at once. The squadron's shift officers apologized profusely and then sent them on their way.[16]

A few hours later, four Iraqi soldiers wandered across the border and into B Troop's sights. After a scout section fired a few rounds of machine-gun fire in their direction they stopped, raised their hands, and waved a white flag at the approaching Bradley. While they claimed to be deserting, they had weapons with them and had buried several hand grenades before the Americans arrived. So, the squadron's officers did not accept the Iraqi explanation and suspected that this was a long-range patrol sent south to discover what was on the other side of the border. Again, there were some interesting moments as the division and corps figured out how to process prisoners, obviously a task the senior headquarters had not planned on performing so early in the deployment.[17]

With dawn, things quieted down, but that night at around 1830 hours the activity along the border resumed. A ground surveillance radar squad identified vehicles moving toward the screen line. Taking no chances, Rhame ordered the aviation brigade to deploy Apaches to the 1-4 Cavalry's sector. At 2045 hours, after a briefing by Wilson, LTC Ralph Hayles led a team from his battalion on a sweep forward of the cavalry screen line.[18] As Hayles and his wingman flew near CPT Bills's sector and prepared to return south of the squadron, they received radar warning signals from their on-board sensors that there were anti-aircraft systems in the vicinity. He reported the coordinates to the squadron command post and requested permission to engage. Wilson, monitoring events in the TOC, denied his request and asked both ground troops to confirm their outpost locations. He ordered Hayles to take up positions behind Mike Bills's M3A2. Hovering behind Bills, Hayles soon reported an unidentified movement about 500 meters forward of the screen line. As the troop commander stood up in his turret for a better look, a burst of green tracer arched up towards the helicopter hovering behind him. Hayles shouted a warning and took evasive action, backing off from the line. Bills still could not see where the fire was coming from, but when he heard the rounds bouncing off his vehicle, he too dove for cover. Then the fire ended as quickly as it had begun and an eerie quiet returned to the screen line. The Apaches continued to pick up movement in and around the screen line but the reports could not be confirmed by the OPs.[19]

While Wilson waited for the troops to verify their locations, he cross-referenced the reported enemy location on his map. Soon he determined that the alleged enemy unit identified by Hayles was an A Troop vehicle. He was furious and scolded the troop first sergeant, who had been monitoring the situation, for not knowing the actual location of his unit and for not making sure that the aviators knew they were friendly. Thus avoiding a potential fratricide incident, the squadron commander directed the Apaches to cease-fire and move out of the area. From that moment forward, Wilson made it standard procedure to always be on the command net when Apaches were passing through or operating within the squadron's area of operations.[20]

Early the next morning, B Troop noted more movement toward the screen line and its scouts fired two TOW missiles, both of which missed the targets. In addition to the Iraqi patrols, there were other indications that the Iraqi forces were interested in this sector. As LTC Hayles was returning from his engagement around 0300 hours that morning (February 2), he noticed a break in the border berm. Another Apache flight after dawn confirmed the break that opened onto a primitive road into Saudi Arabia. In front of the gap were several "dragon's teeth" or cement blocks designed to slow vehicle movement. Soon, patrols discovered other gaps and an Iraqi bulldozer hard at work tearing into the berm. A squadron Cobra helicopter destroyed the offending bulldozer that morning, scattering the Iraqi soldiers working in the area. Cavalry reconnaissance patrols later found three additional gaps in the berm with new antitank ditches in front of them. The 1st Division Intelligence Officer (G2), LTC Terrance Ford, believed that the Iraqis were be-coming bolder with the recent departure of the Saudi border guards, and were about to begin operations in the division's sector.[21] The situation was becoming far more extensive than Wilson could manage with his small unit and staff. He decided to ask for help.

7   Combat Command Carter

Even before Wilson asked for help, MG Rhame was discussing the situation with the corps commander. The battle at Khafji at the end of January and numerous reports of Iraqi movements since, caused the generals to reconsider the security arrangements for the corps logistics base. Certainly, a similar effort near the Wadi al Batin could have disastrous consequences.[1] From a tactical perspective, the 1-4 Cavalry was beyond American artillery support and would be unable to stop a determined Iraqi raid on the growing logistics installation. The recent Iraqi troop movements opposite the squadron suggested either possible Iraqi probes or an improvement of their defensive positioning along the border. Either way, it was essential to change the nature of the operation and improve the corps's defensive posture in this critical sector. Therefore, on January 31, Rhame issued orders to form a small brigade task force under his Assistant Division Commander for Maneuver (ADC-M), Brigadier General (BG) William G. Carter III. Called Combat Command (CC) Carter, it would assume command authority for the sector and add additional combat power to the security force.[2]

LTC David Gross's Task Force (TF) 3rd Battalion, 37th Armor; LTC Harry Emerson's 1st Battalion, 5th Field Artillery; and the division's tactical command post or DTAC would join the Quarter Horse on the line.[3] With this ad hoc command, Carter's mission was to conduct security operations to protect DSA Junction City and screen the movement of the division's maneuver brigades into the sector. As part of this organization,

80

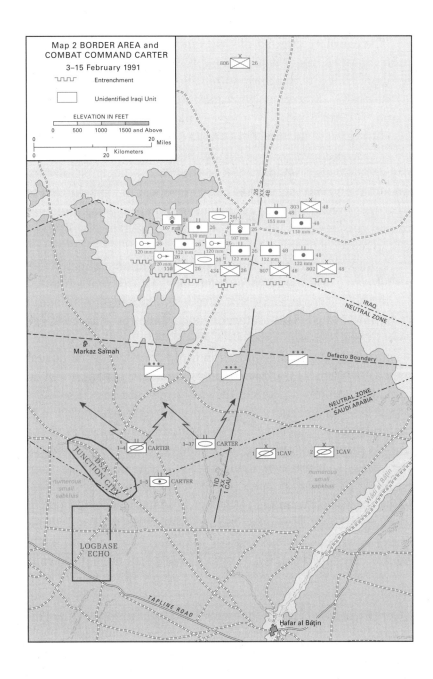

Map 2 BORDER AREA and
COMBAT COMMAND CARTER
3–15 February 1991

the squadron would continue to gain proficiency, prepare for the upcoming corps offensive, conduct border patrols and surveillance activities, and conduct small-scale raids and attacks.

The combat command's advance party arrived on the morning of February 3 and the main body followed the next afternoon. Along with armor and artillery, the DTAC brought its sophisticated radio and telephone equipment to allow the command to communicate with the remainder of the division. It also brought the most recent version of the division attack plan, called Scorpion Danger, which planners had continued to refine since the squadron had moved to the border. The division continued to prepare for its attack and periodically MAJ Burdan or LTC Wilson returned to TAA Roosevelt to discuss the details of the operation with COL Lon E. (Burt) Maggart, the 1st Brigade Commander, and the division staff.[4]

Combat Command Carter's primary mission was security and this role dominated most of its effort. MG Rhame reminded Carter not to engage in combat unless attacked and to avoid electronic and physical detection since the entire chain of command, from Rhame through General Schwarzkopf, did not wish to draw the Iraqis' attention to this portion of the border area. LTC Gross's task force, with three tank companies and an infantry company, took over the eastern twenty-five kilometers of the line on February 4, reducing the squadron's sector to about thirty kilometers. Like Wilson, Gross was one of the army's rising stars and destined to achieve the rank of general officer. For the next two weeks the two units policed the Iraq-Saudi Arabian border. Tank and Bradley crews occupied observation posts and used their systems' powerful thermal sights to monitor activity along the berm. Ground surveillance radar crews monitored possible Iraqi avenues of approach, while mortar sections occupied firing positions behind the forward screen line. The command used its Cobras and OH-58C helicopters to investigate any possible activity to avoid disclosing the presence of American ground troops. In support, as required, were also the 4th Brigade's OH-58D, a more sophisticated version of the OH-58 with target acquisition sensors and a laser range finder mounted in a sphere above the main rotor, and AH-64 helicopters with their night operations capability.[5]

With Gross's task force now in the sector, Wilson was able to pull one platoon at a time from each troop off the screen line and back to the assembly area. There the unit commanders supervised the training these platoons would need during the assault, including conducting a zone reconnaissance and a hasty attack. These skills were perishing while the troopers occupied their stationary observation posts. This training was especially important for CPT Pope who had only worked with his platoon leaders for a short period of time, and would pay great dividends later. Combat crews continued preparing for their upcoming assault, rotating back to a firing range in the rear. There, the tank crews finally had the chance to calibrate their guns with their optical sights and fire 120-mm service rounds for the first time. Mortar squads practiced adjusting their indirect fires, and scout crews, in their new M3A2 Cavalry Fighting Vehicles, practiced acquiring, and without actually pulling the trigger, engaging targets. It took time to work out all of the little problems in the new systems. The air troops also used this time to train their troopers. The troop commanders and their platoon leaders worked with their pilots to develop the scout-weapon teamwork needed to ensure survival on the battlefield. Daily air patrols along the screen line helped to establish the needed routines and coordination requirements between flight operations, the squadron tactical operations center, and the ground/air troops. As a rule, the squadron tried to match C Troop aviators with A Troop and the D Troop aviators with B Troop. CPT Pete Smith's aircraft maintenance teams did a masterful job of supporting all of this air activity by keeping the squadron's aircraft repaired and serviced. This was not an easy task as the flow of repair parts was not as steady as it was stateside and the flying environment was far more hostile.[6]

One of the most serious equipment problems encountered by the squadron during this period was with the Bradley's TOW missile systems. One night, a large explosion startled the command and everyone went on alert. Rather than enemy soldiers, however, a CFV driver in the maintenance area had caused the commotion. As he turned on the vehicle's master power switch, the two live TOW missiles suddenly launched and flew north, exploding harmlessly in the desert. At first, the leaders believed it was a mistake by the crew. However, as CPT Morrison and CSM Cobb continued their investigation, it became obvious that other squadron Bradleys were having the same problem. The CSM, an experienced soldier who had taught gunnery at Fort Knox, contacted a civilian Bradley technician who happened to be in the squadron area that day. Of course, this manufacturer's representative was convinced it was crew error and there was no need for further investigation. Cobb persisted, and pointed out that it would be bad public relations if the media were to discover that soldiers were going to war with defective equipment. After that remark, the representative decided to investigate and discovered almost half of the squadron's new Bradley Fighting Vehicles had defective missile circuit boards! Within a short time, the manufacturer, who now had a sense of urgency, located new boards and installed them in the defective vehicles.[7]

One of the less successful aspects of this phase was the use of the division's Long Range Surveillance Detachment, or LRSD, which arrived in the sector after the corps detachment departed. In theory, it worked for and reported to the intelligence section (G2) back at division main command post. As in the case of the corps unit, it was supposed to conduct independent reconnaissance and surveillance missions. Its soldiers were supposed to move stealthily to hidden observation posts well forward of the friendly security zone. There, these small teams would remain, motionless, observing enemy activity. Then at the appointed time, the division would extract them surreptitiously and return them for a debriefing by the intelligence specialists. However, it did not work out quite that way. Because the division commander was concerned about taking needless casualties, its employment was not as bold as the original doctrine writers had envisioned. Rather than establishing posts beyond the view of the forward screen line, the teams were within the observation and direct-fire weapons range of CC Carter. This conservative employment created a number of problems. First, the staff chose to use the cavalry squadron for team insertion and recovery, essentially displaying increased activity for observant Iraqi units who would have little problem identifying helicopters and American vehicles. More important from the task force's perspective, the LRSD teams had no communications with the units on the line behind them. Finally, because they were within observation range of armored vehicle thermal sights and ground surveillance radar, Combat Command Carter's ground outposts often picked up their activity at night.[8]

Almost immediately, this poorly conceived arrangement created serious problems. For example, one night a troop observation post reported that it had detected a small patrol to its front. A check of the LRSD positions posted in the tactical command post indicated that if it was an Iraqi patrol in the area, the two groups were near each other. The distance between the screen line and the LRSD team was far enough to make it difficult to determine what was going on, and without radio communications, it could not contact the reconnaissance team. Rather than risk losing this team, the command ordered B Troop to send out a mounted unit and determine the situation. As it turned out, contrary to doctrine and procedures, the team had left its positions and was moving around, not realizing that in the darkness they were being observed. Of course, once the troop's vehicles arrived and compromised the LRSD's location, it was necessary to extract them. Problems with the division's reconnaissance teams continued until they were withdrawn at the end of the border surveillance mission on February 14.[9]

Another frustrating aspect of border operations during this time was the difficulty in getting permission to engage the enemy. Squadron scout weapons teams, backed up as needed by Apache attack helicopters from the Aviation Brigade, routinely flew across the sector to examine areas where the ground scouts could not or were not permitted to go. Like the Bradley crews, they were anxious and ready for action. For example, at 1500 hours on February 4, a combined C/D Troop scout weapons team under CPT Jim Tovsen flying a patrol along the screen line reported a possible Iraqi Panhard AML light armored vehicle armed with a 90-mm gun along the border berm and asked for permission to engage it. The squadron command post then asked CC Carter's command post, which then had to ask the VII Corps command post, taking about twenty-five minutes before receiving approval. Just before WO1s Gary Notestine and Thomas Copeland had to break contact and return their Cobra to the rear for fuel, they engaged the target with a TOW missile at 3,200 meters. Another scout-weapons team replaced CPT Tovsen's element and confirmed the vehicle as destroyed. Unfortunately, while it had appeared from a distance that it was an armored vehicle of some kind, it later turned out that the squadron had destroyed another bulldozer. The apparent gun tube was part of a broken driver's cage that had a leg sticking out at a 90-degree angle from the driver's seat.[10]

Task Force 3-37 Armor on the screen line to the squadron's east was not having any better luck in developing its combat identification skills. That evening, the cavalry scouts and ground surveillance radar teams began reporting a variety of activity in their sector moving across the combat command's front toward the armored task force's sector. Shortly after 2000 hours, radar determined that something was heading towards its Charlie Team. LTC Gross put his unit on alert and directed his reserve tank platoon into a position to assist the unit on the screen line. Everyone waited, ready to respond. The team commander soon broke the silence and reported that the unknown unit was in sight, but was not sure what the rules of engagement were in dealing with a "camel herd, nationality unknown."[11]

The cavalry ground scouts also became involved in this rash of false identification. On February 6, 2LT Tom Karns, a platoon leader with B Troop, reported three vehicles that appeared to be Soviet-made BTR-60s moving towards his location. The squadron was still prohibited from firing at vehicles along the border without permission. Combat Command Carter's command post confirmed that there were no other friendly units in the area and discussed the situation with the division command post. Meanwhile, the "BTR-60s" had turned back to the north and appeared to be looking for a place to cross over the border barrier and head back into Iraq. MAJ Burdan decided to verify that the vehicles were Iraqi and, if so, destroy them before they could get away.

One of Karns's noncommissioned officers, SSG Jimmy Burnett, was a little concerned about the vehicles, having seen new FOX chemical vehicles, which looked similar to BTRs, back in port a few weeks ago. He persuaded his platoon leader to hold fire until he could take a closer look. Moving forward under the watchful eyes of platoon tank gunners, he was able to determine that they were indeed friendly vehicles and notified his lieutenant. It was a corps-level chemical platoon that was lost and trying to find its way to the 1st Cavalry Division on the combat command's right flank. MAJ Burdan drove to the unit and discovered that the platoon's young lieutenant had no maps, no compass, and no GPS receiver. He was completely confused and believed his platoon was on the *north* (Iraqi) side of the border, rather than still in Saudi Arabia. Burdan got him reoriented and sent him and his platoon in the right direction. Had this platoon managed to cross the berm, its new state-of-the-art vehicles would have been a welcome addition to the Iraqi Army's inventory. A similar incident took place on February 5 as a petroleum re-supply unit was looking for a place to establish a fuel dump. Its senior headquarters had given the commander a location north of the squadron's screen line. Forward of the cavalry screen is not the place to store large amounts of fuel and the cavalry sent them back to the rear.[12]

Surveillance operations from February 3 through 6 were generally uneventful. The squadron's daily journal logs, maintained by Captains VJ Tedesco and Scott Sauer in the tactical operations center, indicate that daytime operations focused on sending out aviation SWT patrols, coordinating with flank and supporting units, and gathering the occasional Iraqi soldier who came south of the border berm seeking to surrender. During the hours of darkness, scouts sometimes picked up unidentified movement on the horizon or occasional flares. These variously colored pyrotechnics apparently had some sort of meaning to the Iraqi unit deployed several miles north. The division G2 believed the flares helped orient Iraqi night patrols. From time to time, the squadron requested AH-64 Apache helicopters to fly forward to investigate this or that sighting.[13]

The activity along the border began to increase the morning of February 5. That day, B Troop scouts watched a light armored vehicle move along the border berm. Possibly, the squadron's attack on the bulldozer (the presumed AML) the day before had caused the Iraqi commander to wonder what was going on in his security zone. That night observation posts, LRSD teams, and GSR crews sent a constant stream of reports indicating that enemy forces were operating near the small town of As Samah, one kilometer north of the screen line. Around 0300 (February 6), Wilson sent his two supporting AH-64s forward to investigate. They discovered an Iraqi truck with two three-man teams, one moving north of the berm and another in the town. The division tactical command post told the squadron not to engage these targets, but to go look for another ten vehicles in the area that their sources indicated were near the town. Unable to find the other target, the crews returned, convinced that something was going on.[14]

That morning, LTC Wilson decided to personally investigate and when the crews of the two OH-58C and two AH-1s arrived at the command post for their morning briefing, the briefer announced that rather than their routine patrol, they were going with the squadron commander on an aerial reconnaissance of the village. As they flew over As Samah, they noted many vehicle tracks. It was the post that formerly held the Saudi Arabian border troops, which the squadron had encountered several days earlier. Now many fresh tracks indicated that someone from north of the berm was visiting this area. The observers could see nothing from the air and Wilson directed one of the Cobras to fire a few rounds of 20-mm in the direction of the village. An Iraqi soldier came running out of one of the buildings, frantically waving his arms and trying to talk to the helicopter pilot.[15]

Wilson, who was obviously caught up in the excitement of the event and not wanting to let the Iraqi soldier get away, decided to land and take the man prisoner himself, a task he should have delegated. In the squadron commander's defense, he was the only person who could dismount for this action (the OH-58 only required a crew of one; if the AH-1 Cobra dismounted its front seat passenger, and subsequently needed to engage the enemy, the pilot would have to do so without the assistance of the assigned gunner). Directing the aerial team to provide cover, Wilson had his pilot land the helicopter and headed for the Iraqi who continued to wave his hands like a madman. Approaching with pistol drawn, Wilson heard him shouting at the Cobra "No more . . . no more shoot," as though the pilot could hear him over the noise. Like any good trooper, the squadron commander disarmed, searched, and secured the captive, who indicated that a couple of his buddies were still in the area. Leaving his prisoner bound on the ground under the watchful eye of a Cobra, Wilson flew in his OH-58C to the nearest B Troop observation post to get some help to search the complex and recover the prisoner. Staff Sergeants Jimmy Burnett and Alvin Fugate were manning that OP with their vehicles and crews. They pulled out of their position and followed the commander, still in his helicopter, back to the village, where they secured the prisoner and conducted a hasty search of the surrounding buildings. They investigated each building, but were not able to find any signs of additional soldiers. Finally, Wilson figured they had been there long enough and loaded the terrified Iraqi in a Bradley and headed back to the screen line.[16]

At around 1300 hours, A Troop scouts reported seeing more activity in the village. Wilson decided to send another team back into the town, this time led by his executive officer MAJ Wimbish. Since tracked vehicles were not supposed to be forward of the screen line, as they had been in the morning, he decided to use the squadron's old UH-1 (Huey) to carry a five-man patrol of A Troop scouts led by SSG Wehage. CPT Morrison, upon hearing what was going on, volunteered to accompany MAJ Wimbish and help him out as needed. In addition, Wimbish had air support from an aerial scout-weapons team and both ground troops ready to launch forward if the patrol got into trouble. They landed near the village and the patrol conducted a search of the buildings, taking about one hour. MAJ Wimbish, concerned that they were taking so long, asked CPT Morrison to locate the team and pull them out. A short while later the team returned to the UH-1. While they had found no Iraqis, they did come away with some radios and documents in Arabic that later turned out to be items left behind by the Saudis when they had evacuated their base.[17]

MG Rhame was furious when he heard what was going on in the cavalry squadron's sector. They were supposed to be on the line quietly observing the border area and protecting the corps and division logistics bases. Not only were they out blowing up vehicles on the border, but also they were launching dismounted raids. To make matters even worse, in violation of

corps and army orders, the cavalry was bringing M3 Cavalry
Fighting Vehicles up to the border area, advertising to the Iraqis
that they no longer faced Saudi border guards but mechanized
troops of the United States Army. The last straw was when the
commanding general realized that his cavalry commander was
out acting like a junior patrol leader. Rhame, who would later
command the division amongst its attacking brigades in an
M1A1 tank, understood how important it was to lead from the
front. He also knew that the job of the commander was to fight
his entire command and use all of the material and human assets at his disposal.

The division commander flew out to CC Carter's headquarters to convey his displeasure with Wilson in person. In his
pointed Louisiana drawl, he made it painfully clear that this
was the last time he wanted his commanders emulating Holly-
wood heroes such as Rambo or John Wayne. He had some darn
good soldiers in his squadron and Wilson needed to use them.
"If you go too far forward," Rhame told him, "you run the risk
of becoming personally involved in the fighting and losing
sight of the need to fight the entire squadron, not just the piece
in your immediate vicinity." The commanding general would
make a point of talking to each of his other battalion commanders in the next few days and pass on the same guidance about
commanding from the front. Dave Gross, Wilson's partner in
CC Carter, remembers Rhame telling him to "keep your hand
off the trigger," and "don't break trail," or try to get out in front
of your subordinate units. He made it clear that there were
plenty of other soldiers to do the killing; the commander's job
is to get them to the right place and right time on the battlefield
and let them do their jobs.[18] Rhame liked Wilson and after his
dressing-down sent him back to the Quarter Horse to get back
to work.

There was no question, however, that there was more activity in the border area. During the night of February 7–8, there
was a rash of remotely piloted vehicle, or RPV, sightings
throughout the command's sector. The coalition had used RPV
in the area for several weeks but this time no one at senior headquarters accepted responsibility. As they flew around, observers noted that the small propeller aircraft made a buzzing

sound and had three flashing lights. On occasion it would emit a white strobe, as if it was taking a picture. John Burdan stepped outside the squadron command post that evening and watched as one circled about 200 feet above him and then departed. A short while later he got the word that it was not a friendly aircraft and was quite unnerved as he was sure that the enemy had discovered his location. Judging by its speed, he decided that first thing in the morning the squadron command post would move to a new location. The RPV returned the next evening; however, the division denied both ground battalions permission to engage. With so many different allied intelligence agencies in Saudi Arabia, no one wanted to shoot down a friendly aircraft by mistake.[19]

The unmanned aircraft was one of two big events that caused Carter and his staff to get excited on February 9. The other was the constant electronic interference, or "jamming," that affected radio communications in the area. The cavalry squadron had, on several occasions, noted at least two or more antennas on a building within As Samah. As that was the only covered, protected location in the area, Carter bet that it was the jamming device's location and ordered the cavalry to destroy it. He also gave the order to shoot down the RPV if it came back. Unfortunately, what transpired that night was not exactly an example of American military prowess.[20]

The small, unmanned, and unidentified aircraft returned around dusk. First, the cavalry observation posts shot at it with machine guns but missed, and it continued flying towards Gross's task force. At 2033 hours, based on BG Carter's previous order, the task force's Stinger air defense team fired a missile at it. Again, the Americans missed and the missile exploded when it reached its maximum range. Meanwhile the little airplane continued to chug along impudently, with its red light and flashing strobe, towards the supporting 1-5 Field Artillery command post farther in the rear. Again, the task force fired a Stinger and again, it blew itself up as the RPV flew away. Later that night another Stinger crew also tried to shoot the RPV down, but the missile lost its lock-on and also self-destructed. Why did the Stinger teams miss? LTC Gross believed it was because of the excessive amount of time it took to get permission to fire, which they had to request through air defense channels. Gross also believed that it had to do with it being a poorly re-hearsed action. Of course, the aircraft was also small and diffi-cult to hit under any circumstances.[21] What seems to have been lost on the participants was that if the goal of the Iraqi com-mander was to discover the location of the enemy troops by causing them to react, then his mission had been accomplished.

The cavalry operation to destroy the building with the an-tennas did not go much better. That evening the division sent an AH-64 to destroy the antennas. It fired a Hellfire missile and about 150 rounds of 30 mm ammunition at them. However, the crew failed to destroy all of the antennas. At 1020 hours the next morning, Wilson ordered a Cobra crew to launch an attack. First they fired 2.75-mm rockets at the facility with no effect. Then they tried to engage with the aircraft's 20-mm cannon, but the gun jammed. Finally, in frustration, they launched two TOW missiles that struck the building and caused one of the re-maining antennas to lean.

That night (February 9–10) the RPV flights and jamming continued, and scouts now observed at least five antennas in and around the building. Carter ordered a flight of AH-64 Apaches forward. They engaged with several Hellfire missiles and destroyed most of the building. However, it was obvious to the aircraft crews that the Iraqis were still active. Frustrated with the resilience of this target, BG Carter decided to use a Copperhead laser-guided artillery round, fired from the 1-5 Field Artillery, to destroy the building. Of course, echoing LTC Gross's previous comments, the engagement had not been re-hearsed. The Copperhead was a complex weapons system that required a combination of good weather and visibility, a trained artillery crew, and a trained observer with a laser designator in the right location on the battlefield. Neither the Apache gunner, who would use his laser designator to identify the target, nor the artillery battery that had to prepare and shoot the round, had ever practiced this kind of engagement before. The helicop-ter gunner initially identified the wrong building and then, *af-ter* the 155-mm Copperhead round was in the air, asked if he needed to continue designating the target (which he did!). LTC Gross recalls scared tank commanders slamming their hatches shut throughout the sector in anticipation of a short round. That is exactly what they got as the round landed short and to the right of the target, followed by a second round that also missed. The next evening, COL Stan Cherrie, the VII Corps G3, told the division to "knock it off" and stop shooting rockets and drawing Iraqi attention to that sector.[22]

For the next couple of days Iraqi activity in and around As Samah continued. During a discussion in Wilson's command post on February 13, the squadron's leadership decided to ask for permission to clear As Samah of Iraqi troops. The 1st Infantry Division, along with the entire VII Corps, was scheduled to begin moving on February 15, from its tactical assembly area, west across the Wadi al Batin, and into designated forward assembly areas in preparation for an attack into Iraq. As part of the preparation for that operation, the division planned to form a task force, under the control of the 3rd Brigade, to establish a screen line north of the border, inside Iraq beginning February 15. The squadron was concerned that with As Samah not secure, an enemy scout could watch the Big Red One's movement to the border and cause the Iraqi high command to react. Therefore, Burdan contacted his counterpart at 3rd Brigade headquarters and conveyed the background of that sector and the squadron's concerns about As Samah. That afternoon, the division command post ordered the clearing of "the town" once and for all. Gross's D/2-16th Infantry supported by Wilson's mortars and medics would clear the town. The concept of operation would be briefed by the infantry company commander to BG Carter.

The squadron's clearing operation on the fourteenth did not go well. The infantry company attacked into As Samah with A Troop prepared to support by fire if required. The company commander used one platoon in support while two dismounted infantry platoons swept through the cluster of buildings. His rules of engagement directed the soldiers to fire only if fired upon by the enemy. Unfortunately, these infantrymen had never actually trained in clearing a built-up area. Even in the case of a small village, urban assault is a difficult task that requires training and rehearsals in advance. Once inside the village the soldiers started shooting, without provocation, and throwing

grenades into the buildings. When it was all over, the infantrymen had wounded three American soldiers and no Iraqis were
in sight. Fortunately, the covering infantry platoon and A Troop
held their fire or the incident could have been worse.[23]

Wilson was in a position to listen to and partially observe
the attack. Once he realized what was happening he ordered
the company to cease-fire and hold in place. He then ordered
the company commander to report; when asked what happened, the company commander said he lost control when the
shooting started. A Troop's executive officer, 1LT Jon S. (Scott)
Raynal, called in a medical evacuation helicopter while the
troop medics treated the wounded. It turned out that the evacuation helicopter did not have the secure communications
equipment that the squadron used. This made it very difficult
to guide it to the pick-up point. The danger was that the Iraqi
Army could monitor open communications and direct artillery
down upon the hapless company at As Samah. The squadron
and the medics worked around the problem, but it was another
example of the kind of difficulties that can happen when units
do not train to combat standards. It was not a good way to end
the final hours of Combat Command Carter. [24]

At 1615 hours that afternoon, the squadron came under operational control of the 3rd Brigade. The brigade had the mission of breaking across the border, creating gaps in the berm,
and setting up a screen line a few kilometers on the other side.
After three weeks of operations, Wilson and his cavalry troopers had adjusted to operations in the desert. As with any unit,
the squadron had had its share of bad reports, confusion, and
wrong decisions. Stories of camel attacks and wisecracks about
the "killer" bulldozer would continue long after they returned
to Fort Riley. However, Wilson and his leaders could look back
on the preceding weeks with pride. The squadron had done its
job with its only unfortunate casualties belonging to the attached infantry company. Ground vehicles and aircraft were
operational and ready for combat. They would now begin to
expand their operations across the border and into Iraq.

8   Task Force Iron

The 1st Infantry Division's 3rd Brigade, commanded by Colonel David Weisman, provided the headquarters for Task Force Iron. Based in northern Germany near the ports of Hamburg and Bremen, it was a relic of the Cold War when planners feared that large armies from the Warsaw Pact would overrun NATO defenses before they could send reinforcements. Formally designated the 2nd Armored Division-Forward, it was now assigned to the 1st Infantry Division bringing the Big Red One up to the normal complement of three brigades. In its role as Task Force Iron, it consisted of two ground battalions (1st Battalion, 41st Infantry and the 1st Squadron, 4th Cavalry). The 4th Battalion, 3rd Field Artillery had the direct support role, backed by sixteen additional battalions of artillery prepared to provide indirect fire support and counter-battery fire. Attack helicopter support came from the 1st Battalion, 1st Aviation, and support for tearing down the berm came from the 317th Engineer Battalion.[1]

Task Force Iron had a two-part mission that would require it to advance north of the border into Iraqi territory. First, it had to win the counter-reconnaissance battle in the sector where the 1st Infantry and the 1st (UK) Armoured Divisions would enter Iraq. These kinds of engagements normally include destroying or repelling the enemy's reconnaissance elements and denying the hostile commander any observation of friendly forces.[2] In this case, it was essential that the Iraqi commander not discover the actual attack's location. If he found out, he could react by maneuvering forces to the area and attacking troop concentrations and combat engineer units with direct and indirect fire. While the American forces would still prevail, the division's attack would be much bloodier and slower than need be. The second part of the task force's mission was to cut gaps in the border barrier to allow the assaulting forces to cross it without delay.[3]

Task Force Iron began its operation at 1100 hours on February 15 as the squadron launched two scout-weapons teams, placing one under the operational control of Task Force 1-41 Infantry and the other in direct support of the squadron. At 1130, the 155-mm self-propelled howitzers from the 4-3 Field Artillery fired at a trailer and a few trucks in the Iraqi sector that could observe the American advance. Simultaneously, the two-battalion-sized task forces advanced, with the 1-4 Cavalry on the left and TF 1-41 Infantry on the right. Within the squadron's sector, CPT Pope's A Troop advanced on the left while CPT Bills's B Troop moved on the right. As soon as they reached the berm, the engineers began tearing down the wall with their M9 Armored Combat Earthmovers. Within fifteen minutes, combat vehicles were moving through the gaps and into Iraq, A Troop claiming credit for being the first divisional unit across the border.[4] Its tanks, led by SFC Ed Cyphers, pushed through the narrow gaps first, followed by the lighter-skinned Bradleys.[5]

Shortly after noon, all of Task Force Iron began moving north. At the border berm, the units conducted standard defile drills[6] and then crossed into Iraq. As they advanced on a front almost thirty kilometers wide, gunners identified Iraqi vehicles in front of them, but the enemy withdrew as the ground units advanced.[7] In the cavalry's sector, A Troop initially had no contact with Iraqi troops as it crossed the border. However, in the B Troop zone, the 3rd Platoon received small arms fire as it worked on the berm. The shooting came from an outpost that looked like a small earthen fort with a small trailer inside. In a few moments tank and Bradley shells destroyed the structure and its occupants. The troop also spotted some Iraqis in a white pickup firing mortar rounds at them. When they returned fire, the Iraqis managed to escape to the north unharmed.[8] In the outpost the soldiers found a logbook with daily entries, which the Iraqi scouts had maintained since August. Unfortunately, it was unreadable and sent to the rear with other documents.

As A Troop fanned out to cover the north side of the breach sites, 1st Platoon sighted some dismounted Iraqis running over a ridge. A quick search of the area located a dug-in outpost within sight of the berm. It was quite crude, with only a large hole dug into the ground and no overhead cover. The only amenities were spaces for cooking and storage. However, it was well camouflaged and the scouts could not see it until they were almost on top of it. The platoon leader, 2LT James Copenhaver, sent dismounted scouts to clear the area around his platoon and police up the gear left behind by the surprised Iraqis. The squadron also discovered other evidence to prove they had not been imagining their enemy while conducting their screen the previous few weeks. Just beyond the berm were several bunkers full of communications equipment, mortar ammunition, and grenades and it was obvious that Iraqi soldiers had been operating on both sides of the border. The squadron commander could not resist personally inspecting some of the hastily abandoned bunkers, and LTC Wilson and the crew of HQ-66, his Cavalry Fighting Vehicle, acquired an Iraqi flag that is now on display in the Cavalry Museum at Fort Riley, Kansas.[9] By 1430 hours, both units had established a screen line two to three kilometers north of the border. The engineers had cut eight good breaks in the berm and continued to improve the traffic lanes over the next few days, widening some gaps to almost 100 meters across and wide enough for the large division and corps support vehicles to drive through.

It was clear to the soldiers up front that the Iraqis knew that the Americans had crossed the border. The most telling evidence came from A Troop after one of the platoon leaders, 2LT Mitchell A. Osburn, was called back to CPT Pope's location for a meeting of the troop's leaders just after he arrived at the screen line with his platoon. According to Pope, Osburn often complained about having to come in for these impromptu gatherings and this time was no different. A few minutes into the meeting, the officers heard some artillery fall in the general direction of Osburn's platoon. CPT Pope decided that they had to spread out, so he rushed the operations order he was issuing and sent the troop's platoon leaders back to their units. When the lieutenant returned to his original location, he discovered a crater and black smoke marking the location where he and his Bradley had been only an hour or so earlier. Osburn called Pope on the radio and promised his commander that he would never again complain about coming to his location for another meeting.[10]

As the troops moved their vehicles into the best firing positions they could find in the open desert, they rotated crew duties so everyone could get a little sleep. Some turned on their portable radios to monitor what was happening in the outside world. Chaplain Lou Parker remembered chuckling upon hearing President Bush state that the United States had no soldiers in Iraq. From the squadron's perspective, the war was already underway.[11]

By late afternoon TF Iron began to slowly push the screen line northward into Iraq. Troopers watched as Air Force A-10 close support aircraft attacked the Iraqi positions to the north. LTC James L. Hillman's TF 1-41 Infantry made physical contact with the 1st Cavalry Division on its right flank and informed them of Task Force Iron's new location. Squadron aviators screened the task force's exposed left flank.[12] By nightfall, the two units had moved a total of five kilometers into enemy territory and were arrayed along the division's Phase Line Minnesota.[13] The next day, the sixteenth, was spent in clearing the sector and improving Task Forces Iron's posture. This included the placement of ground surveillance radars in observation posts to cover both wheeled and infantry avenues of approach.[14]

General Ahmed Ibrahim Hamash, the Iraqi VII Corps commander responsible for the defense of southern Iraq, probably knew by now that something was afoot in his sector. It is ironic that corps-sized units with the same number, VII, confronted each other along the border. From the Wadi al Batin to the west, there was enemy activity. Holes had been torn in the berms and unknown armored vehicles had crossed over to his side of the border. His subordinate units were also receiving artillery fire and were now subject to precision air attacks. It was time for him to investigate and develop the situation. That evening, several groups of Iraqi vehicles appeared to observe the Americans and were driven away by indirect fire from the 4th Battalion, 3rd Field Artillery.[15]

The squadron and TF 1-41 Infantry spent February 16 inspecting the ground behind them and watching the area to their front. At 2151 hours that evening, Task Force Iron reported the movement of an approximate platoon, six vehicles, from the northeast. Whether by coincidence or design, these vehicles were close to the boundary line between the 1st Infantry and 1st Cavalry Divisions.[16] As the Iraqis were beyond the fire support coordination line, the graphic control measure that allows for unrestricted indirect fire beyond it, Task Force Iron prepared to engage them with artillery fire.

Twenty minutes later, another three vehicles were observed six kilometers to the west. As the tanks attached to TF 1-41 Infantry prepared to fire, the Iraqi vehicles disappeared from sight. At 2230 hours the task force reported to division headquarters that the vehicles appeared to be wheeled armored personnel carriers, probably Soviet-made BTRs, accompanied by a tank. They had taken good hull-down positions and were now difficult to observe. For the next hour Task Force Iron fought a small series of battles with the Iraqi reconnaissance elements that mimicked the tactics of a Soviet reconnaissance battalion.[17]

At 2340 hours, the cavalry squadron, still located on the western flank, spotted another group of vehicles moving from west to east towards the center of the task force's sector. At the same time, almost forty kilometers to the east, TF 1-14 IN fired TOW missiles at a group of vehicles that it had spotted along the boundary with the 1st Cavalry Division. It reported destroying one tank and engaging the remainder of the vehicles with artillery fire. As expected, the difficulty of positively identifying friend or foe in the difficult terrain at night prevented more vigorous action.[18]

Into this fragile situation the Task Force Iron commander, COL David Weisman, called for Apache support. A platoon led by the 1-1 Aviation's battalion commander, LTC Ralph Hayles, took off soon after midnight. The AH-64's night fighting capabilities appeared ideal for the task at hand. The division tactical command post quickly ordered Task Force Iron to turn off all ground surveillance radars so they would not interfere with the aircraft's electronic systems. At 0031 hours (February 17) the flight passed over the TF 1-41 Infantry. LTC Hillman coordinated directly with Hayles to identify the friendly line of troops. Nine minutes later, 0040 hours, COL Weisman shut off all artillery fire so the Apaches could move forward.[19]

At 0055 hours, an on-board alarm warned Hayles that unknown radar had momentarily acquired his aircraft. It is possible that this signal came from one of the American ground surveillance radars that had not yet been turned off. Later, the division discovered that these radars actually reflected the same warning profile as a Soviet-built ZSU 23-4 anti-aircraft system. Hayles continued on his mission, now concerned about his flight receiving enemy fire. Moments later he reported sighting two vehicles about a half-mile north of the troop line. Weisman immediately ordered them taken out. The aviation battalion commander hesitated as he attempted to positively identify the targets. A moment later, with more emphasis, Weisman again ordered Hayles to destroy the target. The aviation commander drew a bead on the vehicles and at 0059 hours, tried to engage one of them with his 30-mm cannon, hoping to test the target vehicle's reaction. In the back of his mind was the concern that they might turn out to be American troops. The weapon jammed. With even more emphasis, Weisman again ordered Hayles to destroy the targets he had acquired. At 0059, remarking, "Boy, I'm going to tell you its hard to pull this trigger," he personally fired a Hellfire at each of the two vehicles.[20]

Listening to the radio nets of both the infantry battalion and the division, Rhame realized that Hayles's targets were 1st Infantry Division vehicles. The infantry's scouts immediately reported on the battalion net that two of its radar vehicles had just been destroyed. Troopers from the 1st Cavalry Division also sent the same report over the corps's radio net. Rhame ordered the engagement broken off, sent the Apaches back to base, and later directed a formal investigation into the incident.[21]

The division commander had told all unit commanders to let their soldiers do their job and not get personally involved in the battle. Hayles had violated Rhame's instructions and, within forty-eight hours, the general relieved him of his command and returned him to the United States. The discussion and recriminations over the killing of two soldiers and wounding of six others would last long after the division returned to Fort Riley.[22] The stress of Task Force Iron's night across the border did not end with that engagement and for the next two hours, enemy operations continued. An Iraqi mortar position was identified and its crew subjected to direct and indirect fires. Finally, soon after 0300 hours, the Iraqi probing ended.[23] The squadron now settled down to its combat routine.

The squadron's tactical command post crew, located near the berm and centered on the two troops, monitored and coordinated squadron activities. Like other command posts in the desert, one of its most important problems was to adapt to living and working in a combat environment. The simple question for many was where to sleep when they were not working their twelve-hour shift. SGM Ken Shields lived and operated from the Diazo trailer, designed to carry the squadron's reproduction machine of the same name. When they could, the crews set up GP (General Purpose) tents to live in. Of course, during this period they were worried about incoming artillery and the possibility of having to displace rapidly. So, the TOC crews set up a couple of cots beside the M577 and slept on them during their off-cycle. They also dug out a small trench beside it so that they could roll over into it in the event of an artillery barrage. Although it was rather uncomfortable, this arrangement was flexible and very convenient. Flight Operations was deployed near the Squadron TOC with a stinger team, as well as its slice of logistics support from both HHT and CPT Smith's E Troop.[24]

Things were not different with the ground troops. The armored crew members lived in, on, or alongside their vehicles. When possible, they set up a cot. Usually, there were at least two crew members awake and manning the weapons and optical sights at all times. When it was time to replenish the vehicle with fuel, food, water, and ammunition, the crew guided it out of position and drove it a few hundred yards to the rear. There they linked up with elements from 1LT Matt Vanderfeltz's support platoon and replenished their supplies. With all lights off, it was not uncommon for a crew occasionally to get disoriented. Fortunately, there were no major problems during this period. The squadron's service support operated from either the combat trains or the logistics support area where they lived in tents or in their vehicles. The air troops, along with E Troop, remained in the Aviation Brigade's assembly area where CPT Pete Smith coordinated all aviation activity since Flight Operations was now deployed forward. When not flying, air crew members performed routine maintenance on their helicopters with the help of the brigade's aviation mechanics, conducted crew training, and slept on cots inside tents.[25]

While on the screen line, another field-grade officer arrived to augment the squadron. There were excess officers throughout the U.S. Army in Southwest Asia. The squadron headquarters was authorized two majors, but had three for most of Operation Desert Storm. Large command posts, such as for a division, could have a field-grade excess of twenty or thirty percent. MAJ John S. Dinnell, a West Point classmate of John Burdan, joined the squadron and went to work in the command post. Captains Tedesco and Sauer immediately began joking about each having their own field grade to supervise them. Of course, as soon as Dinnell arrived, the division pulled him away and directed him to conduct an investigation on the incident at As Samah, so he was unavailable for other duties.[26]

About mid-afternoon on February 17, the squadron scrambled for cover when a field artillery target acquisition battery detected Iraqi mortars firing from positions just north of B Troop's screen line. CPT Tedesco in the squadron TOC notified the troop, which sent a scout section to investigate. The section, led by SSG Alvin Fugate, discovered two Soviet-made BRDM scout cars and engaged them with TOW missiles, but missed when the vehicles retired on the far side of a ridge. CPT Mike Bills, on his way back from the squadron TOC when the original alert arrived, sent out a second patrol, which he essentially led, supported by an aerial scout-weapons team. They found trash at the location identified by the radar but not much else.[27]

This incident had several important results. It gave the ground and air teams another opportunity to practice together. It was also a drill that allowed the squadron command post to react to a changing situation and assist in actually commanding the squadron. Finally, it was another exercise that helped to season its leaders at all levels. As an example, after the patrol returned, its platoon leader 2LT Tom Karns approached his commander and told CPT Bills it was his job to run his platoon, and the troop commander was out of line taking charge unless he really had to. Bills realized that his young platoon leader was correct. Like all leaders, it was difficult for him to stand back and watch his subordinates. But the B Troop commander knew he had to and would keep this exchange in the back of his mind for the remainder of the campaign. That discussion says a great deal about the climate of the squadron: the young officer felt comfortable confronting his commander, and the captain was mature enough to listen and agree.

By the afternoon of February 17, LTG Franks was concerned about the task force's activity north of the border. He ordered Rhame to reposition it to the southern side of the berm the following morning and observe the cuts without being quite as provocative. As if to confirm the wisdom of his order, that night an American vehicle lost its way, crossing in front of the task force's line. At first, it appeared to be an Iraqi reconnaissance vehicle and only good fire discipline by vehicle commanders prevented a repetition of the previous night's mishap. The next morning Task Force Iron returned to the south side of the border and conducted a rearward passage of lines through the 1st and 2nd Brigades, which had taken up defensive positions behind Task Force Iron. The squadron passage points and lanes were through COL Maggart's 1st Brigade. As the squadron began moving back through the 1st Brigade, it used D Troop with a mix of C/D Troop scout weapons teams to screen its activities.

While CPT Roy Peters, the D Troop Commander, was talking on the radio trying to direct a new scout-weapons team into position, he noticed a couple of explosions in the distance. As he continued talking, he watched a few more explosions, each approaching closer to his position. Realizing that his group had been spotted, probably by Iraqi radio intercepts, he decided to move. After he flew his helicopter a few kilometers south, Iraqi artillery hit the ground where he had only recently been hovering.[28]

A short while later, as A Troop was completing its rearward passage of lines, the squadron flight operations received a distress call from a scout-weapons team: its OH-58C scout helicopter, with 1LT Tom Schwartz (an attached pilot from Ft. Hood) and SPC Steven Dunn, had crashed. The first fear, fueled by the pilot's distress call, was that it was downed by hostile fire. Since the aircraft was downed in the sector previously occupied by A Troop, CPT Philbrick immediately contacted CPT Pope and alerted him to the situation. Pope jumped into his Bradley and led a team back to the crash site to assist the crew in the event they were injured and secure the helicopter at the crash site so it could be evacuated. He was quite relieved to see them standing by their downed helicopter as he arrived.[29] A few moments earlier, WO1 Gary Notestine, flying the Cobra that was part of the team, and CPT Peters in his helicopter, had also arrived at the crash site. As they circled the location, they could see that the wreckage was strewn over a large area. Glad that the crew was safe, the aviators were also impressed by the ground troop's rapid response. Although they had discussed many times in briefings how they would respond to a downed aviator call, this was the first opportunity they had to execute this mission. The crew of the downed helicopter was safely evacuated and by late afternoon the helicopter was recovered. Later, an investigating team determined that the aircraft's crash occurred because of an engine failure and not hostile fire.[30]

The rearward passage of lines was completed in the late afternoon with the recovery of the OH-58C, and the squadron gathered in an assembly area called AA Respite just behind the 1st Brigade. The two ground troops formed their own small enclaves and the air troops flew to the 4th Brigade area approximately twenty kilometers to the rear. Now Wilson and his leaders began planning for the attack in earnest.

Once they passed to the rear, the tired cavalrymen gained a few days to rearm, refuel, and relax, the squadron's first opportunity since mid-January to stand down and rest. Since its deployment almost a month earlier, the cavalry had been on a war footing. While newspapers at home focused on the air campaign, the squadron had conducted their own deadly game. The time on the border had been invaluable; soldiers at every level became more proficient and disciplined, comfortable with their equipment and competent. The leaders developed a level of trust and confidence among themselves that would pay important dividends in the days ahead.

9   Final Preparations

On February 18, as Task Force Iron was completing its mission north of the berm, Secretary of Defense Richard Cheney approved General Schwarzkopf's recommendation that the ground campaign should begin on February 24.[1] Across the theater of war, artillery, army helicopters, and close-air support aircraft began shifting their strikes away from targets in the heart of Iraq to those enemy units defending along the border against the coalition arrayed in Saudi Arabia. At 1100 hours the morning of February 18, the division commander placed the 1-4 Cavalry under the operational control of COL Maggart's 1st Brigade.[2]

The Iraqi Army had more than 300,000 soldiers in and around Kuwait to meet an American-led offensive. Expecting the main thrust to follow the Wadi Al Batin, the Iraqis arrayed their forces in a series of echelons. Along the border were standard infantry divisions, usually deployed with two brigades forward and one to the rear. They had almost no mobility and had the mission of defending the border and absorbing the initial allied attack. Ironically, it was the Iraqi VII Corps, with four infantry divisions, that prepared to defend against the U.S. VII Corps. Behind these static units was a heavy division, the 52nd Armored, acting as the Iraqi corps's mobile reserve and designed to counterattack against the initial American penetrations. Located in depth, astride the Wadi Al Batin, was the theater reserve, the 10th and 12th Armored Divisions. Called the Operation Jihad Corps, its mission was counter-penetration and counterattack. Finally, positioned farther to the rear was the Iraqi Army's strategic reserve, the Republican Guard Forces

Command. The heart of this force consisted of three heavy divisions: the Medina and Hammurabi Armored Divisions and the Tawakalna Mechanized Division. These units were the linchpin of the entire Iraqi defense in Kuwait and perhaps Saddam Hussein's entire regime.[3]

On the ground, the allied coalition arrayed essentially five corps with over 472,000 soldiers against the Iraqi Army. In the east, two small Arab corps and a two-division Marine expeditionary force attacked into Kuwait with the intent of focusing the Iraqi commander's attention to the south. In the far western portion of the sector, the U.S. XVIII Airborne Corps, reinforced by the 6th French Light Armored Division, had the mission of attacking toward the Euphrates River to secure the coalition's left flank. The U.S. VII Corps, reinforced by the 1st British Armoured Division, was to conduct the main attack in the center of the line.[4]

The VII Corps's chain of command now began executing its war plan: Operation Desert Saber.[5] LTG Frederick Franks organized the VII Corps attack as two operations. In the western portion of the sector, the 2nd Armored Cavalry Regiment would lead the 1st and 3rd Armored Divisions in an envelopment of the exposed flank of the enemy army and drive deep into Iraq in search of the heavy divisions of the Republican Guard Forces Command. In the eastern portion of the corps area, the 1st Infantry Division would attack, or "breach," the defenses of the Iraqi 26th Infantry Division, opening up a direct supply route to the corps troops moving into Iraq, and pass the 1st British Armoured Division through the lanes it cleared. The British mission was to attack to the east to clear out the Iraqi forces defending along the border and defeat the expected counterattack of the Iraqi 52nd Armored Division. The Big Red One would then, if able, join the remainder of the corps in its battle with the Republican Guards.[6]

The Iraqi 26th Infantry Division defended a sector of approximately thirty-five kilometers directly opposite the U. S. 1st Infantry Division. Only two of its brigades were on line. Its third was almost fifty kilometers to the rear, arrayed to prevent a coalition flanking movement. The front-line brigades were weak, with probably less then fifty percent of their authorized strength, and supported by only one battalion of old Soviet-made T-55 tanks. This division was no match for the modern, over-strength, Big Red One.[7]

MG Thomas G. Rhame arranged the 1st Infantry Division and the 1st Brigade on the western portion of the attack zone and the 2nd Brigade to the east just beyond the border berm. Its task was to secure a semi-circular phase line called PL Colorado, which generally corresponded with the rear of the Iraqi defensive positions. On order, the 3rd Brigade would pass through the 2nd and expand the penetration to Phase Line (PL) New Jersey, well to the rear of the 26th Iraqi Division's defensive line. Once it achieved its objective, the command's primary task was to move the 1st British Armoured Division's brigades and all of their support equipment through specially marked routes to their attack positions (called "forming up points") just behind PL New Jersey. To ensure security on his western flank, Rhame placed the 1st Squadron, 4th Cavalry under the operational control of COL Burt Maggart's 1st Brigade. Rhame envisioned the operation lasting two days. On the first, the division would clear the security zone to the edge of the Iraqi defenses (PL Wisconsin). On the next, it would continue the attack to PL New Jersey and pass the British through in the late afternoon.[8]

Maggart's detailed plan, worked out in close coordination with the 2nd Brigade and the division commander, corresponded to the general scheme of maneuver, with an attack in zone to clear all Iraqi reconnaissance and security elements between PL Vermont to PL Plum, which lay just south of the Iraqi main defensive line (PL Wisconsin). The Quarter Horse would conduct a zone reconnaissance in the western half of the zone, clear out any Iraqi recon and security elements, and maintain contact with the 3rd Squadron, 2nd ACR on the division's right. TF 2-34 AR would be on the squadron's right and would be responsible for clearing the Iraqis from the eastern half of the brigade's zone. When Rhame gave the order, the brigade would breach the Iraqi defenses and attack to PL Colorado and continue on order to PL New Jersey, where it would then become division reserve. The Quarter Horse would initially follow TF 2-34 AR through the breach and then attack north while protecting the division's western flank and maintaining contact with the

2nd Cavalry advancing in that area. On order, it would continue to PL New Jersey, and then defend until ordered back to divisional control. Once through the breach, the Quarter Horse's initial task was to destroy a small armored reserve located to the rear of the main line of resistance and labeled Objective 15K, located in the Iraqi 26th Division's support area. The 1st Brigade staff believed that this armored reserve was no larger than a reinforced platoon, with three to six old T-55 tanks.[9]

For this operation, LTC Wilson decided to organize his squadron with A Troop in the west and B Troop in the east maintaining contact with TF 2-34 Armor. Two scout-weapons teams (SWTs) would fly under squadron control on the flanks and just behind the ground troops to maximize the advantage that altitude could give their weapon systems without needlessly exposing the aircraft to an unknown anti-aircraft threat. The western SWT would have the responsibility to maintain visual contact with the advancing elements of the 2nd ACR. The squadron commander's M3A2 Bradley would follow CPT Bills's B Troop while MAJ Burdan would trail CPT Pope's command. It was normal for the commander and S3 to split across the sector, ensuring that the squadron's leaders could see the whole battlefield while minimizing the potential for both becoming casualties simultaneously. Trailing the lead units would be the tactical operations center led by MAJ Wimbish. The tactical operations center would act as the information hub, connecting the cavalry troops, squadron command group, adjacent units, and the brigade headquarters. CPT Christopher Philbrick's flight operations section, which controlled C, D, and E Troops, would trail the tactical operations center by eight to fifteen kilometers and stop just south of the berm. They would remain there until the situation dictated a move. He would have a couple of five-ton cargo trucks for ammunition, some fuel HEMTTs with JP8 for the aircraft and diesel for the vehicles. He also had an aircraft maintenance team headed by CW2 Daniel Hunter and SFC Dennis Demille who would be able to provide limited, on-site repair of the aircraft.[10]

Mechanized war requires an extensive combat service support organization. Each ground troop was followed by its own collection of medical and maintenance vehicles, called "trains" in army terminology. Following behind the troop trains were the squadron combat trains, led by the S4, CPT Steve Harmon. These contained essential support items that were of immediate concern: repair parts, fuel, ammunition, and medical support. The squadron organized the larger field trains into two elements for ease of control and rapidity of response to demands from the fighting units. CPT Doug Morrison would lead a forward support element with most of the fuel and ammunition, which followed directly behind the combat trains. Farther to the rear would be the rest of the field trains under CPT John Maloney, the HHT executive officer. They were located in the 1st Brigade Support Area and moved with them. The air troops remained collocated with the 4th Brigade and moved with them. CPT Philbrick would relay instructions for the squadron's air elements through Pete Smith, E Troop commander, and the squadron's senior captain on site. In the absence of any contrary instructions, Philbrick told Smith to launch two SWTs each morning and send them to Flight Operations for the day's mission.

As part of the final preparations, each crew thoroughly readied themselves and their vehicles or aircraft for combat, and after several weeks on the line, there was much to be done. They emptied each tank, personnel carrier, aircraft, or truck of all of the trash and unneeded personal gear and restored it in accordance with the squadron's loading plans. They cleaned all of their weapons, optical equipment, and chemical detection devices. They loaded up cases of MREs (Meals Ready to Eat) and supplementary off-the-shelf rations such as canned beans and franks, lasagna, and ravioli. Every vehicle was to have at least one five-gallon can of water on it and, in the way of modern American-style war, cases of soft drinks and Gatorade.[11]

Then they opened the crew maintenance manual, known as the "-10," and began going down the checklist, inspecting and servicing each item in turn. These checks addressed everything from oil levels to track tightness. The air troop crew chiefs performed similar tasks and coordinated with E Troop for any needed repairs. In most cases, the crews or helicopter crew chiefs fixed minor problems and were ready to go by the next day. In B Troop, however, 1LT Gerald Danussi's crew discovered a crack in the hull of its M3A2 Bradley. It was quite severe and extended from the right rear all the way to the left front. In no time, squadron and direct-support maintenance crews were joining in the discussion. There was not much a tactical unit could do to solve this kind of a problem, since it requires a factory rebuilding, so the division sent one of its "float" or extra Bradleys forward as a direct exchange. This vehicle turned out to be a M2A2, the improved infantry version of the Bradley that had more room for an infantry squad and fewer storage racks for the TOW missiles. Using this extra space, CPT Bills decided to assign his Stinger air defense team to Danussi.[12]

Iraq had a record of using chemical munitions and was suspected of experimenting with biological ones. As a result, the army tried to protect its soldiers from these terrifying weapons as best it could. Everyone had a protective mask and chemical protective suits. Vehicles had chemical alarms and all soldiers were trained to react to a chemical attack. In case of nerve agent contamination, soldiers had atropine injectors to counter its effect. In advance, they were supposed to take "PB" pills that contributed to the effectiveness of the atropine.[13]

Biological agents require different kinds of protection and one of the most effective is vaccination. In preparation for the advance, the medics began giving shots that were designed to ward off botulism. Although the Food and Drug Administration had not approved the vaccine, the army's leadership felt it was safe to provide it to the troops in the field. Not everyone shared that confidence and one of the squadron's aviators refused to take it. LTC Wilson and others in the chain of command counseled the aviator, but to no avail. Wilson had little choice but to ground him. Other than this one case, everyone else grudgingly took his medicine and completed their preparation for combat.[14]

Chaplain Lou Parker visited the crews as they prepared for battle. An army chaplain is not only a religious leader, but often acts as the soldier's counselor and advisor. As he circulated among the crews, some broke away from their daily activities to spend a few minutes in prayer or conversation with Parker. At each stop the soldiers quietly talked about their fears and worries, the kind that have always bothered young men on the eve of battle: how would they act under fire and could they kill a fellow human being? They also talked of family concerns, and what might happen to them if they got hit. Parker did his best to calm their fears and concluded each of the group sessions with a prayer.[15]

Behind the scenes, squadron leaders dealt with other concerns. Wilson pulled CPT VJ Tedesco aside and told him that if something happened to one of the ground troop commanders, he was going to take his place. On the one hand, he felt honored since he had only been in the squadron for a short period of time. On the other hand, it made him quite uncomfortable knowing that his route to professional advancement might occur over a friend's dead body.[16]

Another example concerned the leadership in A Troop, where CPT Pope was unhappy with his first sergeant. After a final incident involving his first sergeant and one of his troopers he decided to take action. After a discussion with Wilson and CSM Cobb, Pope and the other leaders decided to move newly arrived MSG Gary Parkey into the job. When Cobb asked him, Parkey jumped at the chance and pulled his old first sergeant diamonds out of his duffel bag. He arrived at the troop command post as it was preparing for the final order briefing. In less than twenty-four hours he would be in combat and senior noncommissioned officer of a unit he was just being introduced to.[17]

Now things began to happen with an increased intensity and sense of purpose. On February 22 the squadron changed its radio call sign from "Dragoon" to "Quarter Horse" to prevent confusion with the 2nd Armored Cavalry Regiment on the division's left flank. The 2nd Cavalry sent over a liaison officer to maintain contact between the two units. Brigade engineers began removing the concrete dragon's teeth that had blocked the roads at the old border crossings. Supporting and attached units checked into the squadron area. One of these was a psychological operations team that brought along its capability to play music over loudspeakers. These blared in the command post area, picking up the soldiers' morale and starting good-natured arguments over the merits of country music versus rock and roll. Meanwhile, leaders rehearsed their combat actions and the command post streamlined the complex operation order into a handy guide commanders could use during the fight. Due to the number of changes to the operation order, called fragmentary orders or "FRAGOs" that the brigade issued during this period, keeping the plan organized turned out to be quite a task. Captains Tedesco and Sauer worked all night prior to the squadron rehearsal to produce what was referred to as the operational narrative. They, along with the other members of the TOC, also prepared fresh copies of operations overlays, issued final orders, reviewed recent aerial photographs, and refined the intelligence available on the Iraqi defenses. After the final rehearsal on February 23, Chaplain Parker held one last prayer meeting and had a picture taken of the squadron's leaders.

That night the sky filled with flashes as the division completed its artillery raids on the Iraqi forces and began bombarding the forward defenses. For the first time in their professional lives, leaders saw artillery battalions firing en masse. Batteries of new MLRS rocket launchers moved among the squadron's positions and unleashed their potent weapons. Of course, it was a good thing that the Iraqi counter fire was almost non-existent, since many of the firing units set up right next to squadron encampments.[18]

Few of the squadron's almost eight hundred soldiers slept that night. Artillery firing, vehicles coming and going, last minute packing and checking kept them all awake. As before any battle, soldiers thought of home and family. They also fought their own fears. We should not forget, now, after the fall of the Hussein regime, that the Iraqi Army appeared to be a serious, formidable force in 1991. Many of its soldiers had been in uniform for over a decade and one had to give them the respect they had apparently earned. For the American soldiers then, the prospect of battle was simultaneously frightening and exhilarating. Fortunately, LTC Wilson and his leaders had used their time wisely since the notification to deploy back in November. Both ground troops were ready to go, equipped with their new Bradley Fighting Vehicles and Abrams tanks. The helicopter crews were comfortable with flying in the desert and working with the ground soldiers. It was time to put it all together.

10   The Breach

We now know to what extent the Big Red One out-classed its Iraqi opponent. The few thousand poorly armed, deployed, and equipped soldiers of the Iraqi 26th Infantry Division were simply not prepared for what was to come. Operating the most sophisticated and lethal weapons in the world, and backed by the largest concentration of artillery the United States had employed since the Battle of the Bulge over forty-five years earlier, the 26,000 soldiers of the 1st Infantry Division could not be stopped by the paltry Iraqi defenses. But, we know this today. At the time the division's soldiers looked back to previous assaults at Catigny, France (1917), Omaha Beach (1944), and Junction City (Vietnam, 1967) as indicators of how bloody battle could be.

The largest attack the United States Army had conducted in almost fifty years began on a rainy, overcast morning. The showers continued until about 1000 hours, but the visibility continued to decrease as fog and blowing sand dominated the soldiers' view. Winds were fairly strong with gusts up to twenty-five knots during the day. The horizon began showing traces of light in the eastern sky at 0531 hours and sunset was to come at 1753 hours.[1]

American forces made up over sixty percent of the 472,000 coalition troops beginning their offensive. An attack by United States Marines and Arabic forces into Kuwait was supposed to fix the attention of the Iraqi high command. Then, LTG John Yeosock's Third Army would attack in the west with LTG Gary Luck's XVIII Corps heading for the Euphrates River and LTG Frederick Franks's VII Corps maneuvering against Saddam's

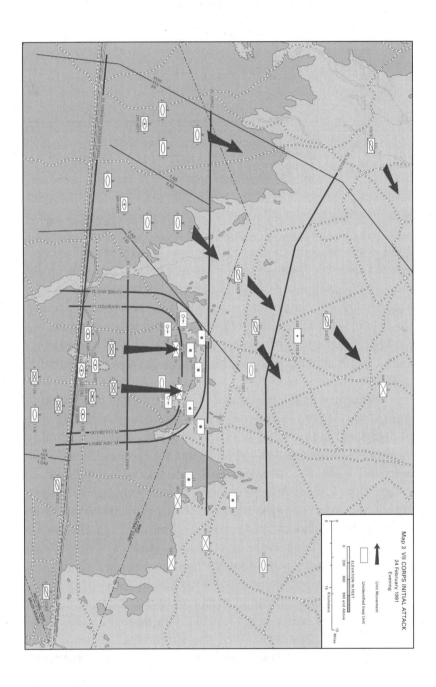

best troops, the Republican Guard Forces Command. Franks's divisions, including the 1st Infantry, were not scheduled to participate in the initial coalition attack. Their role on Ground Attack Day, or G Day as it was called, was to make contact with the Iraqi defenses, get as much of their combat units as possible across the berm, but not actually start their attack until dawn on February 25, or G+1. The specific unit tasks were different on the corps's breach zone on the right (1st Infantry and 1st [UK] Armoured Division) and the envelopment zone (2nd Cavalry, 1st and 3rd Armored Divisions) to the west. However, because of the allied success along the coast, General Schwarzkopf would direct the Jayhawks to change their plans and attack much earlier than anticipated.[2]

The 1st Infantry Division's 1st Brigade's initial task was to secure the left half of the division sector from PL Vermont, the border berm, to PL Plum, two to three kilometers from the Iraqi defenses. The distance between these two lines was about twenty-five kilometers and was already well known to the division's aviators. Other than a few reconnaissance vehicles and deserting Iraqi soldiers, the leaders did not expect any significant engagements. Shortly after 0500, February 24, scouts from the 1-4 Cavalry and TF 2-34 AR began moving in their M3 Cavalry Fighting Vehicles to PL Vermont, designated as the line of departure. A scout section from each of the 1-4 Cavalry's ground troops was part of the advance. These scouts generally had two missions: first ensure that the crossing lanes were clear of Iraqi soldiers or other obstacles and second facilitate the passing of the remainder of the unit through the berm's narrow lanes. Since it was still dark outside, they relied on GPS, thermal sights on the vehicles, and night vision goggles.[3]

Shortly after 0530 hours, the entire 1st Infantry Division commenced its attack. COL Maggart's 1st Brigade, reinforced by the 1st Squadron, 4th Cavalry, attacked on the left while COL Anthony Moreno's 2nd Brigade attacked on the right. COL David Weisman's 3d Brigade remained south of the border, prepared to exploit the breach.[4]

The squadron TOC packed up and was ready to move by the early morning hours. CPT VJ Tedesco began the day as the Track Command of HQ 33, the S3 section's M577. He had put

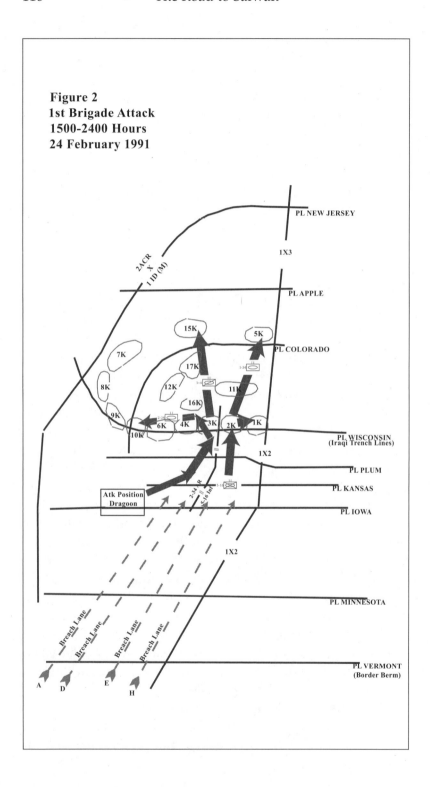

Figure 2
1st Brigade Attack
1500-2400 Hours
24 February 1991

on his flight suit and over that he had put on his chemical suit. He wondered whether he would be too hot. Later in the day he had to take his flight suit off. He strapped two AT-4s to the generator to his front and borrowed the SPC Mark Aide's M16A2 rifle. Since there were no crew-served weapons assigned to HQ 33, CPT Tedesco put the M16A2 on automatic and set it on the deck beside him. He and the crew were concerned that as they advanced behind the ground troops they would be vulnerable to small arms attack and/or attack by lightly armed infantrymen. As he climbed up into the track commander's hatch to begin the day he found himself surrounded by four "Jerry Cans" of gasoline that were needed to power the command post's generators. In addition, the camouflage nets and the soldiers' personal gear were piled high all around him. He found he had to sit a good distance up in the hatch in order to see where they were going and even then he could see only straight ahead. He realized that even with his NOMEX suit he would have no chance if the gas cans got hit by small arms fire. However, at this late point there was nowhere else to put them. They stayed where they were as the TOC rolled out following the ground troops.[5]

As the sun came up, CPT Morrison had the field trains finish packing. He then moved them over to the location of the 101st Forward Support Battalion. He reported in to his commander and then departed with the forward area support team (FAST) to link up with the combat trains. He would remain near and then follow the combat trains for the next few days. CPT Maloney, 1LT Vanderfeltz, and 1SG Collangelo were the senior soldiers left behind with the field trains.

Not everything went as smoothly as perceived by the public and postwar commentators. For example, while observing the troop's M577 command post and the combat trains as they pulled out of their assembly area, A Troop's new first sergeant, Gary Parkey, discovered they were heading in the wrong direction. Getting nervous, he called his executive officer, 1LT Jon S. Raynal, who was inside the command post track taking reports. After Parkey's call, Raynal popped out of the track commander's hatch, checked his GPS, and confirmed the first sergeant's fears. Parkey drove his HMMWV to the front of the column and helped turn it around and send it off in the right direction: north into Iraq.[6]

B Troop also had a problem after crossing into Iraq. Mike Bills's eastern platoon crossed the berm and hooked a right into Task Force 2-34 Armor's column and joined its advance. Apparently, a combination of a malfunctioning GPS and confusion on the radio led to this mix up. It took the troop's executive officer, 1LT Gerald Danussi, about thirty minutes to get everyone heading on the proper azimuth.[7]

However, such incidents were few. As the squadron traveled through the border berm and into the open area beyond, MAJ Burdan trailed Ken Pope's A Troop and LTC Wilson followed Mike Bills's B Troop. The farther north they went, the more difficult it became for the troops to communicate with the squadron command post still located along the border berm. Wilson and Burdan kept the advance under control, and when necessary, relayed information back to the squadron and brigade headquarters. It also helped that there was a great deal of "cross-talk," a term in vogue at the time, between the two troop commanders, thus improving coordination between the units.[8] In addition, as the sun rose, around 0645 hours, Wilson directed an aviation scout-weapons team to fly just behind each of the two ground troops to provide extra security, monitor the advance, and maintain visual contact with the 3rd Squadron, 2nd Cavalry on the left and Task Force 2-34 Armor that was on the right.[9]

Most soldiers were concerned about Iraq using chemical weapons. They all knew Saddam Hussein had a reputation for employing them in his previous wars and fully expected a chemical strike sometime during the conflict, a prospect no one welcomed. The first indication of chemical use came through intelligence communications channels a little after 0800. Apparently, Marines attacking into Kuwait had encountered mustard gas mines in their sector. Prudently, the command post warned the troop commanders to be on the look-out for mines in the brigade's sector. A half hour later, the squadron TOC received an update from division that the Iraqi mines had not detonated, and that it was not clear that they were really chemical weapons. These messages reinforced the old adage that the first reports, even in an age of sophisticated equipment, are usually wrong.[10]

As the squadron continued its zone recon it ran across various small enemy units. TF 2-34 to the east also encountered scattered mounted reconnaissance elements as they attacked north. In every case the Iraqi units rapidly fell back in the direction of their main defenses. Things were strangely silent. The squadron expected the enemy to call artillery upon the lead elements but they did not. The cavalry did run across a few signs of the enemy in places where CPT Seelinger, the S2, had initially predicted their location. This was the case throughout the division zone of advance. As the squadron closed in on the Iraqi main defensive belt it began to encounter more of the Iraqis who wanted to give up. In general, they surrendered in groups of ten to twenty soldiers. Other 1st Brigade units began capturing Iraqi soldiers as early as 0730 hours in the morning as they closed in on PL Minnesota, which was about fifteen kilometers from the expected main enemy defensive positions.

By 1000 hours, the entire brigade was arrayed about four kilometers south of the Iraqi positions (PL Wisconsin). On the front line, cavalry scouts set up on a low ridgeline and watched the Iraqi soldiers across a shallow valley a little less than two kilometers away. The troopers sensed that the defenders seemed a bit surprised to be located across from American forces. At this point, the squadron (and the remainder of the brigade) was almost nine hours ahead of the schedule laid out in the 1st Brigade's operations order timeline.[11]

While the combat units consolidated their positions, the squadron's command post and combat trains moved across the berm and close to the front line. The command post stopped approximately 1500 meters behind ground units and the combat trains another 1200 meters farther to the rear. These elements were now in position to support the attack that would take place during phase two.[12] CPT Morrison, who had been following closely behind the combat trains, had been waiting for the opportunity to bring the squadron fuel vehicles forward. Fuel was always a serious concern in units like the Quarter Horse. Tanks needed it first, and they normally had to refuel every six to eight hours of operation. Next came the Bradleys, which could operate for a whole day without refueling. The procedure, worked out many times, was for the support platoon leader 2LT Matt Vanderfeltz or CPT Doug Morrison to bring the fuel trucks forward to a release point just behind the ground troops. Then, unit first sergeants came back, picked them up, and moved them to troop refuel points. As part of an often-rehearsed drill, individual vehicles backed off the firing line and drove over to the waiting fuelers.[13] Taking advantage of the lull in the attack, CPT Morrison got permission from Major Wimbish to bring the fuel vehicles forward. The refuel operation went off without a hitch and was completed by 1130 hours.

While the squadron waited for further orders, the aviation troops began to take things into their own hands. CW3 Craig Winters began edging his scout-weapons team out over no-man's land to see what would happen. With no indication of active air-defense artillery units, he continued to fly forward. Soon he was above the Iraqi positions, with soldiers emerging from the bunkers waving white cloths as if asking to surrender. The squadron then had its psychological warfare team play audiotapes over its loud speakers, urging the somewhat surprised Iraqi soldiers to drop their weapons and give up. By noon the brigade had over 350 prisoners, with about thirty of those in squadron hands.[14]

CPT Jim Tovsen's team replaced Winters's aviators shortly thereafter. As Tovsen's helicopter flew over an enemy bunker, he noticed an Iraqi soldier with binoculars observing the squadron. Since this Iraqi could have been able to direct artillery fire against the squadron, he was considered dangerous. After receiving the aviator's report, CPT Mike Bills had his first platoon fire at the bunker with coax machine guns and 25-mm Bushmaster cannon. This was to no avail, as the Iraqi continued to stick his head out and observe the Americans. Bills then ordered the platoon to take the bunker out with a TOW missile. The TOW flew straight into the bunker and destroyed everything in it.[15]

So, the squadron waited for orders. LTC Wilson began to grow impatient to learn what the division's next move was going to be and he instructed the TOC to monitor the division command net. This was not normally done as the squadron was OPCON to the 1st Brigade and not working directly for the division commander. In this case, however, the move paid dividends. The squadron became aware that the division was considering pressing the attack early. Shortly after 1130 hours, the corps commander, based on a conversation he had had with the Third Army Commander, asked MG Rhame if the division could continue. Rhame, of course, said yes and then double-checked with his brigade commanders, who passed the same question down to the battalions. All battalion commanders in the brigade were eager to continue.[16] While the chain of command planned its next move, the squadron continued watching the Iraqi front line. Shortly after noon, Jim Tovsen, who was still in the air, again flew over the Iraqi positions. He was specifically looking for the armored vehicles he had seen in pre-attack photographs. Near one objective, named A10K, he discovered three tanks that the artillery or air support had already destroyed. Then he discovered one, apparently intact, French-made AML. This is a wheeled, lightly armored vehicle, with a 90-mm main gun, primarily used for reconnaissance. Tovsen destroyed it with 100 rounds of 20-mm cannon and two TOW missiles, a bit of overkill for so light a weapons system. Iraqis in the area dove back into their bunkers as soon as the Cobra began shooting.[17]

Finally, a little before 1300 hours, the corps commander ordered the division to continue the attack at 1500 hours: two hours later. While this three-hour wait was necessary and made sense at senior echelons, it was immensely frustrating for the soldiers who were motivated to continue.[18] For the next hour the front line units in the Big Red One's zone remained in position watching the Iraqis while the remainder of the division prepared for the attack. There was little enemy activity, other than Iraqi soldiers coming out of their trenches and surrendering.[19]

At 1400 hours, the squadron began moving to its attack position, called Attack Position Dragoon, behind the 1st Brigade's lead battalion task forces. Wilson continued to rotate the aeroscout weapons teams along the brigade's flanks to watch for Iraqi counterattacks and to maintain contact with adjacent units. With the E Troop commander, CPT Peter Smith, controlling overall aviation maintenance operations and assisting with the control of the air troops from south of the berm, CPT

Christopher Philbrick had not waited for the word to reposition. He had already moved flight operations north of the berm to better coordinate helicopter operations with ground activities. At one point during the day, communications had become so poor because of the extended tactical distances that Philbrick had to mount a large RC-292 antenna on the front bumper of his van. The antenna gave him the necessary range to communicate to both the TOC forward of his position and the aviation assembly area in the rear. This quick fix worked quite well and he was now able to provide the continuous SWT support that Wilson needed.

As the squadron repositioned, the troops passed numerous artillery battalions that were now ready to fire the artillery preparation and support the assault. Friendly vehicles were moving and preparing for action. The scale of this artillery commitment was unprecedented in the post-Vietnam War era U.S. Army. Almost five full brigades of self-propelled artillery and multiple rocket launchers moved through or up to the berm. Once in place, this massive artillery force, essentially an artillery division, would fire the "prep" and support the breaching operation that the division would conduct at 1500 hours that day. For the first time in years, the entire Big Red One was coiled and ready to strike.[20]

At exactly 1430 hours the artillery preparation began and lasted for thirty minutes as corps' and division artillery battalions fired over 11,000 rounds of tube and rocket artillery across the entire zone of attack. It was an amazing display of firepower, certainly the most impressive demonstration ever witnessed by this generation of soldiers. When the fire stopped, the two lead brigades of the Big Red One lunged forward. The 1st Brigade, in the west, attacked with 2nd Battalion, 34th Armor on the left and 5th Battalion, 16th Infantry on the right. The 2nd Brigade, in the eastern zone, struck with 3d Battalion, 37th Armor on the left and the 2nd Battalion, 16th Infantry on the right. All four battalions were organized as combined-arms task forces. To the defending Iraqis, they must have appeared as a solid wall of fire and iron as the assaulting battalions opened fire with 120-mm volleys from their tank platoons. Tank and Bradley-mounted machine guns poured rounds into all possible positions, while smoke rounds marked assault sectors and isolated Iraqi positions from each other.[21]

As the lead elements approached the trenches, the Iraqis could see that many of the tanks pushed plows and mine rollers in front of them. Combat engineer vehicles with their short but lethal 165-mm guns and plows, and the new armored combat earthmovers, called ACEs, also headed for trenches and bunkers. Behind this 6,000-meter-wide wall of iron came the remainder of the battalions, especially the Bradley Infantry Fighting Vehicles, with soldiers ready to fire from the ports on the side and rear. In the turrets, the gunners prepared to engage with 7.62-mm coaxial machine guns and 25-mm Bushmaster automatic cannon. Five hundred meters south of the enemy trench line, the assaulting task forces dropped their plows from their carry position. They continued north at fifteen kilometers per hour, firing coaxial machine guns and 120-mm cannon into the trenches. Trailing the four lead maneuver and two engineer task forces were the three exploiting units: 1st Squadron, 4th Cavalry, and 1st Battalion, 34th Armor, from the 1st Brigade and the 4th Battalion, 37th Armor from the 2nd.[22]

Although enemy resistance was generally limited to uncoordinated small-arms, rifle propelled grenades (RPG), artillery and mortar fire, the Iraqis did not simply quit. In the 1st Brigade sector, LTC Gregory Fontenot, the 2nd Battalion, 34th Armor task force commander, and one of his teams were forced off a low ridge by Iraqi artillery. The 5th Battalion, 16th Infantry task force took fire from an Iraqi platoon and used concentrated coaxial machine gun and Bushmaster fire to capture the position and its twenty-five survivors. In the eastern part of the sector, the 2nd Brigade's movement went faster and met little opposition. Iraqi soldiers continued to fight from their trenches and bunkers, obviously expecting a friendly counterattack to drive the attackers off. Mounted fire from approaching American armored vehicles was not enough to defeat the defending Iraqis.[23]

Finally, the attacking battalions reached the trench lines. The Iraqis probably anticipated dismounted American soldiers assaulting their ground positions, but the 1st Infantry Division commanders had no intention of playing by the Iraqi rules. Once across the trench, tanks equipped with menacing multitoothed plows turned either right or left. With blades down, these tanks moved along the back of the trenches filling them in as they went. Behind the Abrams tanks were mechanized infantry, who dismounted only to gather the Iraqi soldiers who poured from their positions with hands high in the air. Some Iraqis tried to run away, but were either killed or captured by the following American assault elements. A few fought to the death. The Big Red One soldiers did not, however, dismount. It was an unequal battle as tanks pushed the soil back on top of the resisting Iraqis. When RPG and small-arms fire bounced off the tanks, most Iraqis realized that they had no choice but to give up. The U.S. infantry dismounted and gathered them according to the drills they had practiced since they came in the army. Then the grisly process of filling in the trench line, burying those who resisted, continued. Probably fewer than 200 members of the 110th Brigade, the unit from the Iraqi 26th Infantry Division defending against the 1st Brigade's assault, chose this method of resistance. Most were content with surrender and removal to the POW cage in the rear.[24]

The 1st Brigade commander ordered the cavalry to commence its movement through the lanes in the trench lines shortly before 1530 hours. Mike Bills's Troop B led as the squadron moved through the lanes, each clearly marked with a large panel at their entrance. The tanks and Bradleys often bunched up as each tried to get into line for their designated lane. Once in column, the units moved with steady speed though the smoke and dust. With all the fear and confusion around them, the large number of combat vehicles and the sound of friendly artillery firing reassured the cavalry troopers as they headed for their attack zones. On occasion a track would break down, only to be attended to by the ever-ready maintenance teams, with most crews continuing on their journey after an hour or so of repair work.[25]

Once the combat troops moved forward and gained contact with the Iraqi forces, the maintenance and supply units followed in the plowed, mine-free, lanes. With so many vehicles on the move, some problems were bound to arise. For example, one of the squadron's HEMTT cargo trucks broke down, stopping traffic. Fortunately, a maintenance crew led by CW2 Gerald Kovach and SSG William Ball was just behind them. The truck turned out to have an engine problem that could not be repaired on the spot. They got another HEMTT truck, hooked up the broken one to it, and supervised its towing through the lane. Within an hour, the truck was operational and delivering its badly needed supplies.[26]

The support troops also had one of the first enemy contacts when the A Troop M88 Tank Recovery Vehicle crew, lead by SSG Ernesto Infante, saw three Iraqi soldiers climbing out of a bunker. The maintenance sergeant stopped his vehicle and fired his .50 caliber machine gun at them, causing the Iraqis to throw their hands in the air. Unfortunately, this engagement took place inside one of the narrow breach lanes, causing the following combat equipment to bunch together and stop. SFC William Molitor jumped out of his vehicle and ran up to Infante and ordered him to quickly disarm the prisoners, send them to the rear, and get moving.[27]

At 1600 hours, Fontenot's Task Force 2-34 Armor reported clearing its objectives (3K and 4K), thus opening the way for Wilson's troopers to begin their attack towards their objective 15K. Meanwhile, TF 5-16 Infantry cleared objective 1K and linked up with the 2nd Brigade on the 1st Brigade's right flank. A short time later, COL Maggart judged that the situation amongst the trench lines was clear enough for the cavalry and LTC Patrick Ritter's 1-34 AR to commence their attack.

As B Troop emerged from the breach and began passing 2-34 Armor, it spotted two trucks filled with Iraqi soldiers trying to escape north. The tanks engaged each of the trucks with the 120-mm sabot rounds they had already loaded in their tubes. Each round passed through the light-skinned Iraqi vehicles, with the concussion from the impact killing everyone on board. An M3 fired a TOW missile at another light armored vehicle about 2,000 meters away, destroying it with one shot. The troop also attacked through an artillery position, and as they did so almost a hundred Iraqi soldiers came out of their bunkers to surrender. 1SGT David Rooks, 1LT Gerald Danussi, and the mortar platoon rounded up the prisoners and sent them to the rear. CPT Bills remembered watching these events as if each transpired in slow motion. For just a moment, he felt he was an observer, monitoring his sergeants and lieutenants taking charge of their platoons and vehicles and performing exactly as he had prepared them.[28]

On the squadron's right flank, A Troop moved out of the passage lane and encountered sporadic resistance. MAJ John Burdan, a key figure in developing the attack plan, followed behind A Troop's lead platoons. He was struck by the primitive nature of the Iraqi defenses. He had expected to find elaborate defenses along the lines of World War I battlefields, complete with wire and mutually supporting firing positions. Fortunately disappointed, he discovered little more than shallow ditches and small mounds. What serious dangers he did discover were caused not by the Iraqis, but by American troops.

First were the unexploded munitions or "bomblets." As Burdan traveled in his Cavalry Fighting Vehicle over to the contact point to meet a representative from 1-34 Armor on the squadron's right flank, he kept hearing popping sounds that resembled small-arms fire. He asked his gunner, SGT Bradley Carpenter, to scan to see if they were taking fire; they were not. Just then another M3 drove by and Carpenter pointed out the little explosions near that vehicle's tracks that were crushing the little shiny balls on the ground. A large portion of the munitions fired by army artillery and dropped by supporting aircraft were not the high-explosive rounds of previous eras, but canisters that dispensed a wide array of miniature munitions on the battlefield. Because of the soft sand, many had not exploded on impact, and now constituted a hazard to friendly as well as enemy soldiers. While most of the bomblets the troops encountered were not powerful enough to hurt an iron track, they were a serious danger to unsuspecting soldiers on the ground. Ultimately, the small shiny cylinders would be a serious cause of death and injury among soldiers and civilians alike.[29]

The second problem was friendly fire. This is nothing new, as any student of war knows. The accuracy and lethality of modern weapons make it all the more frightening for those receiving the fire. As John Burdan waited at the contact point, he watched 1-34 Armor , the exploiting battalion on the squadron's right flank, move out of its passage lanes and begin its attack to Objective 5K. Suddenly it became dangerous as the tanks began firing into each and every foxhole and bunker they passed. Burdan noticed that the western-most company was heading in his direction and continuing to shoot at anything its crews considered hostile. Just as he reached for his hand mike to remind the battalion command group that he was waiting at the contact point, the approaching armor let loose a stream of machine-gun fire in his direction. Cursing, as bullets were pinging off his vehicle, Burdan dropped into his hatch and began yelling repeatedly "Cease Fire! You are shooting at friendly units to your west!!" over the brigade command net. LTC Patrick Ritter, the battalion commander, reacted within seconds and got the tank company under control.[30]

Even as darkness began falling, the Iraqis continued to resist, firing artillery and mortars at the lanes cleared through the forward positions. Now the loss of those hours of daylight when the division waited became critical. Evening found the 1st Brigade still in the process of clearing the Iraqi fighting positions on the western part of the objective. The 2nd Brigade had cleared its sector on the eastern side and had reached PL Colorado. The 3rd Brigade was ready to begin its attack. However, just after dark, a soldier either stepped on a mine or detonated one of the many unexploded bomblets on the ground. His death added to the concern MG Rhame had about continuing his attack with the 3rd Brigade after dark. This was the same force that had formed the core of Task Force Iron and had suffered the resulting casualties from the Apache strike. It had not trained at the National Training Center and therefore had little experience in night combat operations. In addition, there was still much work to be done as American engineers had still to mark lanes for the following 1st (UK) Armoured Division.[31]

The corps commander also had concerns about continuing the attack in the dark. He wanted three divisions and his armored cavalry regiment concentrated ready to strike the Republican Guard Forces Command like a strong fist. He feared that dawn would find his left wing strung out and the breach area was not yet clear enough for the logistics units to begin moving forward. After talking to his senior commanders, including Rhame, Franks gave the order to hold in place for the night.[32]

By 1800 hours, the squadron was on its objective and had

completed its coordination with 1-34 Armor on its right and TF 5-16 Infantry, which had moved between the squadron and TF 2-34 Armor, on its left. The night was cold and rainy and illuminated by burning Iraqi ammo dumps and vehicles. By now the squadron had collected over 100 Iraqi prisoners. They were consolidated in the vicinity of the combat trains under the control of CSM Cobb. He was sure that it would be too dangerous to attempt to move them at night through the unexploded bomblets back to the prisoner-of-war collection area. The enemy was fleeing or surrendering all around and there was no sign of any kind of counterattack. With the division's attack halted for the night, it was now time for the combat service support activities to begin. The thousands of unexploded munitions still in the area made the resupply operation very dangerous. The support platoon leader, 1LT Matt Vanderfeltz, and his drivers performed exceptionally well in a very confusing situation, moving their large ammunition and fuel trucks into positions, in the dark, where ground units could rearm and refuel. Along with the necessities came the mail. Of course, not all was well. In B Troop, a tank commander had his knee smashed by the main gun's breech. Evacuated that night, he was headed for the hospital and ultimately a medical discharge.[33]

In A Troop, CPT Pope discovered that two vehicles were missing from 2LT Palmieri's platoon. It seems that a Bradley and another vehicle were inadvertently left behind when the attack began, one with a broken track and the other to lend assistance. Palmieri had instructed them to get the vehicle fixed and then join with the troop's maintenance section. Pope asked 1SGT Gary Parkey to retrace the day's route and try to find them and return them to the troop. Just in case, Pope gave him the grid coordinates for the next day's anticipated route of advance, in the event the mission took longer than expected. Parkey and PV2 Shawn Witherspoon, his HMMWV driver, began what would become a long separation from the rest of the unit.[34]

Finally, shortly after 2200 hours, the order came to the 1st Brigade to commence phase three of its attack at 0600 hours. This phase of the attack completed the penetration of the Iraqi defenses and established a half-circle line called PL New Jersey. The 3rd Brigade would join the attack and position its units between the 1st and 2nd Brigades. Once in position, MG Rhame would call the corps commander and report that his sector was clear and he was ready to begin passing the British armored division through the cleared lanes to the northeast.[35]

LTC Wilson convened a quick "orders group" late that evening consisting of the squadron staff, the troop commanders, and CPT Philbrick to discuss the day's events, determine current combat status, and brief the order to continue the attack to PL New Jersey. Everyone was in good spirits and by 2330 hours they were on the way back to their units. Burdan left the squadron tactical operations center, now located with the squadron on Objective 15K, shortly after midnight and crawled into the back of his HMMWV. His driver had laid the seats down and there was just enough area to stretch out. As he fell asleep he could scarcely believe the squadron's good fortune. The attack had succeeded beyond anyone's wildest hopes.[36]

Not all of the Iraqi troops were gone, however. A Troop's 1st Platoon watched from a distance as some kind of Iraqi unit, probably a headquarters or supply installation, prepared to leave. The platoon leader 2LT Jim Copenhaver and SFC William Molitor continued to ask the troop commander for permission to fire, which was denied because of the growing concerns over fratricide. Finally, when a few Iraqi trucks rolled up on the position and people started to get in them, the platoon received permission to engage. They fired and destroyed the trucks, one of which was apparently hauling ammunition as evidenced by the explosion. The Iraqi soldiers who had not yet boarded the trucks fled back into their bunkers where they remained the rest of the night. Few in the platoon slept that night because they were so close to the Iraqi soldiers, and because that ammunition truck continued to burn and explode for the next four hours.[37]

As morning broke, the squadron resumed the attack to PL New Jersey. A Troop immediately flushed the Iraqis out of the bunkers they had been observing during the night. It turned out to be an artillery battery and, as the Iraqis emerged with their hands in the air, SFC Molitor stopped his vehicle next to the dazed enemy. Almost immediately, he found himself talking with the Iraqi artillery commander who spoke some English. The Iraqi told Molitor that his whole unit was ready to surrender. As they were talking, the remainder of A Troop passed by. As the trailing reaction platoon moved through the area, they saw Molitor's M3 stopped and Iraqis moving around it. Assuming the worst, the American tanks began engaging the Iraqis who jumped back into their bunkers. The American now realized how inexperienced he was, as everyone else was scurrying for cover while he remained standing. Seeing the tanks heading his way and still firing, he too hit the ground and followed the Iraqi officer into his bunker, where the two waited for the commotion to subside. After a minute or two, the firing died down and Molitor climbed back out and told the reaction platoon that the Iraqis were surrendering. Next time, he decided he would make sure the rest of the platoon and troop knew what was going on before he dismounted. Molitor's section finished disarming the Iraqis and sent them to the rear. He then hurried to catch up with the rest of his platoon.[38]

When B Troop arrived along PL New Jersey, it found itself on a series of abandoned Iraqi positions on top of a low bluff that commanded the approaches from the south. These defensive positions were well positioned to inflict serious damage on the advancing Americans. The strength of this complex impressed CPT Bills, who looked back across the valley to the ridgeline he had occupied at mid-morning the day before. He knew they would have been hard to assault if the enemy had not already been defeated by air and artillery. While Bills observed the countryside, his troopers began to clear the bunkers. They found headquarters bunkers, underground kitchens, and ammunition storage points. Without informing most of the soldiers, the engineer platoon accompanying the troop, with Bills's permission, destroyed the ammunition. The explosion startled all and the troop commander made a note to pass the word before he let that happen again.[39]

Soon afterwards, A Troop reported that it had arrived at PL New Jersey. From the high ground on the bluff, the cavalrymen were able to watch the 3rd Armored Division, in battle formation, move in brigade columns on the northwest side of the phase line. This division, along with the 1st Armored on its left flank, trailed the 2nd Armored Cavalry Regiment that was advancing north and east in search of the Iraqi Republican Guard.

The thousands of vehicles on the march were impressive and gave the soldiers a sense of invincibility. Within thirty-six hours, the 3rd Armored Division would be locked in a heavy fight with the center of the Tawakalna Mechanized Division's battle line.[40]

Shortly before 1130 hours, the division arrived on PL New Jersey. Now the squadron began the task of organizing the battle positions. This included moving more than sixty prisoners to the rear, under CSM Cobb's control, and destroying all non-American equipment. The engineers approached the task of equipment and bunker destruction enthusiastically, and brought forward a couple of bulldozers to help do the job. Not having the means to transport the captured Iraqis to the rear, the ever-resourceful Cobb borrowed the empty flat-bed trucks that had carried the bulldozers forward and loaded them up with the Iraqis. He then moved them to the prisoner-of-war collection point in the brigade support area.[41]

Numerous enemy bunkers and vehicles were in the squadron battle position, many of them belonging to artillery and support units. Despite the terrific bombardment from land and air, a large number of the Iraqi bunkers appeared to be untouched. The troops spent some time looking through them and found a varied assortment of equipment, binoculars, radios, maps, and night vision goggles. Much of it would find its way back to the Cavalry Museum at Fort Riley. Of special interest to the American soldiers were the living conditions of their opponents. The structures were small but livable, with old mattresses, lanterns, water cans, and even books. Some had little notches in the wall that held a picture of the family they had left behind. It brought a human face to war and a sense of how terrible it really was.[42]

Majors Bill Wimbish and John Burdan took some time to examine this complex while they were out inspecting the squadron. Those they saw were all below ground level with a raised roof that allowed the occupants to scan the terrain around them and fire at someone if necessary, and you could stand upright in most of them. The roofs were made of thin sheets of corrugated steel over a set of wooden rafters. The builders had piled only eight to ten inches of dirt on top of the metal, and it was obvious the roof could not withstand a hit by a mortar or artillery round. Each structure had a small kerosene burner intended to heat food, but apparently also provided the bunker's only source of heat. Each bunker had a rusty, five-gallon metal can for water. The liquid inside had an oily smell and contained bits of rust and other matter.

The two field-grade officers located what they believed to be the unit's kitchen facility. It was larger than most of the other structures and contained several burner units and a container of kerosene. Inside was a long wooden table, probably used to prepare food, and sections of the dirt wall hollowed out for shelving. Nearby were approximately twelve fifty-pound bags of rice, but few of the pots, pans, and utensils that one would find with a typical American mess section. Continuing their search, Wimbish and Burdan also found the unit command bunker. Inside were several old radios and various kinds of hand microphones and headsets. The generators to run the radios were in holes outside and connected by buried cables. They also found several crates, with "Jordanian Army GHQ" stenciled on them, containing radios, antennas, and other communication equipment. They were surprised to discover this facility because they had seen no signs of any antennas that would normally be associated with a command post. Following one cable from the back of a radio set to see where it would lead, they traced it outside to a six-inch deep trench that ran for about one hundred and fifty meters to an antenna. It was single mast, thirty-foot pole that was lying in the open on the ground. Three small cables, with stakes at each end, connected to the top portion. Apparently, the Iraqis left the antenna down on the ground except when needed. At the designated time, they would pull on the wires, erect it, and stake it down. Once they had completed their radio transmissions, they would then pull the structure back down to avoid American detection. Inside the bunker the majors found maps with operational graphics, written in Arabic, which seemed to indicate that the squadron now controlled the location previously occupied by the 110th Brigade of the Iraqi 26th Infantry Division. Burdan compared the map with the squadron intelligence template and determined that they had done a pretty good job of targeting the actual enemy locations.[43]

Meanwhile, 1SGT Parkey continued his search for the missing A Troop vehicles, after spending the night with the combat trains. As he and PV2 Witherspoon drove south through the breach and searched for the lost vehicles, they were amazed at the number of Iraqis who were still in the area trying to surrender. They arrived back at the original troop assembly area around 1030 hours but could not find the missing vehicles. Parkey decided to remain for awhile and see if he could contact SFC Steve Kuder, the missing Bradley's commander.[44]

By noon the division was in place on PL New Jersey and Rhame notified the corps commander that the area was ready for the British to begin their passage of lines. By 1330 hours the lead elements of the famed "Desert Rats" were moving through the lanes marked by the engineers. The Iraqi 26th Infantry Division no longer existed. Its equipment was scattered in the desert and its soldiers either dead or on their way to prisoner-of-war holding cages back in Saudi Arabia. While eating an MRE and watching the Desert Rats pass, the support platoon leader Matt Vanderfeltz was approached by a hungry British soldier riding in a Land Rover. After a short chat the two allies arranged a swap. In return for an MRE Vanderfeltz got a stuffed British bear. He later gave the bear to one of the troop first sergeants who passed it on to his daughter when he got home.[45] The forward passage of the British was uneventful, and as they commenced their attack, the 1st Infantry Division reverted to the role of corps reserve. However, it would not rest for long.[46]

11   Objective Norfolk

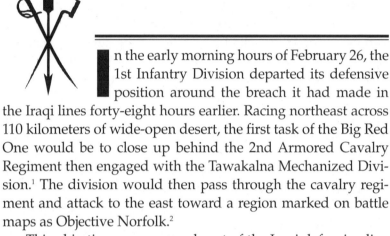

I n the early morning hours of February 26, the 1st Infantry Division departed its defensive position around the breach it had made in the Iraqi lines forty-eight hours earlier. Racing northeast across 110 kilometers of wide-open desert, the first task of the Big Red One would be to close up behind the 2nd Armored Cavalry Regiment then engaged with the Tawakalna Mechanized Division.[1] The division would then pass through the cavalry regiment and attack to the east toward a region marked on battle maps as Objective Norfolk.[2]

This objective encompassed part of the Iraqi defensive line that they had scrambled to establish on February 25 after they became aware of the VII Corps's attack from the west. The Iraqi 18th Mechanized Brigade from the Tawakalna Mechanized Division and the 37th Mechanized Brigade from the 12th Armored Division defended this sector that contained a large number of supply depots for units assigned along the border and in western Kuwait. It was also the intersection of several roads, most importantly the IPSA (Iraqi Petroleum Saudi Arabia) pipeline road that ran northeast towards Basra. It was the Iraqi Army's main supply route to support units defending along the Saudi Arabian border.[3]

The 1-4 Cavalry continued to consolidate and reorganize on PL New Jersey on February 25. Shortly after 1400 hours, word arrived that MG Rhame wanted to see his commanders at the division's forward command post. At 1630 hours while Wilson was still at the meeting, the division staff issued a warning order for Contingency Plan Jeremiah II. This plan, which was one of several that had been worked out by the division planners earlier, had the squadron returning to division operational control and leading its advance from its current location, northeast to an area just behind the 2nd Armored Cavalry Regiment. On order, the division would then conduct a forward passage of lines and fight the Iraqi forces around Objective Norfolk. As Burdan and the squadron staff pulled out the contingency plan's map overlay, all were amazed at the distance they were now going to have to travel. It was over 100 kilometers just to link up with the 2nd Cavalry and then another twenty to thirty kilometers of fighting to secure their objective. It was now also obvious the squadron did not have enough 1:250,000 maps.[4]

At the division meeting, LTC Wilson had learned that the VII Corps had encountered little resistance as it continued to plunge into the Iraqi desert and it appeared that the Iraqis might not yet be aware that they were about to be trapped inside Kuwait. The 1st and 3rd Armored Divisions and the 2nd Armored Cavalry Regiment were continuing toward the expected location of the Republican Guard Forces Command, around Phase Line Smash. LTG Franks designated the 1st Infantry Division as the corps reserve and ordered it to move to the northeast. The division staff could provide almost no information as to the enemy situation, the friendly situation on either flank, or where the VII Corps would make contact with the Iraqi main force. Remaining flexible, MG Rhame planned to move the 1st Infantry Division in two columns, with the 1st Brigade on the left (north) and the 3rd Brigade on the right. The 2nd Brigade, without Task Force 2-16 Infantry, which Rhame wanted left in the breach area for security, would follow the 3rd Brigade. The cavalry's mission was to conduct a zone reconnaissance in front of the division main body, and to report and then bypass any pockets of enemy resistance. The division's movement would begin at 0500 hours the next morning.

Wilson departed the division command post at 1700 hours and radioed back to the tactical operation center to have the troop commanders and staff ready for an orders-group briefing at 2000 hours. He arrived back at the TOC at 1730 hours and met with his staff. After a quick mission and course of action analysis discussion, he issued his guidance for the squadron order. Wilson planned to use the air and ground scouts together to find the enemy units in the division's zone and pass on their location to the following brigades. In response to the division scheme of maneuver, Wilson organized the squadron with A Troop in the north in a zone about eight to ten kilometers wide maintaining contact with the 3rd Armored Division, and B Troop in the south in a slightly larger zone. Because of the different axes of advance between the 1st Infantry Division about to move to the northeast, and the 1st British Armoured Division in the south, moving eastward, there would be a growing gap between the divisions and more potential for discovering bypassed Iraqi units. Hence, the decision to place B Troop, with its three more tanks, on the southern route. The aeroscout weapons teams would work with the ground units to help speed the recon effort and to provide flank security for the squadron. The squadron logistics elements would follow the lead troops in the zone of advance.[5]

After the TOC sent instructions to the troop commanders to report for orders at 2000 hours, the staff officers began the process of developing a fragmentary order to guide the squadron's movement. Essential to this phase was graphically displaying the scheme of maneuver on paper and reproducing it on sheets, called overlays, that subordinate units could place on their own battle maps. However, the map problem now became serious. Up to now, the squadron had been able to work from detailed maps in the area around the breach. This new mission required them to travel a great distance and there were simply not enough operational (1:250,000 scale) or more detailed tactical (1:50,000) maps for all the soldiers who needed them. In addition, the graphics themselves reproduced by SGM Shields and the S3 shop on the Diazo machine were hard to use at the squadron/troop level. Now the value of the Global Positioning System became obvious. The staff developed a series of checkpoints, or predetermined locations. These locations, which were entered into each GPS, took precedence over the less accurate hand-drawn graphics. As a result, the orders handed out at the meeting were quite simple, with only checkpoints, unit boundaries, phase lines, and Objective Norfolk indicated on the attached map overlays.[6]

With the warning order came the requirement for a task reorganization. The squadron needed to ensure that those elements that no longer belonged to them got to the units that they were to work for in the next phase of the division's attack. CSM Cobb took charge of returning these units, such as the psychological operations team that had helped to process the squadron's captured Iraqi soldiers, to the 1st Brigade.[7]

The troop commanders, with CPT Philbrick representing the aviation units, began arriving at the command post soon after 1930 hours. The briefing began on time with CPT Seelinger, the S2, presenting an overview of what the division knew about the Iraqi forces they would encounter on the move. MAJ Burdan then briefed the details of the operation, to include the movement of the remainder of the division, major phase lines, and the probable course of action after they made contact with the 2nd Armored Cavalry. MAJ Wimbish and CPT Harmon then addressed the plans for ammunition, fuel, and maintenance support. Harmon would continue to control the combat trains while CPT Morrison would form a small Forward Support Element that would bring supplies forward from the squadron field trains and keep them closer to the ground troops than normal support doctrine prescribed. Through an agreement with the 1st Brigade, the squadron field trains would remain with its field trains and receive supplies from them. LTC Wilson closed the meeting by trying to describe what was going to happen over the next few days. The meeting ended soon after 2130 and everyone returned to his unit. Time was short as the squadron had to pull out of its defensive array and move into consolidated attack positions shortly after midnight.[8]

Once Wilson was done with his order, the troop commanders needed to translate this guidance into their own plans. CPT Bills recalled that it was difficult getting back to his command post in the rain and he needed his GPS to navigate the seven kilometers between locations. After he arrived at his headquarters, he and 1LT Gerald Danussi, his XO, drafted a plan to implement the squadron's order. They relied on the troop's standard operating procedures to shorten the process. Once his leaders joined him, Bills issued his version of the order, which broke down the squadron mission into tasks that the platoon leaders could accomplish. He emphasized that the platoons needed to maintain visual contact with each other and developed a series of waypoints to keep them on line. He ended the meeting as promptly as possible so that his subordinates could develop their own plans.[9]

It was a cold night, with almost no visibility because of the rain and overcast skies, making standard night-vision goggles almost useless. The squadron began repositioning shortly after midnight. To keep from bumping into each other, vehicle commanders used their thermal imagery sights and watched the black-out drive lights on those vehicles in front. The drivers and vehicle commanders were also exhausted and often fell asleep in their seats whenever their column stopped. There were also minor collisions and the normal array of maintenance problems. Lieutenant Dave Palmieri's Bradley, for example, dislocated its track from its drive sprocket (called "throwing" a track) just as he was receiving the fragmentary order over the radio from CPT Pope. He had to change to his platoon sergeant's vehicle and leave his behind for repairs after first light. The ground was still dangerous with scattered unexploded munitions. This was just one more worry for Pope who was increasingly concerned about 1SGT Parkey, who had not returned from his mission of finding A Troop's missing vehicles and he realized that Parkey would have to catch up on his own.[10]

It was no easier for the squadron's logistics units. Captains Harmon and Morrison, each leading a portion of the combat trains, were attempting to find each other in the dark. They were arguing with each other over the radio and voicing their frustrations over the squadron command frequency for all to hear. Wilson finally intervened and ordered them off his frequency and told them to continue their conversation on the squadron administrative-logistics net. Ultimately, without further broadcasting their confusion, they found each other in the dark.

Meanwhile CPT Mark Johnson, the squadron motor officer, was busy leading the maintenance section toward the line of departure and found the going very difficult. As other unit convoys rolled through the area, some sleepy soldiers suddenly awoke and mistakenly tried moving their vehicles to join the wrong unit. In one well-remembered example, the motor officer was on the ground ensuring that all the vehicles were present when one of the squadron's M88 Recovery Vehicles suddenly pulled out of line and inexplicably joined another unit's convoy. Of course, the driver had fallen asleep and woke up convinced his unit was moving out without him. Johnson had to spring back into his HMMWV and race after the confused fifty-eight-ton tank retriever in the dark, try to get the driver's attention in the noise and darkness, and redirect it back to his proper convoy. It took Johnson almost ninety minutes to finally get everyone heading in the right direction. His section eventually linked up with CPT Harmon and rest of the combat trains in time to depart as a group.[11] As a result of all of this friction, it took until the early morning hours for Wilson's command to travel the short distance to its attack positions.

At 0428 hours the squadron reported crossing the line of departure as planned, approximately ninety minutes before the rest of the division. Because of the darkness, a dearth of global positioning systems, and an uncertain enemy situation, its pace was slow. After the first half hour, the squadron had progressed only a few kilometers over relatively open terrain. Wilson began urging Captains Bills and Pope to pick up the pace, since he knew that the remainder of the division would rapidly catch up with the squadron and its value to MG Rhame as a reconnaissance element would then be lost. Despite his urgings, the squadron's speed would not increase until after dawn. By 0611 hours, the division's lead brigades had closed the gap and were just in front of the squadron's support trains.[12]

Major Wimbish's command post actually crossed the line of departure with the advanced units from the 1st Brigade, a dangerous situation as the lightly protected vehicles were in close contact with the brigade's heavy armor. As dawn broke, the command post and CPT Harmon's combat trains began to race to get ahead of the brigade's lead units and rejoin the squadron farther forward. Wimbish later remembered thinking it a bit strange for his unarmored support vehicles to be darting out ahead of the 1st Infantry Division's combat power. By 0900 his column had passed the 1st Brigade's lead scouts and was out in the open.[13]

The weather did not improve after the sun came up and a dense fog developed, making visibility even worse. The aviation scouts got into the sky for a short period, but the fog and

cloud ceiling made it too dangerous and CPT Philbrick pulled
them back in. That meant that the ground scouts would be unable to locate anything until they were almost on top of it. The
weather, however, did not stop COL Mowery from flying out to
the squadron to confer with Wilson. Mowery had a difficult
task in finding the squadron's command group and had to be
vectored in by MAJ Burdan. Although they could hear him flying through the area the low ceiling prevented them from seeing him until he dropped to within 100 feet of the ground. Once
he landed, the brigade commander told Wilson and Burdan
that he had directed Philbrick to get the aircraft flying despite
the weather. He felt it was essential that the aircraft be available
to support the recon effort.[14]

The Quarter Horse arrived in the 2nd Armored Cavalry's[15]
rear area by 1000 hours and immediately began to refuel and
prepare for whatever mission the division would demand.[16]
The 2nd Cavalry had located the Tawakalna Division and was
attacking it in what would be called the Battle of 73 Easting.
Early in the afternoon, LTG Franks ordered the Big Red One to
pass through the engaged cavalry regiment and attack the
Iraqis defending on Objective Norfolk. His staff directed the
2nd Cavalry to select coordination points on the 62 Easting.[17]
Given these points, one for each of the two 1st Division
brigades, leaders from the squadron, the division and the 2nd
Armored Cavalry would work through the innumerable details
of the operation and Rhame ordered Wilson to supervise the coordination.[18] At 1530 hours MAJ Burdan traveled to the 2nd
Cavalry's command post to confer with the deputy regimental
commander and began working out the details of the passage
of lines.[19]

Not since World War II had a United States Army armored
or mechanized division conducted a passage of lines in combat. Yet, in the space of only two days, the Big Red One had the
opportunity to do it for the second time. The first time it was
the stationary unit passing the 1st (UK) Armoured Division to
the east. Now it was the passing unit in an operation that required the utmost unit and personal discipline. Twelve battalions of armor, mechanized infantry, and supporting artillery
(1st Infantry Division) approached three armored cavalry

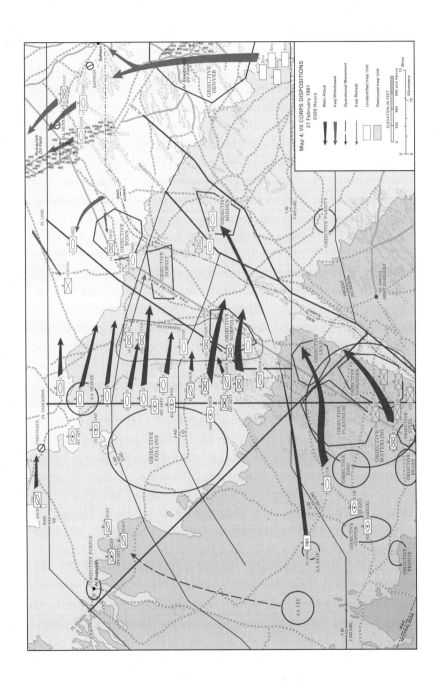

squadrons with its supporting artillery that were locked in battle with several Iraqi brigades. This time there were no rehearsals. At precisely the right points in the desert, the passing units needed to move through the lines of the exhausted cavalry troopers, turn their gun tubes towards the enemy and continue the battle. Simultaneously, all artillery systems within range would come under the control of the 1st Infantry. As the brigades of the 1st Infantry Division, "Devil" (1st), "Iron Deuce" (3rd), and "Dagger" (2nd), passed forward into enemy contact, the 2nd Armored Cavalry would stop shooting. From that point on, the regiment could only engage targets it positively identified. Any mistakes in either the approach, passage, or battle hand-off would spell disaster.[20]

To preclude engaging each other by mistake, and to minimize the natural friction of an operation to be conducted at night by tired soldiers, the leadership of both units tried to conduct the operation by the book. It was, however, a hasty passage, with little time for all of the procedures spelled out in the army's field manuals. Friction, the cumulative effect of tired soldiers and leaders, darkness, great distance and little time, began to interfere with the operation. The original plan had envisioned Wilson's squadron making the appropriate coordination, and then leading the 1st and 3rd Brigades forward through the designated passage lane. However, the line of contact between the regiment and the Iraqis was fluid. Although the 2rd Armored Cavalry was on the 70 Easting when the 1st Infantry Division started moving towards them, it ended up closer to the 73 Easting and in contact with at least two more Tawakalna battalions as the actual time for the passage approached. Furthermore, Rhame had second thoughts about trying to fit his relatively light cavalry squadron between the 2nd Armored Cavalry and the defending Iraqi armor. Once the squadron led the 1st and 3rd Brigades to the passage lanes, the brigades would then have to pass through the regiment to bring their firepower to bear on the enemy. Essentially, it would have been a double forward passage in the face of the enemy. Therefore, keeping with the American Army's adage of KISS ("Keep It Simple, Stupid"), Rhame directed the two brigades to pass directly through the regiment in the passage lanes coordinated by 1-4 Cavalry. Shortly after the brigades began their passages through the 2nd ACR, Quarter Horse would conduct its forward passage of lines and establish a flank screen along the division's northern boundary. While the change made tactical sense, especially in this dangerous environment, it drove the 1st Infantry Division's brigade and battalion commanders frantic. As COL Maggart, the 1st Brigade commander, remarked:

> It is difficult to describe how complicated it was to redefine the direction of attack and to change formations while bouncing across the desert (in a tank or Bradley) in the dead of night at high speed using a 1:250,000 scale map. Even with the Magellan (a brand of global positioning receiver), this was an incredibly difficult undertaking. Notwithstanding the problems of changing the plan en route, the brigade modified the zone of action and continued toward the passage point.[21]

Through the afternoon hours, the squadron command post was busy. MAJ Wimbish and the staff worked with Wilson to develop the plan for the squadron's part of the attack. The Quarter Horse was going to conduct its passage of lines through the 2nd Squadron. It had two passage lanes, one for each of the ground troops. At 1730 hours the XO gathered the troop commanders and CPT Philbrick to issue the revised order. With the passage of lines beginning at 2130, there was little time for the troop commanders to develop and issue their own plans. Captain Bills, for example, sketched out his own concept and passed it to his XO, 1LT Danussi, to transmit to the platoon leaders on the radio.[22]

Shortly before 2100 hours, the 1st Brigade's two lead battalions headed for their passage lanes opposite the Iraqi 18th Mechanized Brigade. Maggart soon realized that the passage arrangements again needed to be modified as a result of the rapidly changing battle. The brigade commander now ordered both lead units, the 1st and 2nd Battalions, 34th Armor, to pass through one passage lane instead of two. That change simplified movement forward and limited the direct coordination and exchange of information between divisional, battalion, and regimental squadron commanders.[23] Colonel David Weisman's 3rd Brigade, moving in the south, coordinated a separate passage

lane for each of his three battalions.[24] Throughout, Burdan remained with the 2nd Armored Cavalry and helped to work out
any coordination difficulties between the division's brigades
and the regiment.

As the 1st Infantry Division soldiers approached their designated lanes, they passed the wreckage of an Iraqi mechanized
brigade whose burning tanks and fighting vehicles marked the
way to the front lines. They drove by batteries of American
MLRS and M109 systems firing at targets a dozen miles to the
east. As the division's tank and Bradley crews neared the passage lane, main-gun and machine-gun tracers shot through the
darkness just above the ground. The horizon, in Iraqi territory,
was filled with blazing fires and massive explosions.[25] Approaching the rear of the 2nd Armored Cavalry's defenses, they
could see the many multi-colored chemical lights that each regimental vehicle had affixed to the back of its turret.[26]

Shortly before 2130 hours, 1st Infantry Division brigade and
battalion S3s and executive officers, moving slightly ahead of
their main bodies, jumped down from their vehicles and conducted last-minute coordination with their regimental counter-
parts. It was suddenly quiet across the thirty-kilometer front, as
the stationary unit held its fire. Scouts on the forward line fired
green star clusters to mark the exact passage lanes. Then, moving past the 2nd ACR soldiers and burning T-72 tanks, the 1st
Infantry Division assumed responsibility for the battle. The regimental squadrons remained in position to assist the 1st Infantry units in their passage.[27] During the next several hours,
Rhame's tanks, Bradleys, and field artillery would eliminate the
two brigades of Iraqi defenders who stood in their way in what
came to be called the Battle of Norfolk.[28]

Some of the fireworks the approaching 1st Infantry Division soldiers saw that night were caused by their own 1st Battalion, 1st Aviation's attack helicopters. LTC Ronald Richelsdor-
fer's Apaches attacked the 9th Armored and 18th Mechanized
Brigade's second tactical echelon at about 2100 hours.[29] At least
two battalions of the Tawakalna Division and one from the 12th
Armored Division were deployed along that line. In addition,
there were dozens of artillery batteries, command and control
facilities, and much of the Iraqi tri-border logistics complex lo-

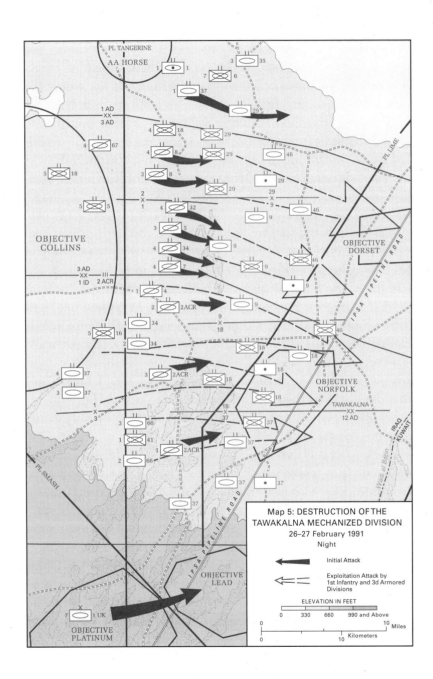

Map 5: DESTRUCTION OF THE
TAWAKALNA MECHANIZED DIVISION
26–27 February 1991
Night

Initial Attack

Exploitation Attack by
1st Infantry and 3d Armored
Divisions

ELEVATION IN FEET

0   330   660   990 and Above

0   10
                                Miles
0   10
                                Kilometers

cated there. The helicopter attack continued the pressure on the
Iraqi commander and his artillery, preventing him from inter-
fering with the 1st Infantry's passage of lines.

By 2230 five heavy battalions and the Quarter Horse had
passed through the 2nd Cavalry and advanced onto their objective. As the 1st Infantry Division took control of the sector, the
210th Field Artillery Brigade added its reinforcing fires to the
1st Infantry Divisions artillery.[30] In the 1st Brigade sector, LTC
Patrick Ritter's 1st Battalion, 34th Armor, a pure M1A1 battalion led by its Bradley-mounted scouts, moved through the single passage lane. Soon after passing the 2nd Cavalry's positions, it ran into a battalion of the 18th Mechanized Brigade.[31]
Iraqi gunners destroyed two of the American reconnaissance
vehicles, probably silhouetted against the fires of burning Iraqi
vehicles. Ritter immediately pulled his scouts back and moved
his tank companies forward. These Iraqis intended to fight, unlike those encountered by the Americans in the breach.[32]

LTC Gregory Fontenot's Task Force 2-34 Armor followed
Ritter's tanks through the passage lane. As Fontenot's four
companies moved through the lane, the two northern units
strayed off their axis and began moving north, rather than
east.[33] With all the postwar celebration of technology, commanders on M1A1 tanks still had no sure way of knowing in
what direction they were heading while on the move since they
had no vehicle mounted compass or navigation system. The
world's most modern tank did not even have the old azimuth
indicator that tankers had used for years as navigation aids.
Unable to locate his two teams, and sensing they were heading
in the wrong way towards possible annihilation by the friendly
2nd Cavalry in the rear or the 3rd Armored Division in the
north, Fontenot called the leading C Team commander. After a
short radio discussion with the battalion commander, C Company's Captain Robert Burns jumped off his tank to determine
his actual direction of movement. Not knowing how close the
enemy was or the condition of the ground, Burns moved away
from his M1A1's protective mass of metal and pulled out his
trusty Lensatic Compass. Quickly realizing his directional error,
he figured out his correction and returned to his tank before
taking fire, friendly or enemy.[34]

Colonel Maggart, following in Fontenot's sector, received the reports from his two battalion commanders. Although dismayed that his attack had come to a quick halt, he had worked with both Ritter and Fontenot for a long time and he knew there was little he could do but calmly urge them to sort their problems out, and both promised to resume their attacks soon, while Maggart notified the 2nd Cavalry that one of his task forces was "pirouetting forward of their positions."[35] Within forty minutes, an extremely long wait for Maggart, both battalions were back on line and ready to resume their advance. The third battalion of the brigade, Colonel Sidney "Skip" Baker's Task Force 5-16th Infantry, was moving up quickly behind the northern task force.[36]

The passage of the 3rd Brigade began much more smoothly as the brigade moved though three separate, well-marked passage lanes. The leading units made almost immediate contact with the Iraqi defenders, two battalions of the 37th Armored Brigade.[37] Almost immediately after their passage, the northern battalion, LTC Taylor Jones's 3rd Battalion, 66th Armor, ran into a T-55-equipped Iraqi tank battalion. Colonel Weisman, the brigade commander, believed the constant pounding by army aviation and air force attack had blinded the Iraqis to the reality of a ground attack and the attack caught many Iraqi tank crews on the ground in their shelters. This situation, however, made a more organized battle difficult for the Americans. Many Iraqi tanks, for example, did not show on the M1's thermal sights because they had not been manned or their engines started.[38] This part of the objective had been an Iraqi supply depot and underground storage and living bunker complexes were everywhere. Constructed by non-RGFC soldiers, these were organized as mutually supporting defensive positions with tank ditches and a limited amount of wire and mines. The Iraqi fighting positions, however, were still poorly prepared and required a soldier to expose his head and shoulders in order to fire, a sure target for tank and Bradley machine gunners.[39]

Although this position appeared to contain nothing other than burning or destroyed vehicles, hidden among this array were operational T-55 tanks. With their engines off, concealed in revetments and invisible to the Americans' thermal sights,

they were supported by Iraqi infantry units. A slightly mis-ori-
ented Bradley platoon, attempting to follow the M1 tanks,
moved across the front of these Iraqi positions, illuminated by
burning vehicles behind them. The Iraqis took advantage of
this excellent target and opened fire from three directions. The
initial volley hit a Bradley, killing three American soldiers.[40] An
American tank company trailing the lead units observed the
Iraqi fire and joined the melee, quickly destroying three T-55s
before they could get off another shot. At the same time, several
small antitank rockets hit some of the other tanks and Bradleys.
From the perspective of the tank gunners looking through the
thermal sights of the approaching M1 tanks, these flashes appeared to be T-55 tanks shooting at them. The young and exhausted American gunners, convinced they were fighting
against a determined enemy, opened fire, hitting three more
American vehicles.[41]

When the confusing melee in the 3rd Brigade's sector was
over, 1st Infantry Division crews had destroyed five of their own
tanks and four Bradleys. Six brigade soldiers perished in these
attacks and thirty others were wounded. Rather than "press the
attack" as those at Third Army and Central Command were demanding,[42] Weisman decided to pull his unit back, consolidate,
and use artillery to destroy the aggressive Iraqi infantry.[43] Once
on line, they would be prepared to continue.

By 0030 hours (February 27), one hour after the attack had
begun, the two attacking brigades of the 1st Infantry Division
were arrayed along the 75 Easting.[44] For the next three hours,
they methodically crossed the remaining ten kilometers of Objective Norfolk. The 1st Brigade commander, following just behind his lead battalions, thought he was "watching a vintage
black and white movie. Everything seemed to move in slow
motion." Such was the thunder of battle that "there was no no-
ticeable sound that anyone could recall."[45] As they slowly advanced, M1A1 tank commanders acquired the thermal images
of the Iraqi tanks or infantry fighting vehicles long before they
were themselves spotted. Platoon leaders, team commanders,
and even battalion commanders issued unit-wide fire commands. Before the defending Iraqis had any idea what was happening, their whole line of vehicles exploded.[46]

Shortly after the brigades began their passage of lines, LTC Wilson and his 1st Squadron, 4th Cavalry began its own movement through the 2nd Cavalry. Initially behind the defensive line established by the 2nd Squadron, each troop moved through a designated passage lane into the division's zone. CPT Bills was a little uneasy as his troop approached the lane. He did not have the frequency of the unit they were passing through and had to rely on the squadron TOC to notify the 2nd Squadron headquarters of his unit's movements. As it entered the passage lane and moved through it, the units on the north side of the lane ceased firing. The 2nd Cavalry units on the south side of the passage lane, however, continued to engage targets to their front, creating some confusion for the passing troops. As the ground troops entered the division battle zone, the eastern horizon was aflame with tracers and explosions. Captains Bills and Pope essentially had their troops execute a left face and traveled north in column towards their assigned sectors, with A Troop leading the way. Shortly after the passage, while the Cavalry Fighting Vehicles headed northeast to establish the screen line, the command's always-thirsty M1A1 tanks moved towards a refuel point established by CPT Morrison. Once the tanks were "topped off," they traveled to rejoin their platoons, none getting lost in the darkness and confusion.[47]

The sector the squadron occupied was adjacent to the 3rd Armored Division's 4-7 Cavalry, a unit that had been shot up earlier in the day when it had made initial contact with the Iraqi battle line and got caught between the enemy and approaching friendly tanks.[48] Now, in the ten-kilometer gap between the 1st Infantry and 3rd Armored Divisions' main combat troops, these two cavalry squadrons struggled to maintain contact and identify any further Iraqi threats. Each unit's use of different scale maps and the 4-7 Cavalry's lack of GPS receivers accentuated these problems. Throughout the night, MAJ Bill Wimbish and the TOC crew worked to resolve movement problems between the two units.[49]

While maintaining contact with the 4-7th Cavalry to the north of the 1st Infantry Division zone, the squadron established a screen line north and west of Objective Norfolk, with B Troop assuming the western sector and A Troop the east. Each platoon occupied its portion of the line by conducting a zone reconnaissance to clear a zone between it and the division to the south. Bills's command occupied its portion of the screen line without incident.[50] Captain Pope's A Troop encountered Iraqis as it moved into position and the troop's Bradleys destroyed an ammunition truck, a few other vehicles, and several supply tents, arriving on its sector sometime after midnight. Shortly after B Troop established their screen line, CPT Bills began to get reports of vehicle movement to their front. He gave the order to engage the enemy vehicles as they appeared. Based upon what he monitored on the squadron command net, Bills began to get the uneasy feeling that they might be in an Iraqi kill zone. This highlighted a problem with operating at night. The Iraqis dug their positions into the ground. The bunkers were constructed so that only about the top eighteen to twenty-four inches showed above the ground. The vehicle positions were dug in with low berms covering them on three sides. Even with the thermal sights it was often difficult to pick out the vehicles that were in those positions at night. If the positions were properly prepared and occupied you might not see the enemy vehicles until you were very close to them. In the midst of all of this activity it soon became apparent that the two troops did not have physical contact with each other. A gap of a couple of unobserved kilometers lay between the two cavalry units.[51]

Once the 1st Infantry Division Tactical Command Post co-located with the 2nd Cavalry's headquarters shortly after 2230 hours, MAJ Burdan received permission to return to his unit, arriving at the squadron's tactical command post around 0130 hours. On the way back to his unit, he saw the tracers and explosions of the division's ongoing battle several kilometers to the south. When he arrived at the TOC, he found it operating in a ramp-up configuration without tent extensions and configured for rapid movement. He walked over to the S3 M577 and tugged open the door. There he found the two watch officers asleep, with microphones in their hands and heads resting on the map boards. He noticed a HMMWV next to the command post and found MAJ Wimbish. The XO said that everyone was dead tired and that he was monitoring the situation while they caught a quick nap. He had seen Burdan drive up but opted not to challenge him. While he was controlling the command radio net, Wilson was awake in the B Troop zone and monitoring the tactical situation. Wimbish then updated the S3 on the tactical situation.[52]

As he updated his map with current unit locations, Burdan noticed the gap between the two troops. Despite assurances from the troop commanders that this sector was covered, at around 0330 hours he and the squadron commander decided to inspect the screen line. With two M3 Bradleys and the M113 carrying the Fire Support Officer, CPT Gary Rahmeyer, the command group headed for the gap between the two troops.[53] Simultaneously, Bills's command began noticing Iraqi soldiers with RPG antitank rockets and tank crews moving towards their dug-in tanks. As he evaluated the reports coming in from his platoons, Bills realized that he was located in an Iraqi kill zone, with only darkness preventing a fire-fight.[54] Now, using the night-fighting capability of the M1 tank, B Troop began destroying Iraqi vehicles, beginning with a T-55 tank that moved out of its hide position.[55]

As the command group reached the end of B Troop's line, it swung northward into the gap between the troops. Wilson made sure both troop commanders knew exactly where he was, to preclude a friendly engagement. Moving very slowly, in the extreme darkness, the group's gunners scanned the terrain to their front. Suddenly, Burdan's driver, Specialist Roland Baker, noticed something out of the corner of his eye: "Sir I thought I saw someone standing on a berm on our left." Startled, Burdan, who had been checking his map, grabbed his night vision goggles and looked over the left side of the M3, discovering an Iraqi crewman jumping into a T-72 tank, which was in turret defilade and not generally visible from the surface. His gunner, Sergeant Brad Carpenter, was scanning the sector away from the enemy.[56]

Shouting "tank" over the intercom, Burdan ordered Baker to back up. After they had withdrawn about fifty meters, it was obvious that the command group had just missed moving into another Iraqi kill zone. Carpenter could see the vehicle's defensive berm, but could no longer see the tank itself. Soon his gunner identified a BMP infantry-fighting vehicle just off to his left and

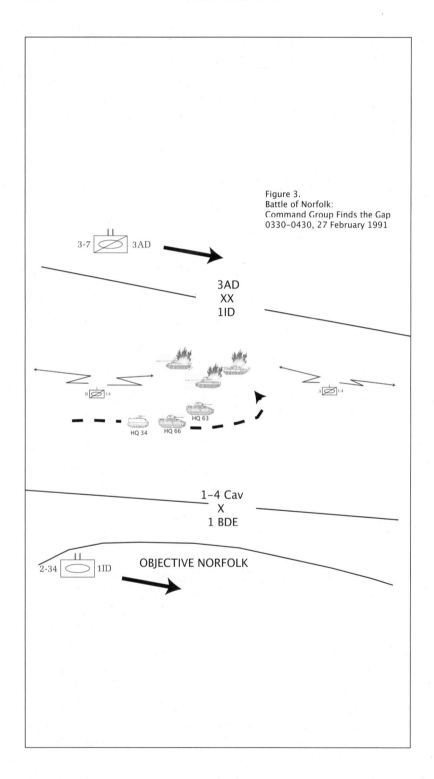

Figure 3.
Battle of Norfolk:
Command Group Finds the Gap
0330–0430, 27 February 1991

possibly a third berm hiding another tank. Iraqi soldiers were also now visible in a number of fighting positions. Apparently, the Iraqi crews could not see the command group but heard them and were coming out of the bunkers. Obviously, there were enemy vehicles in and around the squadron screen line.[57]

Realizing that the command group did not have the firepower to clear this gap, Wilson ordered CPT Bills to send over a platoon in support. 2LT Adrian Lowndes's 2nd Platoon moved forward with two tanks and two Bradleys and his tanks began to "surgically" remove vehicles that were behind the squadron's screen at short ranges of between only 50 to 400 meters.[58] Burdan and Wilson joined the fight also, destroying a BMP, a T-55 tank, and suppressing the dismounted infantry in the area.[59] Although the Iraqis could not identify the precise source of the hostile shooting, they responded with inaccurate but frightening artillery fire on both B Troop and the squadron's supply vehicles. Iraqi green and red star clusters caused momentary concern as American crews, suspecting the use of poison gas, put on their chemical protective masks. A Troop, upwind from the potential strike, continued to monitor the situation. After a few tests, it was obvious that there were no chemicals, and Bills gave the "all clear."[60]

Lowndes's Platoon and the Command Group destroyed five tanks and a variety of other vehicles in that short fire-fight. The troop's other platoons contributed to the carnage, destroying a number of tanks and infantry carriers. Meanwhile, both troops reported other Iraqi vehicles moving both to the front and rear of the squadron's screen line. B Troop, for example, ambushed a small convoy of troop-carrying trucks trying to move over a small ridge to the east.[61]

What the squadron did not know at the time was that they were near the IPSA Pipeline and this line's service road was the fastest and most direct route between southeast Iraq and the Iraqi forces aligned along the western Kuwaiti border. Because the Iraqi high command used this route to support units in both southern Iraq and Kuwait, supply depots, fuel tanks, ammunition depots, and other logistics installations lined both sides of the road. Unfortunately, this road did not appear on any of the squadron's maps. What the squadron faced that evening was a

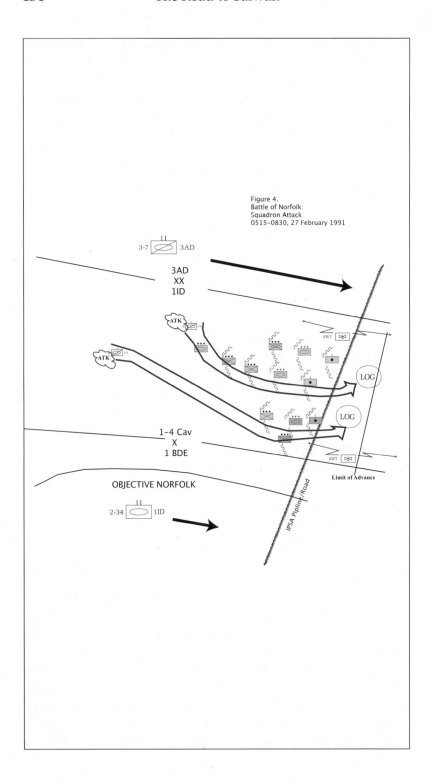

Figure 4.
Battle of Norfolk:
Squadron Attack
0515–0830, 27 February 1991

line of troops, perhaps hastily thrown together, whose mission was to protect the southern portion of the Iraqi Army's logistics supplies and escape route.[62]

Before the first glimmers of light appeared on the horizon, it was obvious that the squadron confronted at least a battalion of Iraqi defenders, many in prepared defensive positions. Wilson decided it was time to concentrate his command and execute a hasty attack either to destroy the troops to his front or, at least, develop the situation. Then he could quantify for the division commander the nature of the threat to his north. He ordered the squadron to pull back from the immediate vicinity of the Iraqi defenses to avoid a pre-dawn fire-fight with Iraqi tanks fighting from prepared positions. The command group then moved behind B Troop.[63]

While Wilson contacted division headquarters and briefed Rhame on the situation, MAJ Burdan developed a plan to attack through the zone. He wanted to get the fragmentary order out early, so the squadron could launch the attack while the limited visibility hindered the Iraqi defenders. The concept was simple: at 0600 hours two ground troops would attack abreast, each with a zone of operations and a limit of advance. In addition, each troop would have operational control of an aeroscout weapons team consisting of one OH-58C and two AH-1 Cobra gun ships. However the SWTs would not arrive until approximately 0645 hours because they were a long way from the ground troops and there would not be enough light for them to fly until about 0630 hours. Shortly before 0600 hours, the squadron was ready to begin.[64]

CPT Ken Pope's A Troop attacked on the left flank. He arrayed his command with two cavalry platoons forward and his reaction platoon in reserve to the rear. Its initial contact was with two T-72 tanks that it destroyed immediately. Tank main-guns provided the power to penetrate the defensive berms and destroy dug-in Iraqi armor. Continuing forward, the troop encountered a dug-in infantry platoon and had a short but intense fire-fight. With machine-gun, rifle, and tank rounds whizzing through the air, Pope and his other vehicle commanders decided to drop back down inside their turrets for safety.[65]

Leaving 2LT Jim Copenhaver's 1st Platoon behind to disarm the Iraqi infantry, CPT Pope had 2LT David Palmieri lead his 3rd Platoon into line and the troop continued to advance to the east. 2LT Michael Osburn's 2nd Platoon, moving on the southern portion of the troop's zone, also encountered an Iraqi infantry platoon. At first, they could only identify the bunkers. Suddenly, the Iraqi troops decided not to fight and poured out of their positions with their hands in the air. One Iraqi soldier even jumped on Osburn's Bradley, allegedly trying to surrender. The lieutenant stuck his 9-mm pistol in the Iraqi's face, encouraging him to get back on the ground. Meanwhile, his platoon continued to destroy a number of vehicles including BMPs, BTRs, and a variety of artillery. At this point, A troop's SWT arrived on station and quickly expended its initial load of ammunition and left to be rearmed and refueled. 2LT Palmieri estimated the depth of the defensive positions they were fighting through to be approximately five kilometers, beginning with tanks and BMPs in the initial positions and ending with artillery in prepared positions. Beyond the artillery further east were cargo trucks and trailers including full tankers with fuel.[66]

As CPT Pope's troop neared its limit of advance, he realized his unit was in a pre-planned artillery zone as Iraqi fire began creeping in from the north, across his position. Fortunately, the fire swept behind the troop's position and inflicted no casualties on the American cavalrymen. As the artillery fire ended, A Troop's second aeroscout weapons team, led by Chief Warrant Officer Wayne Grimes, C Troop, arrived and began searching for any Iraqis that the ground troop had missed during its advance. They slowly worked their way in front of the troop and on to its flanks. As his scout aircraft cleared a small ridgeline to their front, CWO Grimes got a report of enemy vehicles just over the ridge to his front. The Cobra cautiously edged forward and observed BMPs, tanks, trucks, and artillery moving rapidly to the east. Grimes quickly relayed a spot report to Pope and asked for permission to engage the enemy. He received an enthusiastic approval. The aviators destroyed a number of vehicles including several BMPs and three T-72 tanks beyond the range of what A Troop could see.[67] Finally, around 0715 hours, the troop consolidated along its limit of advance. Its final positions rested in the middle of an Iraqi logistics area, with many cargo trucks, trailers, and fuel tankers full of petrol.[68]

While Pope's command was cutting through the Iraqi defenders, B Troop attacked with its three platoons on line. Second Lieutenant Thomas Karns's platoon attacked in the south, 2LT Blaise Liess's command in the center, and 2LT Lowndes, who had already attacked along with the command group that evening, moved in the north and maintained contact with A Troop. Moving through the area they had fought in the night before, Lowndes's platoon destroyed any Iraqi vehicles or soldiers that still had some fight left.[69] In addition, CW3 Waymire's SWT from D Troop was supporting the troop from its position on the southern flank of the troop.

As Bills's command crested a small ridgeline, they faced the amazing sight of dozens of burning Iraqi vehicles, the results of the previous evening's fire-fight. As they rolled into the Iraqi logistics site, they encountered numerous bunkers, dug-in infantry, and supply vehicles. By 0715 hours, the troop was at its limit of advance and prepared to continue the attack into Kuwait.[70]

Wilson had followed A Troop while Burdan trailed B Troop. At the end of the fight they linked up and decided to inspect the area they had just fought through during the past few hours. The BMP that MAJ Burdan thought he had destroyed the night before turned out to be a T-55 tank; the Bradley's 25 mm armor piercing round had gone right into its turret. Other vehicles that B Troop had destroyed were still smoking. While he was pulling out of the area, Burdan confronted a hostile T-72 tank, in hull-defilade, at close range. The Iraqi tank commander dropped inside his turret and began traversing in Burdan's direction. Stopping to raise his turret's missile launcher, SGT Carpenter fired a TOW at the target only 200 meters away. They were too close and the missile hit the ground, careening out of sight. Before the tank could return fire, Wilson, a little farther away, shot another missile, destroying it. They were lucky; the Bradley was simply not as effective as the tank in such a fight.[71]

By 0800 hours Wilson ended the attack and directed the squadron to begin the rearm and refuel operations. The Command Group pulled up together just below a ridgeline looking out to the east. The air liaison officer's vehicle had a shortwave radio that one of the crew had brought along and it was tuned into BBC. The command group heard for the first time how successfully the war against the Iraqis was going. It sounded like the Iraqi army was trying to flee Kuwait and get back into Iraq as quickly as possible.

Bob Wilson's mission that night had been to screen the division's northern flank and maintain contact with the 3rd Armored Division. In the process, his troopers discovered part of the force that had fought the 3rd Armored Division's 4th Squadron, 7th Cavalry, the previous evening and knocked several of its Bradleys out of action. While an exact Iraqi order of battle is difficult to determine, apparently two tank companies, two mechanized infantry companies, an artillery battery, and other assorted troops defended against Wilson's troopers. The Iraqi unit's goal was to protect the supply route to its rear and several logistics sites along the IPSA Pipeline road. As part of the 1st Infantry Division's violent assault, the Quarter Horse in a series of defensive and offensive fire-fights that morning, destroyed the tanks, the artillery, many infantry vehicles, and logistics bunkers. The squadron arrived at its limit of advance without a single casualty.[72]

While there are a number of factors, including luck, which contributed to Wilson's success that night and next morning, one of the main reasons was the integration of main battle tanks into the squadron's cavalry platoons. The M1A1's ability to identify and engage multiple, protected Iraqi targets in rapid succession, in the dark, gave the squadron a technological edge over its T-72-equipped adversary. In addition, during periods of heavy combat, the tank's heavy armor allowed the squadron to slug it out with similar enemy vehicles. Without tanks, Wilson would not have been able to launch his hasty attack against the Iraqi logistics base.

By 0800, MG Rhame's 1st Infantry Division had fought its way across Objective Norfolk, leaving nine or ten battalions of Iraqi armored vehicles burning in its wake. Because he had augmented Wilson's squadron with a company's worth of armor, he did not have to divert other combat power to support the cavalry during the fight. It was a textbook example of a cavalry squadron's security operation in the main battle area.

12   The Basra Highway

From Kuwait City, the four-lane road to Iraq heads west, around the south side of Kuwait Bay, for about twenty miles, then due north for another fifty miles to the Iraqi border.[1] After a short stretch on two-lane roads through the border area, it connects with two different highways; one route continues north for another twenty-five miles to Al Basra, the other northwest along the south side of the Euphrates River. On the night of February 25, 1991, the second day of the ground war, as the allied coalition's forces attacked Kuwait from the south and enveloped it from the west, the Iraqi Army began evacuating Kuwait City and withdrawing from its southern defenses. Loaded with every kind of loot imaginable from the Kuwaiti capital, Iraqi soldiers made a run up the Basra Highway trying to get beyond the reach of rapidly advancing American armored and mechanized units. In some cases, this retreat turned into a rout as allied attack aircraft turned this road into a "Highway of Death," destroying hundreds of Iraqi vehicles in their attempt to escape.[2]

By early afternoon on February 27, the coalition's air attack on the Basra Highway ended when General H. Norman Schwarzkopf's headquarters, U.S. Army Central Command, moved the imaginary line intended to prevent accidental air attacks on friendly ground forces east to the Persian Gulf. Its movement was premature as the advancing VII Corps was not yet in position to send its own attack helicopters against the Iraqis streaming north on the Basra Highway.[3] With an unintended reprieve from air attack, and American ground forces still too far away, Iraqi units and individual soldiers continued their retreat north to Iraq. Within the VII Corps's zone, much of

Iraq's remaining combat power struggled to reach bridges at
Basra and safety on the north side of the marshes and the Shatt
al Arab waterway.[4]

Attacking with five divisions and an armored cavalry regiment across an eighty-five kilometer front, LTG Franks intended to finish off the Iraqi forces within his zone of attack
during the night of February 27–28 with a double envelopment.
He wanted the 1st and 3rd Armored Divisions to continue their
attack east and maintain pressure on Iraqi defenders along the
Kuwait border, while the 1st Infantry Division, located south of
the 3rd Armored Division, attacked northeast toward the Basra
Highway. Franks also intended to the use the 1st Cavalry Division, recently assigned to the VII Corps and still moving into
position from its original location along the Wadi al Batin, to
move north of the 1st Armored Division and then attack to the
southeast towards the Basra Highway in northern Kuwait.
Meanwhile, the British 1st Armoured Division was to race due
east to cut the highway just north of Kuwait City. North of VII
Corps, the U.S. XVIII Corps had the responsibility for attacking
the Iraqi units south of the Euphrates River and north of the VII
Corps zone. To the south, the attack by Arab forces and the U.S.
Marines had stopped with the capture of Kuwait City.

In the early morning hours of February 27, MG Thomas G.
Rhame's 1st Infantry Division was reorganizing and refueling
on the eastern side of Objective Norfolk, in southeastern Iraq,
just west of the Kuwait border. In one of the most dramatic battles of the war, and one of the most intense night-time armored
battles in history, Franks's three-division attack had annihilated
the reinforced Tawakalna Mechanized Division, one of the best
units in the Iraqi Army. The 1st and 3rd Armored Divisions had
destroyed the northern two-thirds of the Iraqi defensive line.
The 1st Armored Division then continued to the east and that afternoon destroyed the Medina Armored Division at the Battle of
Medina Ridge. Meanwhile, slicing across the southern portion
of the Tawakalna's battle line, the Big Red One reduced the Iraqi
18th Mechanized and 37th Armored (12th Armored Division)
Brigades to little more than memory, leaving almost 300 tanks
and infantry fighting vehicles burning in the division's wake.[5]

As the southern arm of his double envelopment, Franks

now wanted Rhame to attack southeast for about fifteen miles into Kuwait and then change direction and attack northeast for another thirty miles and cut the Basra Highway. After some initial delays in refueling and re-supplying, the division began its attack at 0915 hours.[6] Prior to its departure, the squadron had to rearm and refuel its vehicles as well as perform required maintenance. In B Troop, one of 2LT Lowndes's tanks broke a torsion bar during the attack. Of course, there were none available in either the troop or squadron combat trains. This meant that the crew would have to "short track" the tank so that it could have some limited mobility. They were not going to be ready in time to join the squadron when it continued with the division. CPT Bills made the unpleasant decision to leave Lowndes and some of his M3s behind to provide security for the crew and mechanics. The troop commander, worried about this loss of firepower, gave his lieutenant all of the information he needed so he could catch up as soon as possible.[7]

At 0930 hours, LTC Robert Wilson's 1st Squadron, 4th Cavalry, resumed the mission it had performed throughout the attack: screening the left flank of the division along the boundary with the 3rd Armored Division to the north.[8] With the division on the move, Wilson moved his unit along the imaginary boundary with the 3rd Armored Division, prepared to intercept any Iraqi units operating between the two divisions. Throughout the campaign in the desert, Iraqi units had executed numerous small-scale counterattacks against American and British forces. While uniformly unsuccessful, many were vigorously executed and could have been effective against an unprepared foe. In addition, senior tactical officers, veterans of the Vietnam conflict, were not yet ready to assume that the Iraqi Army was bereft of offensive options.

A Troop led the way and was followed by B Troop. The squadron's combat trains moved on a path parallel to the ground troops a couple of kilometers to their south. The squadron tactical operations center and flight operations followed in trail in the 2nd Brigade zone. Aeroscout weapons teams, made up of scout helicopters and Cobra attack helicopters, reconnoitered forward and to the flanks of the ground troops. It was an extremely fast move, with the squadron cross-

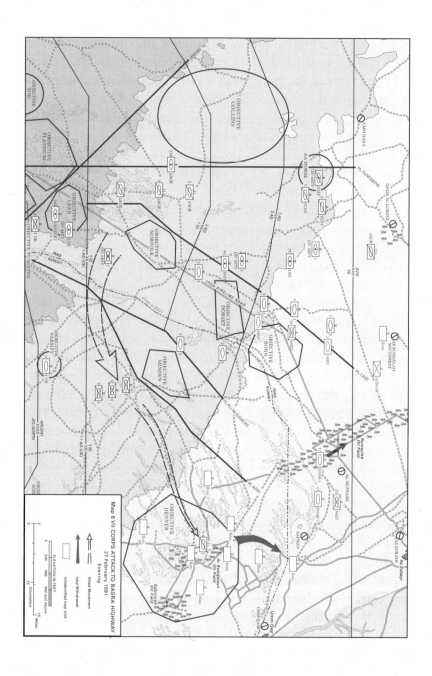

Map 6 VII CORPS ATTACK TO BASRA HIGHWAY
27 February 1991
Evening

ing the border into Kuwait by 1130 and halting about fifteen miles into Kuwait an hour later.[9]

Wilson's axis of advance cut across many Iraqi escape routes to the north. The area was littered with destroyed or abandoned equipment. Leading his supply vehicles through this wreckage and surrendering Iraqi soldiers, CPT Doug Morrison, the Headquarters Troop Commander, struggled to keep the squadron's vehicles full of fuel and ammunition.[10] Thanks to experience, the re-supply task was much easier now than it had been when the squadron first moved out to the desert. After several weeks of combat operations, beginning in the middle of January when the squadron patrolled the Saudi Arabian-Iraqi border, the unit's troopers were now veterans. Conducting re-supply operations was one of the key ways in which they displayed the competence and precision of a seasoned unit. Vehicles backed off the battle line, moved to the fuel tankers, and refueled. They then went to the rearm point where they picked up additional ammunition. Finally, they headed for unit supply trucks where they received an allotment of water, food, and other supplies. Each vehicle then returned to its original position on the battle line, allowing another to replace it in the supply queue. Although tired after almost four days of offensive operations, the troopers' morale was high as they moved closer to the Persian Gulf.[11]

As soon as it completed refueling, at around 1300 hours, B Troop moved forward and destroyed several Iraqi armored vehicles that were trying to pass through the squadron's area. A short while later, the 1st Infantry Division resumed its attack, now to the northeast. The Big Red One's mission was to attack and seize a large objective about fifty kilometers north of Kuwait City, called Objective Denver, which controlled the Basra Highway and numerous small roads that Iraqi units could use in their escape to the north. As the 1st Infantry Division moved out in front of the VII Corps, the 1st Squadron, 4th Cavalry continued its mission of screening the left flank of the division. It needed to destroy enemy reconnaissance elements and provide the division sufficient warning of any possible counterattacks.[12]

Meanwhile the combat trains under CPT Harmon were racing to keep up with the squadron. They had fallen behind earlier in the morning as they worked to repair vehicles and return them to their unit. At approximately 1300 hours they moved through an Iraqi position that they originally thought was un-occupied. However, as they drove through it, several Iraqis came out to surrender. Harmon halted his unit and searched the soldiers to take away their weapons. In the course of search-ing the bunkers they ran across several wounded Iraqis. MAJ Roger Hanson, the squadron surgeon, and 2LT Nathan Butler, the Medical Platoon Leader, with the help of the other medics traveling with the trains, treated the wounded. CPT Harmon flagged down some passing ground ambulances from 4-5 Ar-tillery and directed them to the bunkers. They loaded the wounded Iraqi soldiers and evacuated them to the rear. The combat trains then continued to the east following behind the ground troops.[13]

Franks expected Rhame's armor to be on the objective by nightfall. With the highway cut from the south, the corps com-mander would have the southern portion of his double envel-opment complete and be well on the way to destroying the re-maining Republican Guards units located farther to the north. Rhame promised Franks in a transmission over the division command net that he would reach Denver before the day ended. Bob Wilson, listening to Franks and Rhame talking, had no question as to the importance of his unit's mission.[14]

The division attack, however, did not go as planned. The 2nd Brigade moved forward more slowly than anticipated, co-ordinated through 1-4 Cavalry with the 3rd Armored Division on its left flank while passing the 1st Brigade to its right, and destroying several platoons of Iraqi armor. The 1st Brigade, now in the division's center, ran into a fire-fight as soon as it be-gan moving past the 2nd Brigade. Meanwhile, the 3rd Brigade working on the division's right flank was also in contact with Iraqi defenders. Therefore, for a short time, the division's three brigades were on-line and all involved in several small battles with platoon-sized groups of Iraqi tanks. While there was little serious Iraqi resistance, it complicated and delayed the Ameri-can movement.[15]

In addition, the division was now fighting through these isolated Iraqi defenses in the worst terrain the Big Red One had encountered during the entire war. Although the terrain was normally gently rolling with small hills, heavy mining equipment had dug huge craters throughout a twenty-square-kilometer area. In the 1st Brigade zone, this man-made obstacle had only two trails that would allow the brigade to traverse the area from east to west. On the far east side of this obstacle waited more small units of Iraqi armor and dismounted infantry. As in the past few days, however, the Iraqis demonstrated how poorly trained they were in defensive operations. They did not use mines to limit American movement; they did not mass their tank or artillery fire on the few routes through the sector to destroy American vehicles caught on the narrow trails; and they did not use the terrain to mask their vehicles' silhouettes to protect them from the long-range fires of American tanks. Instead, Iraqi armor often moved to the top of a ridge, firing with little effect and making themselves an easy target for the proficient American gunners. Iraqi leaders lost another opportunity to make the coalition pay for their military gains. However, they still managed to slow down the 1st Infantry Division's advance in what 1st Brigade soldiers called the "Valley of the Boogers."[16]

Meanwhile on the division's northern flank, Wilson's troopers continued moving eastward with little opposition. In coordination with the 2nd Brigade, Burdan had developed a series of checkpoints for the squadron to use as a path toward Objective Denver.[17] Somehow, these imaginary milestones, which he placed well north of the 2nd Brigade's zone of attack, avoided most Iraqi defenders and the rough terrain that faced the rest of the division. Ignorant of the developing situation in the rest of the division, the squadron was now on the way to the Basra Highway.

An aeroscout weapons team from D Troop, led by Chief Warrant Officer 2 Thomas Perkins, reconnoitered the area forward of the moving ground troops to provide early warning as they moved across Kuwait. This team located and destroyed several isolated armored vehicles, but found no serious resistance in the cavalry's path. The ground cavalry units passed several heavily fortified, but unoccupied, defensive positions with reinforced concrete berms, trenches, and bunkers. With the exception of individual tanks or small groups of Iraqi armor generally trying to escape north, the Iraqi troops were gone. Nothing was in the way of the squadron's advance.[18]

As Wilson's troops continued to race across north-central Kuwait in the late afternoon, they could see low-lying dark clouds in the east, the result of Saddam Hussein igniting Kuwait's oil fields. The squadron's speed of advance was very quick, moving as a single unit, advancing across the desert almost in column with its helicopters forward conducting a zone reconnaissance. At around 1500, with its objective nearly in sight, the squadron began to lose radio contact with the division's tactical command post.[19]

Given the hilly terrain and the speed that the squadron was moving, it was normal for communications to become intermittent. In addition, for most of the advance, the headquarters's radio operators could hear radio messages over the division command frequency, not suspecting they were actually losing their ability to communicate themselves. Once they realized that they had indeed lost contact with division, MAJ Wimbish had the squadron command post report their situation through the 2nd Brigade's command post, which was closer. However, no one at 2nd Brigade told them of the division's problems in the Valley of the Boogers, or called the squadron and told them to stop or slow down. Experiencing intermittent contact with his commander, MAJ Bill Wimbish, the executive officer, decided to move the squadron's tactical operations center, consisting of several command post vehicles, various support trucks, and a lone Bradley Fighting Vehicle for security, toward Wilson's location. It left the 2nd Brigade area where it had been operating and headed out along the route taken by B Troop. On the way, it by-passed numerous bunkers and infantry positions, captured three enemy tanks obviously no longer in the fight, and disarmed ninety-three Iraqi soldiers.[20] On a slightly different route, CPT Morrison moved his forward support element, consisting of a small command post, medical teams, ammunition vehicles, fuel vehicles, and maintenance crews, toward the squadron. Fortunately, without any fighting power other than his soldiers' small arms, he had few incidents until his arrival at the Basra Highway.[21]

Soon the cavalry began losing communications with the

2nd Brigade as well. By 1600 hours, LTC Wilson realized he was out of contact with the rest of the Big Red One.[22] Wilson now faced one of those decisions that are reserved for those in command. He had essentially two options. First, he could hold his position and try to regain contact with his senior commanders, planning on accomplishing his mission once he had received more information on the division's progress. Or, he could take advantage of the breakdown in the Iraqi's defenses and continue to his original objective, assuming that the rest of the division would follow shortly thereafter.

Wilson and Burdan, unaware of the confusion at their senior headquarters, assumed that the division would catch up with them shortly. As they continued their advance towards Objective Denver, the leaders sketched out their plan of action. They needed to accomplish two tasks: cut the Basra Highway, as Rhame had instructed, and continue to protect the division's northern flank, in case the Iraqi army attempted to counterattack from the north. Wilson gave A Troop the mission of cutting the Basra Highway, while B Troop would stretch out on line to the west for approximately ten kilometers to block any approach from the north.[23]

The squadron commander discussed his options with Burdan and his two ground troop commanders. They were all comfortable with their mission, knew they could reestablish contact by sending their helicopters south, and assumed that the remainder of the division was on its way. It was obvious to all that organized Iraqi resistance had evaporated. The aeroscouts reported no meaningful enemy activity in the area and no organized units within ten kilometers of the squadron. Of course, cavalrymen by nature are not inclined to wait, and the aggressive Wilson was anxious to accomplish his mission. Therefore, he ordered his commanders to continue towards the highway where they would wait for the arrival of the rest of the Big Red One. They approached the northern edge of Objective Denver around 1630 hours, thus cutting the Basra Highway and accomplishing Rhame's promise to LTG Franks.[24]

As B Troop arrived on its objective at 1630, it moved to establish a thin screen-line stretching west starting about eight kilometers west of the highway. CPT Roy Peters, the D Troop commander, and his aeroscout weapons team scouted ahead of the ground troops and identified Iraqi personnel and vehicles moving north on the highway. His SWT consisted of himself along with W01 Michael Hull, and a Cobra flown by CW2 Daniel Pinkava along with his gunner, W01 Vincent Stella. The SWT observed two Chinese Type 59 tanks along the highway and decided to engage them. Mr. Stella engaged and destroyed both of the tanks with TOW missiles. CPT Peters reported the engagement and the situation on the highway and then had to pull back because his SWT was running extremely low on fuel. CPT Pope was monitoring the transmissions from CPT Peters and notified his platoons of what was occurring and then ordered 1st Platoon to lead, followed by 2nd, 3rd, mortars, and trains. The troopers knew they were approaching the highway as they could see the power lines that were running parallel to the highway in the distance.[25]

At approximately 1650 hours, SFC Molitor got a report from SSG Gerald Broennimann, who was leading the A Troop advance, that there were twenty to thirty soldiers to his front walking northward. Molitor thought he might need some help and he asked SSG Micheal Peters to follow him up to the rise where Broennimann's Bradley was located. When they linked up with the scout sergeant, they realized what he was seeing. Not only was there a small group of soldiers moving, but the entire Basra Highway stretched out below them. Hundreds of soldiers were now on the move trying to escape to the north in military and civilian vehicles. Molitor heard a loud bang to his right and saw the BMP that Broennimann had just shot from his Bradley blow up. Two more BMPs were parked next to a broken-down vehicle, where the crews were trying to take parts and equipment off it. SFC Molitor quickly engaged and destroyed the second vehicle with a TOW missile. The squadron's fight at the highway was now underway. CPT Pope contacted Wilson and reported the mass of approaching Iraqi vehicles and personnel heading north. With those reports in, Wilson ordered CPT Ken Pope's A Troop to attack and seize its objective astride the Basra Highway.[26]

The young captain deployed his unit with 1st Platoon on the left, 2nd Platoon in the center, and his tank and mortar sec-

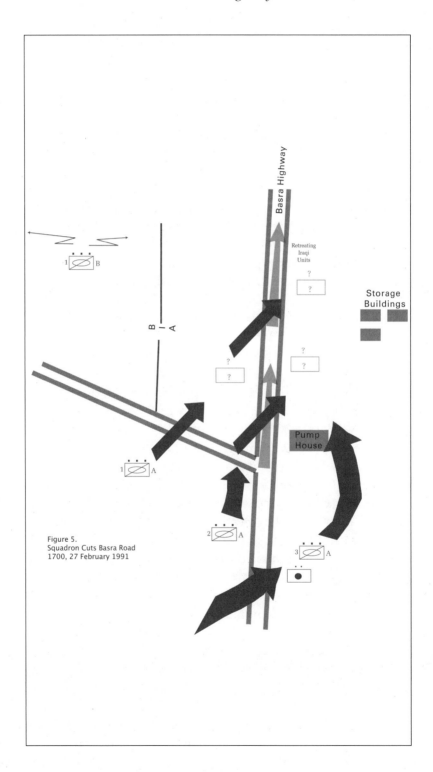

Figure 5.
Squadron Cuts Basra Road
1700, 27 February 1991

tion on the right, or eastern, side of the road. Moving down a low ridgeline, the cavalry attack caught the Iraqis by surprise. One T-55 tank tried to traverse its gun towards the attackers, but an American M1A1 tank destroyed it before the Iraqi ever completed its turn. In the northern part of the troop's sector, 1st Platoon's SSG Gerald Broennimann destroyed the lead Iraqi armored vehicle in the middle of the highway. 2LT Copenhaver, the 1st Platoon leader, detected a tank about 500 meters away moving northward. He stopped his Bradley, raised his TOW launcher and destroyed it with a TOW missile. SFC Molitor detected a tank on a ridgeline in the distance and fired a TOW at it. He controlled the missile from the track commander's position. He thought he was going to miss the tank and then he saw the impact and explosion and the tank disappeared below the ridgeline.[27] With the road now blocked, Pope ordered the two cavalry platoons to continue attacking across the road to the northeast and join his tank platoon in a sweep through the objective. The roar was deafening as the cavalrymen assaulted through the disorganized Iraqi positions. 2LT Osburn, 2nd Platoon Leader, found that he had to pay close attention to the location of all of the troop vehicles in order to avoid firing at friendly vehicles. SFC Molitor saw Iraqi soldiers everywhere. As his Bradley rolled northward as part of the attack, his driver saw some soldiers jump into a stationary T-55. The tank started to traverse its turrent toward them. Molitor again stopped his vehicle, raised the launcher and destroyed the T-55 with another TOW round. When the troop had finished its attack, they left behind a dozen Iraqi vehicles in flames and now had several dozen enemy soldiers under guard. All the platoon's vehicles were operational with the exception of one M1A1 that had run into a mine field and sustained some slight damage. Fortunately, the tank could continue with the troop and would not have to be replaced until after the war.[28]

While B Troop's sector remained fairly quiet, A Troop's activity on the Basra Highway now became increasingly intense. As CPT Pope finished his initial engagement, he could see large numbers of Iraqi soldiers and vehicles heading towards him from the south and east. He dispatched 2LT Jim Copenhaver's 1st Platoon, with its six Bradleys, to the troop's southern flank to hold off the approaching enemy. Within a few minutes, the platoon destroyed several tanks and armored personnel carriers. The Iraqis, however, continued to head towards the squadron.[29]

Just prior to the assault on the highway, MAJ Burdan had established a temporary headquarters several kilometers away to coordinate operations and continued to operate from this vantage point while the two ground troops were conducting operations. As A Troop neared the highway, CPT Peters's helicopters had started running low on fuel. Still out of communications with the division, 2nd Brigade headquarters, and the squadron's flight operations detachment, Peters had no idea where to fly to for re-supply. In addition, while his pilots were trained for night operations, the dark, smoky, desert night made such flying hazardous. Rather than have the aero scout-weapons team fly to the rear and search for the re-supply point, Burdan directed Peters, who was already flying on emergency fuel, to land at his temporary CP.[30] Burdan, of course, still assumed that the remainder of the division was on the way and this would be a safe location for both the command post and the helicopters.

By 1715 hours, almost all of A Troop found itself in a firefight. The Iraqis were obviously surprised to find American soldiers on their planned escape route, and their response was quite disorganized. Some units tried to fight their way through the American position, only to see their vehicles explode and their progress stopped by well-aimed machine-gun or 25-mm Bushmaster fire. Other Iraqi soldiers tried to by-pass the Americans through the burning oil field to the east. Finally, many Iraqi soldiers had simply had enough and came towards the squadron's positions with their hands in the air. In order to control all of the prisoners, Pope ordered 2LT Mitch Osburn's 2nd Platoon to establish an enemy prisioner of war collection point near the highway. Osburn put SSG Terence Favors in charge of the mission and gave him the engineer squad and the troop mechanics to help him. By 1800 hours, Camp Favors, as this concertina-wire-enclosed enclave became known, was soon guarding over 450 Iraqi soldiers. Meanwhile, there seemed to be no end in sight to the enemy forces approaching the American perimeter.[31]

Now the glow of brightly burning Iraqi vehicles began to

mingle with the smoky oil well fires in the approaching darkness. Wilson realized that the waves of Iraqi troops would soon
overpower A Troop, and it was time, in good old-West cavalry
style, to circle the wagons. He ordered CPT Mike Bills's B Troop
to move from its northern screen line to form a defensive
perimeter along with A Troop. His unit defended the western
side of the highway while Pope's troopers guarded the east. In
the center, Wilson planned to assemble the remainder of his
unit near the ever-growing Camp Favors. Bills got his troop on
the move quickly and headed for its portion of the squadron's
perimeter.[32]

Wimbish and his vehicles arrived at Burdan's location
around 1730 hours. As they monitored the situation on the
highway, they soon realized that they would probably end up
stranded outside of the main perimeter on the road. They could
not move the two almost out-of-fuel helicopters until dawn and
they could not abandon them without good reason. In addition,
this was a good location to allow the cavalry squadron, which
had been out of contact for over two hours, to set up a more
powerful antenna and regain contact with the 2nd Brigade. Re-
gretfully, Wimbish therefore established his small command
post, deep in enemy territory, with little tactical security other
than one Bradley Fighting Vehicle. The headquarters's soldiers
began digging in for what could be a harrowing night. As B
Troop arrived at the highway they found A Troop fighting vehicles and Iraqi soldiers located in a pump house to the south
and in a collection of several warehouses to the north. B Troop
took up its initial positions on the west side of the highway and
A Troop took the east side.[33]

Wilson called his two troop commanders to his location on
the highway to discuss the situation. The two young captains
drove up and jumped off their vehicles and climbed onto his. It
was eerie evening, the sun was setting, vehicles were exploding
and burning, and a fire-fight raged all around them. The three
discussed what had occurred and what they were going to do.
Wilson's decision was to keep the squadron on the highway
and in its immediate vicinity while they awaited the arrival of
the rest of the division. They would establish a perimeter with
A Troop occupying from 12-6 and B Troop from 6 to 12. The

troops were to put out security and consolidate their positions. During this discussion, Majors Wimbish and Burdan were having a discussion of their own. At this point, the TOC was located approximately eight kilometers southwest of the highway. They had been monitoring what was occurring on the road, but they too were out of contact with the remainder of the division. The XO and S3 discussed what they should do with the squadron's command post. Since Wilson and those on the highway were not yet in contact with the division or any of the brigades and CPT Peter's SWT was on the ground and not able to safely fly, they decided that the TOC would remain at its present location. It would try to reestablish communications with the division and serve as a relay between it and the squadron on the highway. They contacted Wilson, who had wanted the command post's thin-skinned M577 vehicles brought up into the safety of the hasty defensive perimeter. However, the presence of the SWT's grounded helicopters complicated the situation and he had little choice but to acquiesce to Burdan's recommendation. But, he did need his S3 to help coordinate his fight and directed him to head towards his location on the highway. Burdan set out at once for the highway along with SPC Kenworthy who was driving Wilson's HMMWV.[34]

By 1800 hours, CPT Doug Morrison and the squadron's forward support elements, which now included the combat trains, were approaching the Basra Highway. Morrison had moved his group along a different route from Wimbish's group, and did not run into the command post.[35] From Morrison's perspective, the highway was a scene of total confusion as red and green tracers shot through the air. From the perimeter defenders' perspective, the combat trains merged with other columns of Iraqi vehicles. Morrison reached the B Troop commander on the radio: "I don't know where you are . . . and I don't know where I am, but don't shoot me!" Morrison then left his vehicles on the western side of the highway and began scouting a route into the perimeter and for a location for his support vehicles.[36]

Soon after the headquarters commander departed, MAJ Burdan, who was now en route to the perimeter, encountered a line of strange vehicles in the dark, which turned out to be Morrison's supply vehicles. With gunfire and burning hulks all around, Burdan also began looking for a way to get these un-protected supply trucks into the perimeter. Making contact with the B Troop defenders, Burdan returned to the combat trains and began leading them to safety. Just as they began to move into the area, Doug Morrison returned and resumed con-trol of the logistics elements, guiding them into their evening's positions. Morrison had managed to maneuver this precious cargo through the on-going fire-fight, past Iraqi soldiers, and through areas covered with unexploded munitions without loss. Burdan then remained in the perimeter and joined Wilson in controlling both the defense and the ever-increasing accumu-lation of Iraqi prisoners.[37] As the two leaders stood in the center of the squadron, Wilson commented, "We're either going to get our ass chewed severely for being out here and being on the road, or we're going to be heroes."[38]

After his arrival, Burdan began improving the coordination between the two cavalry troops and brought some order to the confusion within the perimeter. He dismounted his Bradley and made his way to the southernmost contact point between the two troops. The fires from the burning vehicles and oil wells provided enough light that the troops did not need night-vision goggles. The S3 expected to find the road under the firm control of the troops. However, upon his arrival it became apparent that the needed responsibilities had not been worked out. As Burdan was talking to one of the sergeants at the contact point, the sergeant gestured to something behind him. He turned to see five armed Iraqis walking down the road towards him. With his Bradley crew providing over watch, he drew his pis-tol, and along with the sergeant, moved to intercept the Iraqis. The enemy stopped about ten feet from away and threw down their weapons. Burdan had them searched, and while they waited for a detachment from A Troop to take them to Camp Favors, he had a chance to talk with one of the prisoners who turned out to be a graduate of an American college. The cap-tured Iraqi felt that it was proper for his army to have con-quered Kuwait and, although they had been stopped this time, they would be back again. After the Iraqis were escorted out of the area, Burdan contacted the two troop executive officers and had them meet him at the contact point so they could organize how the perimeter was to be properly secured.

Meanwhile, CPT Morrison's Headquarters Troop (the combat trains and the forward support element) took charge of the support activities so that the combat crews could concentrate on combat operations. Taking control of the prisoner of war compound, he established a medical aid station and began providing both the troopers and prisoners with food and water. In addition, his soldiers began moving ammunition and fuel to the vehicles on the firing line. The administrative-logistics center, or ALOC, was set up and later that evening assumed the duties and responsibilities of the squadron command post within the defensive perimeter.[39] By 1830, CPT Pope reported that most of the fighting to his south had died down, and he worked closely with CPT Bills to preclude any instances of fratricide between the two troops as they finished establishing the defensive perimeter.[40]

Contrary to plans, the rest of the division did not follow the squadron that night to Objective Denver. Once LTG Franks realized that the northeasterly movement of the 1st Infantry Division was bringing them across the front of the easterly moving 3rd Armored Division, he decided to make a change. Franks now wanted the Big Red One to stop moving northeast, head east until it crossed the Basra Highway, and then turn due north. While he sorted these instructions out, COL Stan Cherrie, Franks's operations officer working from the VII Corps's Tactical Command Post, ordered the 1st Infantry Division to stop moving some time before 1900 hours. With the entire command strung out by the day's battles and pursuits, he wanted time to coordinate the operations of all the corps's divisions before they became entangled in the rapidly diminishing maneuver space in eastern Kuwait.

Impatiently, the 1st Infantry Division called back to the VII Corps a half-hour later asking to continue, but was told to stand by. Once he finished sorting out the command, Cherrie intended to send a new set of instructions to MG Rhame defining his new avenue of advance. However, he never sent those instructions. Organized around five command post tracks and about two dozen wheeled vehicles, the corps tactical command post, at that moment, was a very busy place.[41] In all the confusion and working on little sleep for the last several days, Cherrie, as he admitted later, simply "forgot to tell them (1st Infantry Division) to start again."[42]

After Burdan departed for the highway, the first thing the TOC did was to erect the large RC-292 antenna so that contact could be made with the division. By approximately 1845 hours contact was established with the 2nd Brigade. The brigade's duty officer informed Wimbish that the corps commander had halted the division's attack due to confusion in graphics with the 1st UK Armoured Division to the south. Since the attack had been halted, the squadron was not only the sole controller of the highway in this area but also the easternmost unit in the VII Corps. When the squadron staff got the locations of the division's major units plotted on the map, it became apparent that the squadron was twenty to thirty kilometers east of the remainder of the division and out of range of any supporting artillery except for perhaps the MLRS, an area suppression weapon. The squadron's leadership realized the precarious situation they were in, beyond the range of friendly artillery and no relief heading their way until dawn.[43] Realizing they could be out-gunned in any serious fight, Wilson directed Burdan to ask the 2nd Brigade for reinforcements. Within a short time, Moreno called back and said that he was not allowed to move any of his units.[44] Of course, if the squadron came under major attack, they could count on support from the division's attack helicopter battalion, if they could get there in time.

Staff problems in the Big Red One had further complicated the squadron's situation. Rhame's fire support officer told the 1st Infantry Division's tactical command post about the cavalry cutting the Basra Highway around 1830 hours. For some reason, the duty officer changed the reported location in his staff journal, the official record of such communications, from the correct location to one ten kilometers to the south.[45] To further confuse the issue, at 1905 hours, the 1st Infantry's command post told the corps staff that Wilson's unit was twenty-three kilometers southwest of where they actually were.[46] Even late as 0130 hours the next morning, when the corps's headquarters identified from various reports an American unit astride the Basra Highway, the division headquarters continued to deny it

was there, in spite of the fact that the squadron had by then re-
gained radio contact with 2nd Brigade.[47] These errors reflect the
fatigue of the division's small tactical command post staff. For
almost forty-eight hours they had been controlling the 1st Infantry's attack without the help of the division main command
post, still moving across the Iraqi desert. Like other headquarters across the battle front, they were simply exhausted.

By approximately 1915 hours the 2nd Brigade Commander,
COL Anthony Moreno, was back in contact with the cavalry
and was preparing to continue the attack toward them. Just as
his commanders were returning to their units from a short
planning meeting, the division commander called Moreno and
told him to *withdraw* twelve kilometers, to comply with the recent orders from corps headquarters. The incredulous Moreno
argued with MG Rhame for permission to continue the attack
to no avail. The best he could get was permission to remain in
place and not pull back.[48] Rhame, who was forward commanding his division from inside a M1A1 main battle tank, did try to
get permission from corps to continue, but as mentioned earlier,
was told to remain in place and he did not, as he later wished
he had, challenge the order to stop directly to Franks.[49] However, with the suspension of hostilities announced at 2245 and
scheduled for 0500 hours the next morning, neither Rhame nor
Franks felt any reason to change the tactical alignment that
night.[50] For the next twelve hours, therefore, the 1st Squadron,
4th Cavalry would be the easternmost, and most exposed, unit
in the entire VII Corps, essentially surrounded by the Iraqi
Army on the Basra Highway.

The problem back at the squadron's defensive perimeter on
the Basra Highway was quickly becoming one of handling Iraqi
prisoners of war. In accordance with standard procedures, the
cavalry troopers segregated the captured or surrendered soldiers into groups of officers and enlisted. The Americans and
Iraqis in the compound now began to interact with each other
in interesting ways. SFC Molitor, 1st Platoon, A Troop, encountered one Iraqi officer who spoke English, and who had been
trying to move his air defense artillery battalion, which had
been stationed outside of Kuwait City, back to Iraq. When he
encountered the squadron, he surrendered but complained

continuously that his surrender was difficult because the Americans appeared to continue to shoot at him and his soldiers when he tried to surrender. He obviously did not realize that many of his comrades in other units did not wish to give up but were trying to fight their way through the squadron's position. In the dark, it was difficult to differentiate one group of Iraqis from another.[51] B Troop's SSG Michael Cowden noticed that the Iraqis continued to try to evade the squadron once they discovered who controlled the road. In one instance he wounded an Iraqi lieutenant with a burst of coax from his Bradley as he tried to evade capture. Cowden and one of his scouts moved out and captured the lieutenant and the men with him and brought them back to the troop medics. CPT Bills was there and recalled that the lieutenant spoke excellent English, and he asked him "Are you now going to shoot me and my men?" Bills replied no and pointed out how the American medics were treating the wounded Iraqis.[52]

Some Iraqi soldiers took precautions before they surrendered. Prior to approaching the American lines they buried their weapons, knives, and the jewels, watches, and other loot they had stolen from Kuwait.[53] Others were still loaded with loot when they stumbled right into the American positions. Among the confiscated items were clothing, radios, and televisions. As night wore on the Iraqis were caught with TVs, radios, and jewelry, looking like they had just looted a department store.[54] One particular Iraqi resisted the standard search. After some effort, the Americans discovered a pack of playing cards illustrated with photographs of scantily clad women. The Iraqi soldier was very embarrassed while the cavalry troopers were quite amused.[55]

As it continued to get dark, Wilson found himself worrying about two separate problems: the rapidly growing numbers of Iraqis he had under guard and the ever-present possibility of an enemy attack from the north.[56] Several divisions of the Republican Guard Forces Command were operating just north of Wilson's location. Most of these units, including the Hammurabi Armored Division, had not yet fought American forces and were still capable of attacking as small a target as Wilson's command. Iraqi units had attacked American forces on numerous instances over the preceding few days, and could easily do so again. The squadron had already demonstrated that it could hold its own in a fight with Iraqi units under normal circumstances. What made this threat more serious were the many enemy soldiers now inside its perimeter.

At 1830 hours, Camp Favors contained 450 prisoners. Less than two hours later, the number had swelled to over 1,000 Iraqis and the squadron now owned a pile of over 700 weapons, including pistols, rifles, sniper rifles, and machine guns. All night the Iraqis continued to flow in. Some gave themselves up. Others surrendered after the cavalry troopers destroyed the vehicles they were riding in. By dawn, the squadron had captured well over 2,000 Iraqi soldiers, most with their weapons.[57] If Wilson's force became engaged in a major battle with an attacking Iraqi force, these prisoners would become a serious liability and could compromise his defensive scheme.

At one point during the night the imprisoned Iraqis began to grumble and appear rebellious. A young American guard, carrying a rifle with a grenade launcher attached, tried to fire some shots over the Iraqis' heads to quiet them down. Instead of his rifle, he mistakenly fired a grenade that exploded just outside the perimeter. Everyone hit the ground, surprised Americans included. From then on the prisoners gave the guards no trouble.[58]

Of course, not all of the squadron's personnel were on or near the highway. Earlier that afternoon, 1SGT Gary Parkey, racing to catch up with A Troop, found himself moving in the same area as scout vehicles from the 3rd Armored Division. After getting permission from the scouts to continue, he headed across open ground to catch up with his unit. As he proceeded through a ravine, he suddenly came upon an Iraqi BMP infantry fighting vehicle. This Soviet-made, heavily armed infantry carrier, mounting a 76-mm gun, an antitank missile, and several machine guns, had its turret pointed directly toward him. He also noticed five or six Iraqi soldiers, obviously the crew, clustered on the ground a short distance from the vehicle. Once these soldiers saw the Americans, they began running towards their combat vehicle. Parkey ordered his driver to get their light truck between the Iraqi soldiers and the personnel carrier. Once they saw what was happening, the Iraqi soldiers threw their hands up and surrendered. As Parkey got out of his truck, intending to search the Iraqis and destroy their armored carrier before continuing, one of the Iraqis grabbed another and said in broken English: "General, General . . . see I give you General." Upon closer inspection Parkey realized that they had indeed captured an Iraqi general. After some tense moments, moving back towards the 3rd Armored Division's lines, he was able to bring his Iraqi captives back to the scout platoon he had left only a short while before. Rather than try to risk movement at night, Parkey decided to remain where he was until morning.[59]

As night approached, B Troop's 2LT Adrian Lowndes and his crew were still back at Objective Norfolk and were not yet done with the tank's temporary repairs. Rather than trying to work under lights, with the possibility of drawing Iraqi fire, he decided to wait until morning to finish the repairs. He felt quite alone, as he had seen no other vehicles since the squadron had departed that morning. He also had no idea what the enemy situation was and thought it best to set up a tight defensive perimeter and wait for first light. He shut his vehicles down and reverted to using only PVS-7 night-vision goggles for security. Later that night they picked up movement as the first of several Iraqi patrols moved through the area. Apparently, these groups were coming down from the north and stopping every now and then to check out a vehicle or bunker. They seemed to be organized, as they were able to rely on some kind of artillery, probably mortars, to support their searches. On one occasion, this indirect fire hit quite close to Lowndes's group and those who were outside their vehicles had to dive for cover underneath them. While several groups of these Iraqis passed by the Americans, they never stopped to investigate. By dawn, the Iraqis were gone and the lieutenant and his band were alone in the desert again. They finally completed the repairs and began trying to find the rest of the squadron. However, It would be almost another twenty-four hours before this band would find their troop again.[60]

Probably no aspect of this operation was more impressive than the way the individual cavalry soldiers made the transition from efficient killers to angels of mercy. Time and again, troopers moved beyond their battle line into the dangerous no-man's land, dodging unexploded munitions and small-arms fire to rescue wounded Iraqi soldiers and, in the process, capture more prisoners. Once back inside the perimeter, they brought the wounded to the squadron aid station. In their urge to help, American soldiers emptied their vehicles of field rations and water, and exhausted most of their medical supplies on the Iraqi wounded.[61] Realizing the danger they were in and because the operation was not yet over, squadron leaders stepped in to stop the troopers from giving away all of their supplies, items they might need during the next day. In spite of the danger of attack, many vehicles reduced their crew to only two combat crew members, as others tried to help keep the Iraqi wounded comfortable and alive.[62] Wilson's troopers were taking a risk, since even a limited Iraqi probe would cause intense confusion within the perimeter.

There were numerous examples of how the troopers sought to aid the Iraqis once they stopped fighting. As the evening wore on, several A Troop combat lifesavers were sent over to help the medics who were treating the wounded Iraqis. One of the Iraqi soldiers, who had hidden behind a tank as A Troop crested the ridgeline above the highway, suffered burns, shrapnel wounds, and a compound fracture when the tank was hit. He was in a state of shock as the A Troop lifesaver and the medics got him stabilized. The transformation of the troop from soldiers intent on killing the enemy to "Red Cross" workers was amazing. It was as if a switch had been thrown and they were now in the help mode.[63]

Chaplain Lou Parker was in the perimeter that night and was able to take a little more detached view of the fight than those trying to defend themselves and supervise the prisoners. He helped MAJ Hansen and his medical team provide care to the many injured Iraqis. As the night wore on, he saw the medics' stress begin to get the better of them and he walked among them coaching and counseling. He was personally moved when Hanson grabbed his sleeve and implored "Don't you leave. You're my moral support." Several Iraqi doctors were taken prisoner who spoke nearly fluent English. They assisted the medical personnel and helped Parker minister by interpreting his prayers. Many of the prisoners recognized the cross on his collar and wanted him to pray for them regardless of the fact they couldn't understand a word he was saying. Some motioned with their hands, many tugged at his collar, and some just cried. One prisoner with a non-Islamic name would not let go of his hand. He spoke broken English and professed to be a Christian. He lamented repeatedly: "Saddam, Saddam, why, why, for nothing!"[64]

Around 2000 hours, the squadron's medics tried evacuate several wounded Iraqi soldiers by helicopter. The squadron's surgeon, MAJ Roger Hansen, believed these soldiers would die if not moved to a field hospital in the rear. The medical helicopter, back behind the division's battle lines, attempted to take off from its base camp over sixty miles away, but was forced back by bad weather and poor visibility. The assistant division commander, BG William Carter, called back to the medical evacuation unit commander and urged them to go forward with the mission. Again, at 2046 hours, the medical helicopter took off, only to return. At midnight, they tried again, but the weather again forced the helicopter back to base.[65] Not until the next morning would the medical evacuation helicopter arrive and begin to shuttle wounded Iraqi soldiers to the rear.[66] Chaplain Parker, the next morning, after talking with the medics and troopers who helped them, estimated that the squadron treated over 450 Iraqi wounded in fourteen hours.

Throughout the night, small-arms fire snapped and tank cannons disgorged a ball of flame with each launch of their dangerous projectiles. Red tracers streaked through the night as the sound of exploding vehicles and ammunition punctuated the smoke-filled air.[67] To the east and south, the sabotaged oil wells filled the horizon with the sights and sounds of dozens of out-of-control torches. By first light, the precariousness of Wilson's situation was obvious. In all directions, living and dead Iraqi soldiers surrounded the squadron. Destroyed vehicles of all kinds—tanks, personnel carriers, military trucks, and civilian vehicles—lay outside the cavalry's perimeter. Safwan Mountain (Jabal Sannam), twelve kilometers to the north, now emerged from the darkness, giving Iraqi observers a good view of the isolated squadron's position. Fortunately for Wilson and his command, the bad weather and poor enemy night vision equipment had hindered the Iraqis' observation during the night. The several combat-ready brigades of the Iraqi Army's Republican Guards (Hammurabi, Adena, and other divisions), stationed nearby possessed more than enough combat power to damage Wilson's troopers in an early-morning attack. Would they have attacked the cavalry if they knew they had the chance for an easy victory? Could Wilson's tired, prisoner-of-war encumbered soldiers have stopped such an attack? We will never know.

At dawn, COL Jim Mowery, the Aviation Brigade commander, arrived in an Apache at the squadron's position. Mowery briefed Wilson on the division's final attack towards the Iraqi border. Soon COL Moreno arrived with his 2nd Brigade and seeing CPT Mike Bills he jumped off his tank and gave the surprised captain a big hug.[68] By noon, the 1st Squadron, 4th Cavalry had resupplied and began preparing for whatever mission the division commander had in mind.[69] Meanwhile, Wilson's staff coordinated directly with the division and began moving the prisoners to the rear on flatbed trucks. Fortunately, it would have no more missions that day. In a controversial decision, President George Bush decreed an end to the fighting on February 28, 1991. The original temporary cease-fire time of 0500 hours was extended in the early morning hours to 0800.

For over fourteen hours the 1st Squadron, 4th Cavalry, had held an important defensive position astride the Basra Highway. Beyond the range of supporting artillery fire, with intermittent communications to its senior headquarters, and with only two ground cavalry troops, the squadron was fortunate that the Iraqis did not mount a major attack against them.

It is something of a paradox that confusion, fatigue, and the friction of war, combined with initiative and a sense of mission, created conditions that allowed the 1st Squadron, 4th Cavalry to attain its intended goal without the rest of the division. The ultimate result was not only the unit's isolation, but also its seizure of an objective that could have been important if the Iraqi Army had chosen to stand and fight in northern Kuwait. MG Rhame's clear intent, and Wilson's understanding of it, allowed the squadron to accomplish the division's mission in the absence of additional orders. Discovering an undefended area between Iraqi units, the squadron headed for the highway.

When out of contact with his senior headquarters, Wilson made the decision to continue his attack toward the Basra Highway, believing that his commander would support his initiative in this confusing situation. Squadron leaders, such as Mike Bills, Ken Pope, Chris Philbrick, Bill Wimbish, Doug Morrison, and John Burdan took the initiative to make decisions in the absence of detailed orders. These leaders relied on their understanding of what their commander wanted accomplished, rather than on more restrictive command and control. Focusing on mission accomplishment, they took risks that resulted in the squadron's success and a harrowing night on the Basra Highway.

*Squadron HHT, fuel tankers preparing to move to the railhead, Ft. Riley,
Kansas, December 1990.* COURTESY CPT DOUG MORRISON

B Troop arrives in Saudi Arabia, January 1991.

COURTESY MICHAEL A. BILLS

B Troop, at the Jay Hawk Firing Range, January 1991.

COURTESY MICHAEL A. BILLS

C Troop in the desert, Junction City, February 1991.

COURTESY STEVE GRUENIG

Final rehearsal by Squadron Commanders and staff prior to the Ground War, 23 February 1991. JOHN BURDAN PHOTO

Squadron Commander and Staff after the final rehearsal, 23 February 1991. JOHN BURDAN PHOTO

Late afternoon, 24 February 1991, 2LT Steve Gruenig and CW3 Greg Schullo have just returned from their second mission of the day.

COURTESY STEVE GRUENIG

Iraqi positions near OBJ 15K, 25 February 1991. COURTESY KEN POPE

C Troop Cobra supporting the A Troop attack on Iraqi positions the morning of 27 February 1991. COURTESY KEN POPE

MAJ John Burdan, after the attack on Iraqi Positions, the morning of 27 February 1991. JOHN BURDAN PHOTO

*According to Steve Gruenig, Mr. Phil Schmiesing of C Troop
investigated this bunker and captured 2 EPWs, 27 February 1991.*

*MAJ John Burdan and the EPWs on the Safwan Highway, morning of
28 February 1991.*

Basra Highway, 28 February 1991.   JOHN BURDAN PHOTO

CPT Pope and LTC Wilson on the Basra Highway, 28 February 1991.
The EPW collection point is in the background.   JOHN BURDAN PHOTO

Basra Highway, 28 February 1991, (left to right) CPT Chris Philbrick,
CSM Mike Cobb, MAJ Bill Wimbish, MAJ John Burdan.

JOHN BURDAN PHOTO

A troop, Safwan Airfield, Iraq, March 1991.   COURTESY KEN POPE

D Troop at Safwan Airfield, Iraq, 2 March 1991, posing in front of a D Troop AH-1, #16198, pilot-in-command (PIC) CW3 Craig Winters.

COURTESY ROY R. PETERS

CSM Mike Cobb and LTC Bob Wilson, March 1991.

JOHN BURDAN PHOTO

Squadron S3 Staff Section, Khobar Towers, May 1991.

JOHN BURDAN PHOTO

Ken and Mary Pope, Marshall Army Air Field, Ft. Riley, Kansas, 10 May 1991.

COURTESY KEN POPE

13   Safwan

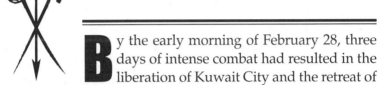

By the early morning of February 28, three days of intense combat had resulted in the liberation of Kuwait City and the retreat of Saddam Hussein's troops from the small sheikdom. With the capital and southern Kuwait in the hands of the Saudi-led Joint Forces Commands and the U.S. Marines, the Third U.S. Army was forcing the remaining Iraqi forces into an enclave opposite the only crossings across the Tigris and Euphrates Rivers at Basra. In the "Basra Pocket," the remnants of the once imposing Iraqi Army were in a position from which they could not, if the Allies chose to block the withdrawal routes to the north, escape.

At 0600 hours, the 1st Infantry Division's 1-4 Cavalry, the northeastern-most unit in the VII Corps, came under the operational control of COL Tony Moreno's 2d Brigade.[1] The entire 1st Infantry Division then lurched forward in one last move up toward Kuwait's northern border. As it moved north, the scene on the Basra Highway reminded some of scenes from the *Road Warrior* movies. The thick smoke of hundreds of fires from the Ar Rawdatayn oil fields blocked the light of the slowly rising sun. Iraqi military and civilian equipment that never made it north littered the highway.[2] By 0800 hours the campaign was over. LTC Bob Wilson, his staff, and commanders used the hours soon after the cease-fire to begin to account for the dead, arrange for the evacuation of the EPWs, and consolidate the squadron.

Gathering the dead around the squadron position was a grisly task. The troopers saw firsthand the results of their handiwork. Troopers pulled dead Iraqis out of their vehicles and placed them in body bags and organized their personal effects together for shipment. As clearly as possible they tried to tag the bodies with the location where they were found. Some of the bodies were burned so badly that they began to fall apart when moved. It was a sobering reminder of the lethality of the profession of arms. B Troop's 1SGT David Rooks established a collection point for the bodies near the road so they could be loaded onto vehicles from division and shipped out. To complicate the task, late that morning dog packs arrived in the vicinity. At first they circled the lines but then as they smelled the bodies they darted in and ran off with body parts that hadn't been collected yet or hadn't been found. The troopers tried to run them off but they remained in the area. By late that afternoon the remains had all been collected and evacuated from the area.[3]

The Iraqi prisoners continued to be a problem and the combat trains, with the assistance of the A Troop engineer platoon, were still in charge of the collection point. With daylight and the population growing, the squadron requested assistance from the approaching division. After its arrival that morning, the 2nd Brigade assigned an infantry company to operate the collection point. Its first task was to count the prisoners so it could estimate the transportation requirements for moving them back to the prisoner of war camps in the rear. By 1000 hours the company commander had determined that the squadron had captured 2,064 Iraqi soldiers. The squadron did not have food or water for that number of additional individuals, so it was important to transfer them as quickly as possible to another unit's control. The division headquarters was initially skeptical about the prisoner count, but promised to send food and water as well as the needed transportation to begin the evacuation. By mid-afternoon the division transportation in the form of five-ton stake and platform vehicles, essentially commercial trucks with open trailers, arrived to begin to take the Iraqis away and also brought a shipment of extra food and water. As the squadron's troopers emptied the prisoner cage, they gave each captured Iraqi soldier a bottle of water and an MRE for the trip to the rear. It took several hours for the squadron to load all the Iraqis on the trucks and move them out of the area.

Finally, the missing elements of the squadron needed to be reunited with the main body. The squadron maintenance platoon was missing an M88 tank recovery vehicle and its crew.

The previous day, SSG William Ball and CW2 Gerald Kovach from the maintenance platoon had discovered a B Troop M113 that had broken down. After an inspection, they determined that it needed to replace a final drive. This was a lengthy process, so they left the broken vehicle with an M88 crew led by Specialist Kevin Lockridge. Kovach ensured that Lockridge had all he needed to finish the job as well as a GPS. After getting the work started, Kovach and Ball raced ahead to catch up with the squadron. After repairing the personnel carrier, the M88 and the M113 headed back to join the squadron. The B Troop M113 crew established radio contact with B Troop but by nightfall, Lockridge and his crew had not arrived and the maintenance leaders began to get worried. The next morning, after the cease-fire, Lockridge had still not shown up and CPT Mark Johnson, the squadron maintenance officer, decided to search for him, taking a driver, extra water, and a case of MREs. Over ten hours later, Johnson returned leading the M88. The young Lockridge had stopped convoy after convoy asking where the squadron was. In addition, he had been asking for fuel, food, and water. With thousands of vehicles heading into Kuwait from hundreds of different units, it is not surprising that no one knew. Johnson had spotted the lone M88 slowly heading in the right direction.[4]

In the aftermath of the 1991 Persian Gulf War, one of the most consistent comments was praise by leaders, at all levels and from all kinds of units, for the incredible dedication and professionalism of the junior enlisted soldiers. Young men and women with only a vague understanding of where they were and the big picture around them consistently performed their duties just as they had been trained. Many were not combat soldiers, but like Lockridge, commanded a maintenance vehicle, drove a fuel truck, or worked as a medic. When faced with the unknown, and in the absence of the leaders they normally could consult, they continued to do what they believed was right. Although only an E4, Lockridge knew what his leaders and the army expected of him and did everything he could to skillfully accomplish his mission. It was not the weapons and super technology that won this conflict, but the judgment, training, and motivation of the soldiers, from youngest private

to senior commander. This conflict also validated the leader-
ship and training programs instituted in the aftermath of the
Vietnam era that continued until the army returned from
Desert Storm.

Other squadron crews and groups began to return. The previous day, Chief Warrant Officer Kirk Waymire's scout-
weapons team, running low on fuel and ammunition, returned
to the squadron's rearm-refuel point located in the vicinity of its
mid-day halt. Unfortunately, Philbrick was out of fuel and sent
his wheeled fuel trucks back to top off. Waymire's team (one
scout and two Cobras), settled down to wait for the fuel trucks.
Soon, the remainder of the squadron's vehicles departed, leaving the SWT with their aircraft and a group of disarmed Iraqis,
without guards, waiting for transportation to the rear. As night
approached and there was still no sign of fuel, Waymire set up
a guard by the aircrews around the aircraft. One of the guards
wore his flight helmet with night-vision goggles and one went
without. Meanwhile, the Iraqis had their own fire going, intending to stay warm regardless of the outcome of the war. Finally, around midnight, Philbrick returned with fuel and ammunition trucks. Once the trucks resupplied the helicopters,
Philbrick left and disappeared eastward into the night, leaving
instructions to fly east in the morning and contact Flight Operations once they were in the air.[5]

At dawn on February 28, Waymire's team tried to take off,
but visibility was initially very poor and they had to land. Soon
after they were back down, an Iraqi officer surrendered to
them. The man was alone and had stripped his patches off his
uniform. He used sign language to indicate he needed food and
water. He did not have any boots and his feet were in very bad
shape. They gave him some food and water and did what they
could for his feet. The weather soon started to break up so they
gave the man a card explaining his conditions that he could
pass on to another American unit and departed. As they flew
off, they noted the ridge where the Iraqi had come from and
saw the officer's weapon and patches discarded on the ground.
By early morning, Waymire was back in contact with the
squadron on the Basra Highway.[6]

1SGT Gary Parkey's odyssey was nearly finished. After

spending the night with the 3rd Armored Division, he decided to make another attempt to find A Troop. Thanking his host scout platoon leader, he headed east toward the Basra Highway. Finally, about mid-morning, he pulled in to the troop's assembly area, after a three-day absence full of adventure. SFC Steven Kuder, the object of his search, also linked up with A Troop that day. Kuder had spent the last few days trying to locate and catch up to the squadron. He and his crew had, like Parkey, even spent time with elements of other units before they finally learned where the squadron was located and rejoined the troop.[7]

However, not everyone was able to rejoin the squadron that day. 2LT Lowndes and his small team of vehicles had still not found B Troop that morning as he had hoped. The broken tank's maintenance problems had proved daunting and he had had to quit working late the previous night. He got his crews up early on the morning of February 28 and finally completed the short-tracking of the tank by mid-morning. They began moving immediately to the east, but could go no faster than twenty kilometers per hour because of the damaged tank's limited mobility. Around noon they ran into elements of the 2nd Armored Cavalry who gave Lowndes a hot meal, fuel, and water, as well as the news of the cease-fire. Plotting his new direction, the lieutenant was again on his way in the early afternoon for Kuwait. The tank's slow speed continued to hinder movement, and with darkness fast approaching, the young lieutenant decided to spend another night in the desert and not risk getting the tank stuck in a ditch or wadi in the darkness.[8]

Late that afternoon the division ordered Wilson's squadron to establish a screen line just north of the positions it had occupied the previous evening. Once again, B Troop moved to the west of the highway facing northward and A Troop set up its line across the highway and off to the east. The squadron still maintained its combat configuration with the air troops remaining with the 4th Brigade, the field trains with the 1st Brigade, and combat trains, flight operations, and the squadron TOC each occupying their separate positions behind the screen line. As evening approached, the squadron prepared to settle in for a well-deserved rest. The commanders were told to get everyone a good night's sleep and to provide for minimal manning of the screen line, telling the troopers that they would definitely not be moving from the area for a few days.[9]

Shortly after midnight on March 1, the 1st Infantry Division's night operations officer had just settled down to what he anticipated would be a routine shift. The Big Red One's headquarters was on the Basra-Kuwait highway just west of the burning fires of Kuwait's oil fields and the night sky had a red glow overlaid with the constant roaring sound of the flaming wells. Troops moved around in the night not needing flashlights. MG Thomas G. Rhame and his principal staff officers had finally gone to bed after almost a week of operations that had begun on February 23. Danger Main's night shift began the routine task of general security and accounting for all soldiers and equipment, and planning for subsequent operations.[10]

Shortly before 0200 hours, the VII Corps tactical operations center's (TAC) duty officer called to ask if the 1st Division had the area around Safwan, a small village in southeastern Iraq, under control or observation. Since he had just confirmed the locations of all units in the division, the duty officer said no.[11] Suddenly, this little town had become extremely important. Over the next eighteen hours, two commands from the 1st Infantry Division would confront Saddam Hussein's army on Iraqi soil in an incident that threatened to reopen the just-concluded conflict.

The problem had begun on February 28 when General Powell ordered General Schwarzkopf to conduct a cease-fire ceremony with the Iraqi High Command. Schwarzkopf wanted this site located deep in Iraq so it was obvious to all who was the victor and who was the vanquished. He also wanted it at a location that the Iraqi delegation could reach by road.[12] He directed his chief of staff, MG Robert B. Johnston, to find a suitable site. Around 2100 hours Johnston called LTG John Yeosock, the Third Army commander, who was at his command post on the other side of Riyadh, for site suggestions. Without contacting either of his corps commanders, who were familiar with the conditions on the ground, he suggested three possible locations: the village of Shaibah outside of al Basra, Jalibah Airfield about eighty miles west of al Basra, and a location across the Hawr al Hammar causeway.[13] Since only one of these, Jalibah, was under American control, it seemed the realistic choice. After Yeosock passed on his suggestions, he ordered LTG Gary Luck and XVIII Corps to prepare the airfield for the ceremony. Later that night Luck told him that Jalibah was not the site to use. It had been the target of a violent attack by the 24th Infantry Division on the morning of February 27.[14] Unexploded munitions and damaged vehicles were everywhere and it could not be cleaned up in time for the proposed meeting. Yeosock now had to call General Schwarzkopf and tell him to change his plans.[15]

Schwarzkopf had already sent a message describing his concept for the negotiations to General Powell, and now he had to call his message back and change the site of the talks. Looking at his map, he selected the airfield at Safwan as the alternate site and redrafted his message to the Joint Chiefs of Staff.[16] The airfield was six kilometers west of the intersection near the village of Safwan. However, Schwarzkopf had never ordered anyone to seize the airfield, although now it appeared as an objective that should have been taken. Neither Schwarzkopf nor Yeosock called Franks ahead of time to ask him for his assessment of the location.

After the fact, later that night, BG Steve Arnold, the Third Army G3, asked COL Cherrie, the VII Corps G3, about using Safwan for the negotiations. It was the first time the corps G3 had heard of the airfield at Safwan and he could not understand why Schwarzkopf had chosen that location. Cherrie told him that it was on the other side of the demarcation line in enemy territory.[17] Around 0130 hours Yeosock called Franks directly and asked him about the status of the Safwan airfield and told him about the upcoming conference.[18] A few minutes later one of Cherrie's staff officers called the 1st Infantry Division's Main Command Post. For almost ten minutes the division's duty officer confirmed to several corps staff officers that no one in the 1st Infantry Division was near Safwan and that unit locations had not changed since the report he had rendered at 1900 hours the previous evening.[19] Finally, an agitated Franks had enough and grabbed the telephone from his staff officer. "Do you know who this is?" He shouted at the stunned divisional staff officer. "Get Rhame on the phone now!" Quickly, the duty officer raced out of the TOC and across fifty yards of fire-illuminated sand to wake his exhausted commander.[20]

Tom Rhame, awaking from his first decent sleep in over a week, at first thought it was some kind of a joke. Throwing on his trousers and boots, he raced back to the command post that he had left only a couple of hours earlier. There, Franks was on the radio wanting to know about Safwan. In a few minutes, Rhame confirmed that Safwan was not under the control of his division and had never been an assigned objective.[21] By now, almost forty-five minutes had gone by since that first call from the corps. Rhame finally asked for his orders. Franks then gave Rhame a mission to reconnoiter the area around Safwan but not to get decisively engaged.[22]

The 1-4 Cavalry now had one last combat mission to perform. Off the phone with the corps commander around 0240 hours, Rhame radioed LTC Bob Wilson.[23] Like other units in the 1st Infantry Division, the cavalry had only a minimum number of soldiers awake and on-duty. For almost a month it had been on a war footing and few soldiers had been able to get any sleep over the previous four days. MAJ John Dinnell, who was running the squadron tactical operations center night shift, took the radio call and walked over to the squadron commander's vehicle to ask him to come over to the TOC. Once Wilson was awake, Rhame told him to move as soon as possible to recon the area near Safwan. MAJ Dinnell quickly put out a warning order to the remainder of the squadron and sent runners out to wake the remainder of the staff in order to prepare the necessary orders.[24]

Franks, meanwhile, had second thoughts about this impromptu mission. At 0308 hours, he called Rhame back and ordered the 1st Infantry Division to stop its movement. At first light, he wanted Rhame to conduct an area reconnaissance to determine if Central Command could use the site as a meeting area. He was to find out if there were any enemy troops in the area, but not to get into a serious fight with Iraqi forces. At 0350 hours, Franks called Rhame again, and laid out his mission for seizing Safwan. "Intent is to not take any casualties." The corps's log read, "If you run into enemy forces, then stop and report to CG VII Corps."[25] Wilson's cavalry still had the mission and it was to move to and seize the airfield near Safwan and occupy .it in preparation for the surrender ceremony. Rhame, passing along Frank's guidance, told him to avoid combat (and re-starting the war) if possible, but to defend himself as appropriate. These orders, from Wilson's perspective, were just what he needed: clear senior commander's intent, maximum flexibility for the ground commander in an unclear situation, and no hint of the tension and politics taking place between division, corps, and army headquarters.[26] Wilson now had a fairly powerful, and veteran, force at his disposal, with two tank-reinforced ground troops, two air cavalry troops, and an Apache attack helicopter company that Rhame had placed under his operational control.[27]

Wilson and the squadron staff rapidly put together the needed orders and finished briefing the command group shortly before 0500 hours. Meanwhile the remainder of the squadron was up and preparing for the mission. The aviators needed little time because they had prepared their aircraft prior to shutting down for the night. The ground troops quickly stowed their gear and began organizing the vehicles into the proper formations. By 0615 hours the squadron was on the move with its two ground troops going cross-country, north-northeast in standard traveling overwatch formation.[28] With the Safwan Mountain (Jabal Sanam) as their guide, A Troop moved in the east and B Troop moved on the western side of the zone.[29] LTC Wilson followed behind B Troop and MAJ Burdan followed behind A Troop. Forward of each ground troop was an aerial scout-weapons team (SWT) consisting of OH-58C scout helicopters and Cobra attack helicopters. One team was led by 2LT Tom Schwartz (a Ft. Hood augmentee) from D Troop and the other by CW4 Bruce Thomas from C Troop. Other SWTs would be rotated in throughout the mission as the morning continued. The AH-64 Apache company was kept on the ground at a holding area ready to respond if Wilson's troopers got into trouble.[30]

Rhame could tell Wilson little about the enemy situation. The 1st Infantry Division's Main Command Post had only recently reorganized after the ground offensive and its G-2 (Intelligence) section was unable to provide the squadron with any information on the Iraqis' composition or disposition.[31] The squadron's aviators, however, were soon reporting dozens of abandoned Iraqi Army vehicles on the way to the airfield. Rhame ordered Wilson not to slow down and destroy any of these vehicles so he could get to Safwan before the Iraqis could react.[32]

At around 0700 hours, as the ground troops approached the mountain, which was off to the side of the airfield, A Troop swung to the east and B Troop moved to the west. The SWT led by Mr Thomas reconnoitered the mountain itself and could find no Iraqis there. However, it did see some to the north of the airfield. As the ground troops swept around the mountain, they had difficulty identifying the small airstrip, as the vehicle commanders had been expecting a large runway. A Troop's soldiers finally crossed what they initially thought was an unfinished four-lane highway that turned out to be the narrow asphalt strip. Realizing their mistake, the ground troops continued their push beyond the airfield and soon ran into the Iraqis. Just as the aviators had reported, tanks, BMPs, and other vehicles occupied revetted positions on the northern side of the airfield, oriented towards the south and west. Behind the dug-in armor, the Iraqis had positioned many more tracked and wheeled vehicles.[33] What the 1-4 Cavalry had found defending about 1,500 meters north of the airfield, was an entire Iraqi armored brigade. Three battalions were on-line and an additional battalion positioned in depth. All of the Iraqi combat vehicles were in prepared positions.[34] Wilson reminded his commanders not to fire unless fired upon or in danger,[35] but to continue in a steady advance to the airfield. The troopers were nervous and some feared that they would be the first casualties in a renewal of the fighting. Courageously, they drove their combat vehicles within the range of the Iraqi weapon systems and occupied the airfield.[36]

With the cavalry squadron on the objective, Rhame ordered Wilson to move his air-scouts to the important road junction about five miles east of Safwan Mountain. As the air cavalrymen continued to investigate, they found the area full of other Iraqi tank and mechanized units. The squadron's scouts watched hundreds of Iraqi vehicles continue to move north and away from the Americans.[37] The squadron had obviously arrived at the southern boundary of the Basra pocket.

Around 0830 hours, Wilson moved forward to the airfield, dismounted from his Bradley, and approached several "well-dressed and well-fed" Iraqi soldiers whose uniforms indicated that they were from a Republican Guard unit. Their equipment appeared in very good shape and Wilson noticed trucks with fresh vegetables and other supplies. Wilson then spoke, through an interpreter, with the senior officer at the site. He told the Iraqi colonel that the airfield at Safwan was under American control and that he must move his men and equipment immediately. Obviously disturbed by Wilson's words, the Iraqi officer left to speak to his commander.[38]

As the officer departed, four Iraqi tanks moved in front of Wilson's command group and lowered their gun tubes at it. The young squadron commander realized this was no time for bravado, and calmly pulled his group south 100 yards. He then alerted his troop commanders who were also negotiating with Iraqis at other portions of the airfield, and directed the Apache company to fly over his location in a show of force. Arriving a few moments later, the greatly feared attack helicopters caused a change in the Iraqi attitude as almost immediately, the Iraqi tanks moved back. With the situation now clarified, Wilson, along with his boss COL Jim Mowery, again moved forward to confront the Iraqi officers. An Iraqi colonel told Wilson that his general said they were to remain on the airfield. Wilson calmly replied that if they did not move out, the entire 1st Infantry Division would attack them within hours. Looking at the hovering Apache helicopters, the Iraqi officer said he needed to speak with his superior and departed.[39]

Similar situations were taking place in the two cavalry troop sectors. Not all the Iraqi soldiers were in as good as shape as the troops Wilson encountered. In many cases the cavalrymen provided rations for obviously hungry Iraqi soldiers, many of whom came out of hiding and surrendered to the squadron's troopers. Just as they had done during the previous week, American troopers disarmed the Iraqis willing to surrender, gave them food, and sent them to the south towards the VII Corps's prisoner of war compounds.[40]

In the A Troop sector at about the same time that LTC Wilson was having his first encounter, an Iraqi Republican Guard

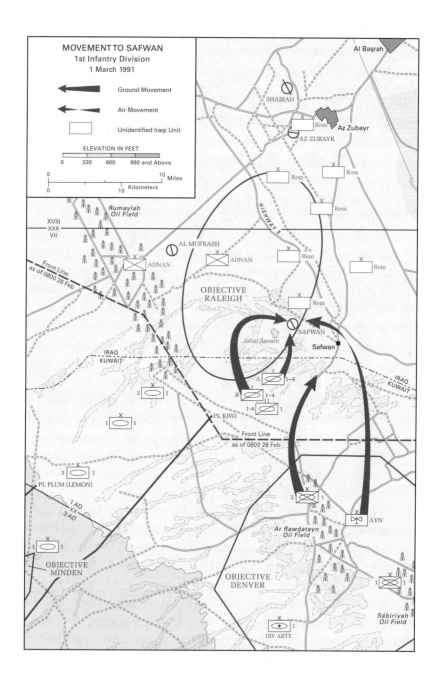

MOVEMENT TO SAFWAN
1st Infantry Division
1 March 1991

Ground Movement

Air Movement

Unidentified Iraqi Unit

ELEVATION IN FEET
0   330   660   990 and Above

colonel approached the American commander. He was angry that they were feeding his soldiers on his land. As a response, he directed his own men to brew some tea for the troopers of A Troop. CPT Ken Pope told the Iraqi officer that they had to leave the area because of the upcoming peace talks. The two leaders exchanged map locations and the Iraqi colonel departed to confer with his superiors.[41] So far, the cavalrymen had accomplished their mission with skill. Their command discipline prevented a tense situation from turning into a needless fire-fight.

Rhame was not waiting for this situation to continue. Now that Wilson had accomplished his reconnaissance mission, he directed COL Tony Moreno's 2d Brigade, consisting of two tank battalions, a mechanized infantry battalion, and a field artillery battalion, to move into the sector. At 1009 hours the Dagger Brigade started to move toward Safwan. Once Moreno was in the area, Wilson's cavalry squadron would come under the operational control of the 2nd Brigade.[42]

At 1020 hours, the Iraqi colonel returned to A Troop and told its commander that he was not going to leave the airfield. Just at that moment, a flight of two A-10 Thunderbolts flew overhead. Pope, knowing the terrifying reputation of these aircraft amongst the Iraqis, told the Iraqi colonel that if he did not move, the aircraft would attack him. This Iraqi colonel again went back to find his superiors, while Pope and several of his soldiers finished the tea prepared by the Iraqis.[43] Meanwhile in another portion of the A Troop area, SSG Donald Wehage was examining the buildings located on the north side of the airfield. He dismounted from his track and motioned it to follow him as he walked in amongst the buildings. Armed with only his pistol, he walked into an Iraqi heavy mortar platoon. They seemed as surprised to see him as he was to see them. Someone in the platoon spoke English. SSG Wehage demanded that they surrender. When they looked at him in confusion, he turned around and discovered that he was all by himself. Somehow he had been separated from his vehicle. Just as he was thinking, "what do I do now?" his M3A2 turned a corner and came to his rescue. The Iraqis surrendered.[44]

In a separate incident, MAJ Burdan intercepted an Iraqi truck that had several soldiers in the back of it, headed to the airfield just as if nothing had happened, with an Iraqi captain and a major in the cab of the vehicle. They seemed totally surprised at the sudden appearance of the Americans and asked the S3 if he knew that the squadron was in Iraq. He smiled and replied yes, and told them they needed to leave the area and asked them what unit they were from. The major smiled this time and replied "Iraqi Army!" refusing to identify his unit. The Iraqis then drove away in a state of confusion.[45]

In CPT Mike Bills's B Troop sector, a similar scenario played itself out. He and a detachment of combat vehicles moved towards the Iraqi defenses. Once close, the young captain dismounted and approached some soldiers asking to see their commander. Soon a lieutenant colonel arrived who, in broken English asked, "Why are you in Iraq? Are you lost?"[46] Bills assured him that was not the case and he was here to secure the site for the cease-fire negotiations. The Iraqi commander told his junior enlisted soldiers to leave and surrounded Bills with about fifteen to twenty officers and senior soldiers. The Iraqi officer then left to confer with his superiors. A short time later he returned with additional soldiers, wearing the black leather jackets, camouflage uniforms, and berets of Iraqi commando units.[47] To Bills, the situation looked as though it had taken a turn for the worse.

However, after a short, tense standoff, this Iraqi unit and all of the others on the airfield received orders from their superiors to leave. By 1200 the entire airfield complex was clear of Iraqi troops. BG William Carter, the 1st Infantry Division's Assistant Division Commander for maneuver, flew to Wilson's location and discussed the new command arrangements, and clarified some of the mission's details. The brigade encircled the airfield with a security zone of tanks and Bradleys. MAJ Wimbish arrived early in the afternoon and set up the tactical operations center on the northwest corner of the airfield. As the squadron was consolidating around the western end of the airfield, CPT Bills got an unexpected surprise. 2LT Lowndes and his team finally linked up with B Troop. They were chagrined to have missed out on the last two days of operations. Bills recalled being told by Lowndes, "Sir, please don't ever do this to me again!"[48]

Soon the division tactical command post arrived and established itself about 400 meters to the east. It now became the focal point of a massive, corps-directed effort to prepare the airfield for a high-profile show as CENTCOM, the Third Army, and VII Corps sent truck after truck of personnel and equipment to this once obscure airfield. BG Carter and LTC Wilson were quite concerned since it seemed as though things were arriving with no plan. Concerned that the show would fail, Wilson directed Morrison to get over to the runway and "organize things."[49]

Morrison headed down to the airfield and found a disaster with the remains of the war everywhere and a growing group of soldiers from higher commands standing around looking confused. He grabbed an M-88 tank retriever and began directing it to haul away broken vehicles, metal containers, and trash of all kinds off the runway so the command could start landing C-130 aircraft full of supplies. Everyone was quite startled as the M88 set off a number of the bomblets that were reminders from the recent campaign. Around midnight a flight of CH-47 helicopters arrived carrying supplies and the first question from the pilots was "did the soldiers have any souvenirs to trade?" The HHT commander and his driver, Specialist Dave Hall, watched the increasingly confused process. Finally Morrison began unloading the new tents, stoves, and porta-johns and began bringing some order to the runway. Around 0300 he fell asleep in his HMMWV, as some sense of order emerged among the crates of equipment and food.[50]

Over the next thirty-six hours the brigade's soldiers transformed the airfield. The corps commander sent another CH-47 cargo helicopter full of tents, tables, chairs, and communications gear. Truck convoys from the 2nd (Corps) Support Command and the 21st (Theater) Support Command arrived with, among other things, refrigerated vans containing fresh meats, fruits, and vegetables. Also in the convoy were a large mess tent and other equipment and furnishings to bring the site to a level fitting for a well-publicized, international conference. Before it was all over, most of the squadron got themselves a good steak meal and a can of "near beer" (non-alcoholic).[51]

The protocol for the meeting was carefully scripted, rehearsed, and constantly revised. The general plan was for brigade officers in armored vehicles, along with interpreters, to meet the Iraqi delegation at a contact point. They would demand that the Iraqis surrender their weapons and transport them in HMMWVs to the cease-fire site. By design, the route would take them through a part of the damaged town of Safwan, and then out to the airfield, past forty-three Bradleys and M1A1 tanks lined up on the south side of the road. With Apache helicopters and jet fighters in the air, the intention was to impress the Iraqi delegation with the combat power available to the American forces. In addition to providing constant patrolling of the security perimeter by air and ground, the squadron provided vehicles for the airfield display and also an escape vehicle for General Schwarzkopf should something go wrong at the site.[52]

The squadron commander directed CPT Bills to provide the Bradley for Schwarzkopf's potential use, and he selected his own track, B66. As directed by the corps choreographers, Bills backed it next to the negotiation tent and placed the squadron's colors alongside the B Troop guidon on either side of the track's lowered ramp. Early on March 3, as Wilson and some of his officers gathered around Bills's track, MG Rhame and LTG Franks came over and praised the squadron for its superb performance over the last week. Franks then asked Wilson to join him inside the tent during the cease-fire negotiations. Soon General Schwarzkopf, who had flown to the airfield with Franks but had gone in another direction, also came over and congratulated Wilson and his troopers. Everyone was all smiles as the commanding general shook each officer's and soldier's hand, thanking them for the great job they did. Of course, this was all captured by the news media and squadron officers found themselves in *Life Magazine*, other publications, and on television for years after.[53]

Soon they received word that the Iraqi representatives had arrived at the contact point. The soldiers immediately manned their vehicles and awaited their arrival. Soon the squadron members saw the AH-64s that were flying above the delegation and monitored its progress by watching the approaching helicopters. Then the procession, two M1A1 tanks, two Bradleys and eight HMMWVs, and two Apaches ten feet off the ground, arrived at the dismount point on the airfield. General Schwarz-kopf and Prince Khalid, the Saudi commander, met them at a search tent. The Iraqis did not look too happy about being searched. They then went into the negotiation tent, followed by the dignitaries including Franks and Wilson. As the rest of the squadron's leaders waited for the group to come out of the tent, they talked with reporters who were covering the events and with friends from within the division and corps staffs who had gotten a ride to the airfield.[54]

Less than an hour after they began, General Schwarzkopf and Saudi Prince Khalid strode out of the briefing tent and up to the podium, with three Big Red One M1A1 tanks as a back-drop. Schwarzkopf gave a short news conference and then turned it over to Prince Khalid who thanked all the soldiers for their sacrifices. Schwarzkopf then disappeared into a tent where he called General Powell back in Washington. Soon after, he and LTG Franks got into their aircraft and flew away.[55]

The squadron's soldiers were all happy that the fighting was apparently over, and they began to think about going home. The news reporters who had covered the conference began talking to the troopers who stood in front of their vehicles. Most wanted to know how the equipment had stood up to the fight. Apparently, some reporters were disappointed with the answers, expecting criticism of the weapons the Americans used. Although the tanks consumed a lot of fuel, they were a quantum leap over the tanks the Iraqis employed and most soldiers had nothing but praise for the Bradley and M1A1 Abrams. Later that afternoon, five reporters who had driven up from Saudi Arabia in a very cramped International Scout, asked to talk to some of the troop-ers. On the way north they had driven past the destroyed Iraqi equipment and were quite impressed with the degree of dam-age they encountered. MAJ Burdan arranged for an interview with some of Ken Pope's soldiers.[56]

Meanwhile, the conference site was torn down as quickly as it had been set up. It had been a very busy three days for the squadron's troopers, as they had found themselves first in the middle of a potential fire-fight, and then at the center of a his-toric meeting between two adversaries. None of the soldiers realized just how tenuous that peace really was and that Saddam Hussein did not consider himself a defeated leader. Twelve years later, American cavalrymen would again pass through Safwan, this time to end Hussein's Baathist regime and begin a combination conventional war and counter insurgency that would last at least five long years. But, that was all in the future. For now, Wilson's troopers began tending to their equipment, cleaning themselves up, and thinking of the trip home. Soon they would discover that trip was not going to happen so quickly.

14   Recovery

During the cease-fire negotiations on March 3, General Schwarzkopf presented the Iraqi representatives with a map showing a temporary boundary line that separated coalition and Iraqi military forces. He directed that until both sides agreed on a permanent cease-fire, opposing units would stay one thousand meters away from this boundary to prevent unintended engagements, such as had taken place the day before in the 24th Infantry Division's sector. There, in a short but intense battle near the Hawr Al Hammer causeway across the Euphrates River, Victory Division's 1st Brigade destroyed most of an Iraqi brigade from the Hammurabi Mechanized Division in an engagement that should not have taken place.[1] With great hesitation, the Iraqi commission agreed to the temporary boundary.[2]

LTG Frederick Franks's VII Corps, including the 1st Infantry Division, assumed control of this military demarcation line, or MDL, as the XVIII Corps that had been in Saudi Arabia since the previous August began heading for home. Soon after the negotiations Franks's command began shuffling around the Iraqi desert. By the end of March, the 2nd Cavalry was patrolling the Euphrates River from As Samawah, east to An Nasiriyah, backed up by the 1st Infantry Division's 3d Brigade. The 1st Armored Division secured the sector from Highway 8 to Ar Rumaylah, while the 3d Armored Division, which had replaced the 1st Infantry Division in the Safwan area, occupied the corps's right flank. Located in the center of the sector, at Assembly Area Allen, was the remainder of the 1st Infantry Division including the 1-4 Cavalry. These arrangements would continue to change until most of the corps withdrew from Iraq in April.[3]

The context of this entire time period, in addition to the be-hind-the-scenes peace negotiations, was the Shi'a uprising in southern Iraq. Although many of the details remain obscure, it began at the end of February, as a protest by regular army soldiers southwest of Al Basra. Apparently, they believed Saddam Hussein and his Republican Guards had abandoned them during the retreat from Kuwait. This protest then sparked a spontaneous, leaderless demonstration of Shi'a Iraqis frustrated with the regime. Mobs broke open the jails and went on a killing rampage against all symbols of the Iraqi government, and soon cities such as Al Zubayr, An Nasiriyah, As Samawah, An Najaf, and Karbella were all involved in heavy fighting.[4]

The rebellion began to fall apart almost immediately. Shi'a radicals took over its leadership and began circulating photographs of Iran's Ayatollah Khomeini. Consequently, moderates, the army, nationalists, and others who could have been instrumental in breaking with the Baghdad government deserted the dissidents' cause. While the revolt caught Hussein's government off-guard, the regime soon recovered. It reconstituted the army, especially the survivors of Republican Guard units, and began a brutal program to destroy all involved. Often, these forces conducted operations in full view of coalition troops, just across the military demarcation line. American soldiers watched as Iraqi tank and helicopter units attacked Shi'a strongholds, in some cases using the chemical weapons they never employed against the coalition forces.[5]

President George H. W. Bush had decided not to participate in this fight, and prohibited United States military units from intervening. Emotionally, American officers would have relished the chance to inflict punishment on Hussein's vindictive troops. However, any overt action could find the U.S. Army engaged in a civil war whose length, cost, and outcome was uncertain. The United States would have gone into Iraq alone since most of the coalition would not have followed. Iran might have intervened on one side or another, further complicating the situation. It was a road down which the United States government did not wish to travel in 1991. The events following the defeat of the Iraqi Army in 2003 have confirmed the logic of that hesitation, as the shine of that victory wore off as American and

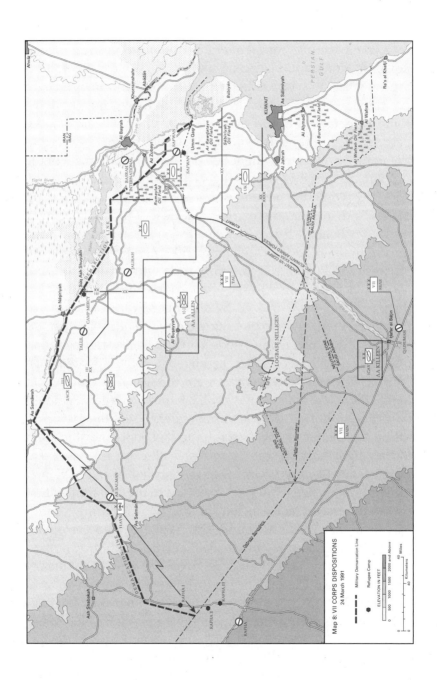

Map 8: VII CORPS DISPOSITIONS
24 March 1991

British troops found themselves in an extended and expensive insurgency. During early March 1991, the 1-4 Cavalry remained under the burning oil well fires of northern Kuwait near Safwan recovering from the recent conflict, conducting operational missions, and beginning to work with the refugees fleeing the retribution of Saddam Hussein's reconstituted forces.[6]

The first thing the squadron had to do was recover from the combat operations of the last month. After Schwarzkopf's departure, the 2nd Brigade, with the 1-4 Cavalry, remained in control of the Safwan area. Right behind the commander, all of the support troops and "strap-hangers" present for the ceremony departed. While the brigade was stuck with much of the clean up, it also had the claim on the great deal of food and refreshments left behind. It was of a quality and quantity which the cavalry troopers had not seen for months, and for two days they ate fresh chicken and eggs, drank soda and "near beer," and lived as close to luxury as they had experienced since they left the port. They were amazed by the apparent life of luxury for those who worked far to the rear in corps and army-level units.[7]

This brief interaction between battle-weary troopers and their rear-echelon comrades highlighted some apparent discrepancies among those who fought the war. For example, in March the squadron's troopers still had problems getting desert boots and uniforms. In some instances, they sent their wives to the post exchange back at Fort Riley to buy boots and ship them to Iraq. In at least one case, a soldier with extra-large feet was using a pair of Iraqi boots, since the Army did not have any available in his size. However, it seemed to the cavalrymen that each and every "rear echelon" soldier was strutting around Safwan in their new desert uniforms. While it was a perception that was not quite true, it was one that stuck with the troops.[8]

Nevertheless, with the campaign over, the quality of life began improving. The mail began arriving with some regularity and CPT Ken Stokes's personnel section began processing individual awards and catching up on the immense backlog of administrative paperwork that had accumulated during the last month, a difficult process in the inhospitable environment. Troops began taking showers, sometimes in improvised stalls as was the case in A Troop where they rigged a diesel engine normally used for pumping water from a well to local fields, to pump water for the troop showers. Everyone also began washing their clothes, getting haircuts, and cleaning equipment.

Sometimes there was the opportunity for amusement, as in the case of A Troop. A sand berm enclosed the unit's defensive perimeter. SFC William Molitor had his soldiers dig a hole in the berm and prepare a small movie room. For the theater, he had a VCR and a TV that ran on a power generator that he had purchased back in the States and carried forward in the S3's cargo truck. They threw a tarp over the top of the structure and began to show movies and tapes of the recent Super Bowl. The soldiers had the first opportunity to see, in private, some of the videotapes made by their wives and families. This popular diversion lasted for only a few days, until the area was inundated with heavy rains and the tarp collapsed, destroying A Troop's little theater.[9]

The environment was exceptionally unhealthy. When Saddam Hussein's troops left Kuwait, they ignited many of the region's oil wells, causing massive amounts of flame and smoke to escape into the air every day. From his position alone, A Troop's 2LT Mitchell Osburn counted forty-seven burning wells. Some days one could look directly at the sun at high noon, as if it were the moon at night. Soot covered everything, and if the wind changed from east to west, it was worse. Soon after cleaning up you were dirty again, as the smoky dirt continued to accumulate. It began to get in troopers' eyes, and it became hard to breathe. Everyone was concerned about the health hazards of working near the oil fires. Wilson and his officers tried to downplay the danger of being in the area. They had little evidence, however, of what effect living in this environment would have on the soldiers' long-term health.[10]

The squadron aviators noticed the operational effects of the fires more than most. In one instance an aircraft flew back to Saudi Arabia to King Khalid Military City, to pick up repair parts for the maintenance crews. When they took off early in the morning, the temperatures were warm and the wind was blowing out of the northwest sending the oil smoke out to sea. When they arrived at their destination, the temperature was above 90 degrees Fahrenheit. Before they left for the return trip, the wind shifted

180 degrees and began blowing the smoke back over the squadron. With the sun now obscured, the temperature at Safwan dropped over twenty-five degrees. As the aircraft entered the blanket of smoke, they had to switch to flying by instruments to keep from flying into Safwan Mountain. Flight operations provided the crew the signals to guide them to the airfield, where the temperature was now in the upper fifties. While the helicopter landed safely, the command decided not to land aircraft in those conditions again. The next time the airfield was smoked in, they diverted the aircraft back to the Aviation Brigade airfield in Kuwait, or some other location, to wait it out.[11]

Heavy rains began on March 5 and lasted almost four days. A small river began flowing through the command post and the staff had to put equipment on wooden blocks to keep it out of the water. The leaders had several meetings at the TOC where they squeezed onto the back ramps of the M577s so everyone would be out of the water. Most soldiers kept their equipment in their vehicles or on wooden pallets inside their tents. In one instance a B Troop HMMWV wandered off the approved path and drove into a tomato field where it promptly began to sink in the saturated ground. The two crewmen were able to get out and retrieve some of their gear before most of it disappeared into the water. The next morning, the B Troop maintenance crews, using an M88 tank recovery vehicle, pulled it out of the water. It took a little cleaning up, and a little work under the hood, but it started up, and surprisingly the troop drove it until it returned home without any problems.[12]

While at Safwan, the squadron continued to get visitors. The division headquarters tasked Wilson's troopers to provide a display of American equipment on Safwan Airfield for a visit by a Congressional delegation. It turned out to be a three-day affair. The first day was spent arranging, cleaning, and preparing everything for the delegation so it looked as good as it could. For the next two days, Congressmen, their staffers, and reporters quizzed the crews on the equipment's effectiveness. Unlike some presentations, the troops did not need to be prepared on how to answer the questions and what was the "politically correct" answer. They were quite proud of their tanks, Bradleys, and helicopters, and they gave their questioners glowing reports on the quality of the American equipment.[13]

In addition to recovering from the offensive, the squadron had two main operational missions to conduct. One was to locate serviceable Iraqi equipment within an area assigned by the division. Some of it, especially the Soviet-made equipment, would go back to the United States for study at schools or technical agencies. Some, especially tanks and infantry fighting vehicles, would find its way to headquarters in the United States to serve as war trophies. The remainder would be destroyed by the engineers to keep it from being recovered and reused by the Iraqi Army after the American forces withdrew. In the course of this mission, the squadron continued to find dead Iraqi soldiers near their weapons and vehicles. Whenever scouts discovered these soldiers, they called the command post so that the appropriate graves registration troops could respond.[14]

The squadron located two vehicles that were eventually placed on display at Fort Riley, Kansas. Doug Morrison's maintenance crews discovered a T-72 tank that appeared to be in excellent condition, although mechanically inoperable. Seeing this as a challenge, the mechanics unloaded all of the ammunition and began identifying what they needed to get the tank back into service. They then searched for other damaged Iraqi tanks and began removing parts (called "cannibalizing" in maintenance terms) that the chosen T-72 required. This restoration project became a good source of diversion for the mechanics who used their American skills to place this Soviet-made tank back into operation. Soon they were able to get it running. Then they found an undamaged BMP Infantry Assault Vehicle and continued the restoration process. For the next two months the squadron dragged or hauled these vehicles along each time they changed locations. Finally, back in Saudi Arabia, Headquarters Troop cleaned them up and prepared them for shipment back to the United States. Today, both vehicles are on display at Fort Riley.[15]

While some Iraqi equipment was sent back to the United States, most was destroyed and rendered unusable. The cavalry organized ad hoc search and destroy teams to support this corps-wide effort. Flying in their OH-58C scout helicopters, the aviators located an abandoned tank, personnel carrier, or artillery piece. Once found the pilot landed the helicopter and the

engineer team on board used C4 explosive compound to prepare the vehicle for demolition. The problem was to ensure
there was enough of a delay after firing the fuse to allow everyone to get back on board the helicopter and depart the immediate area prior to detonation. On one occasion, C Troop's 2LT
Steve Gruenig's engineers had set the charges and were back on
board the helicopter and lifting off as a HMMWV headed for
the vehicle they had rigged to explode. They were apparently
souvenir hunters and oblivious to the explosion that was about
to occur. Fortunately, Gruenig was able to fly by and ward them
off before the explosion.[16]

Like other American units, the squadron also appropriated
some Iraqi equipment to make their own existence more comfortable, such as a few fully functional Iraqi command trailers.
Apparently designed as mobile offices and quarters for their
general officers, the trailers were often outfitted with showers,
latrines, sinks, refrigerators, air conditioners, and flourescent
lights. They also had portable generators mounted on racks.
CPT Morrison's crews hauled them back to the squadron area
and cleaned them up. They were used by LTC Wilson, MAJ
Burdan's S3 shop, and Headquarters Troop for the rest of their
stay in Iraq. Unfortunately, the squadron had to abandon them
before they returned to Fort Riley, since they were not exactly
approved issue for a divisional cavalry squadron.

Iraqi troops abandoned so much equipment that almost
every unit in the squadron found something to use. Many units
and sections found commercial trucks and staff cars to move all
of their equipment and people without having to share the ride
with others. For example, it was the first time CPT Shelby
Seelinger's S2 section had a truck to call its own, after months
of trying to get one through regular channels. In A Troop, SFC
Molitor found a Chevy S-10 pickup truck, with a sabot-round
hole in the wall of the truck bed. He patched it up and it became
his platoon's own special supply truck, nicknamed A17. In all
cases, the squadron used this equipment until it could no
longer run, since the army supply system did not have the repair parts, and abandoned it when they left Iraq.[17]

The troopers were still on guard, as the Iraqi Army was well
armed and dangerous. In addition, one never knew when iso-

lated enemy soldiers might, for one reason or another, continue to fight. On March 11, an officer (allegedly a general) and about 100 men showed up and tried to cross over the cease-fire line into the American sector. Division headquarters ordered the squadron to dispatch a scout-weapons team in support of the 2nd Brigade, who had the mission of turning them around. Chief Warrant Officer Kirk Waymire led the team and linked up with LTC Dave Marlin, commander of 4-37 Armor. Apparently, these Iraqis were trying to gather equipment left behind during their hasty departure. Marlin's battalion and the helicopters overhead convinced them that the cease-fire agreement prohibited any crossing of the boundary, and the Americans were not going to argue with them about it. After a couple of tanks rolled up on the Iraqi soldiers, the unit's interpreters needed to say only a few words before they headed back north.[18]

The next day the squadron was ordered to scramble another scout weapons team to investigate a report that the Iraqis had reoccupied Bubiyan Island in the Persian Gulf. Of course, the division had no intelligence about how the Iraqis were armed, or what the air defense threat might be. Within three hours of receiving the mission, the team was on station and searching the island, which contained of low-lying marshlands and only a few buildings. While getting to the island was no problem, communications were, as it was over forty kilometers from Safwan and beyond normal radio range. They had to rely on their best judgment. To ease the communication problem, CPT Philbrick flew in another helicopter and acted as a communications relay to squadron headquarters and he also provided command and control oversight. After a thorough overflight of the island, the team returned to Safwan. There was no sign of recent Iraqi activity.[19]

The civilian situation bothered most soldiers terribly. Even without the uprising, living conditions for the local Iraqis were still inadequate. In Safwan, much of the town was wrecked and there were damaged cars everywhere. The environment was spooky as the burning oil fields often turned day into an eerie twilight and illuminated the night. Soot and grime from the smoke was everywhere. People were desperate for food, and begging children began to line the streets and roads. American soldiers were inclined to help but it was also dangerous. In one incident a sergeant stopped his HMMWV to pass out candy to some children. When he stopped, others jumped into the back and stole two cases of soda. They could have taken more valuable items or been run over when the truck backed up. Enough of these incidents took place that senior commanders had to order soldiers to stop passing out food because of the danger of theft and injury to the civilians, a tragic but necessary policy. Still many soldiers chose to continue the practice.[20]

The squadron also had encounters with Iraqi soldiers who were returning to homes after the war. A Troop's SSG Donald Wehage had an interesting conversation with one Iraqi who supposedly had spent fifteen of his thirty years in the army. He spoke English quite well and claimed to have participated in the capture of Kuwait, but had run home after the bombing started since he and his comrades did not want to fight the Americans. He also claimed to have attended the University of Michigan, which somehow did not fit into the chronology he had already constructed. Nevertheless Wehage had a good time talking politics and even got some fresh tomatoes from the soldier's field. As in every war, defeated soldiers tried to come to grips with their new situation.[21]

Finally, a few soldiers began to head back to the United States and Fort Riley. Most went home because of family problems that now, after the war was over, could no longer wait. Others were granted leave as a special recognition for a job well done. About twelve troopers left in the first increment. The Fort Riley community and their friends and families welcomed them with big ceremonies and a great deal of fanfare. After a few days off, all reported back to work to start getting the unit billets and facilities ready for the rest of the squadron's return.

Despite the rumors of impending return, the squadron learned that they were going to stay in Iraq for awhile. The corps commander's policy was first in, first out. A lot of commands had priority over the 1st Infantry Division on the shipment home. So after an aerial photograph of the entire squadron arrayed in the desert, it and the rest of the division prepared to continue operations, and move to a location deep in Iraq, Assembly Area Allen.

15　Postwar Operations

ven before the beginning of the ground war, General Schwarzkopf's Central Command had developed two separate but complementary plans to implement after the battle was over. First, coalition forces had to continue to defend Kuwait and help to restore its government to power. In addition to combat service support units to help the Kuwaiti government clean up its land and restore order, the United States intended to keep a division in the country to ensure a stable environment in the postwar period. American troops would also remain in occupied Iraq until Saddam Hussein's government signed a peace agreement. The second operation, which had to be coordinated with the first, was to start pulling American troops out of Southwest Asia as soon as the conflict was over. The U.S. government was determined to bring the soldiers home as soon as possible. Planning for this activity began way back in the first week of February, with the concept ready to go at the end of the month. The number one priority was to get the XVIII Airborne Corps, which had been in country since early August, on its way back home.[1]

Rumors had been running rampant for days after the Safwan meeting that the squadron would be heading home shortly. On March 4, however, LTC Wilson received the first hint that this was only a rumor, and the next day Central Command made the formal decision to start the process of pulling LTG Gary Luck's XVIII Corps out of Iraq. The VII Corps staff began issuing orders to its units to start moving them into the locations vacated by the departing units. First, the 3rd Armored Division, which would be remaining in Kuwait after the bulk of the corps withdrew, exchanged places with the 1st Infantry Division at Safwan. Next, the Big Red One first pulled back to a temporary assembly area in Kuwait and then, from March 19 to 21, traveled west to an area thirty kilometers southeast of Al Busayyah called Assembly Area (AA) Allen. After a short period of rest and recreation, the squadron would then return to the front line to screen the new military demarcation line. All of this movement took place while Saddam Hussein's troops finished off the Shi'a rebellion just to the north.[2]

Moving the squadron to AA Allen was a complicated event as the 1st Infantry Division had to travel west into the desert at the same time the 3rd Armored Division headed east and northeast to the Safwan area. Each division had almost 9,000 tracked and wheeled vehicles heading toward and across the path of each other. It was an operation that required each staff to coordinate and ensure subordinate units stayed on route and on schedule. However, it became even more complicated when MAJ Burdan realized that the route he was given by the aviation brigade for his squadron did not provide a trail for the armored vehicles. Generally, it is not wise to put tracked vehicles on a road, even a dirt one, because of the damage they can cause to the surface. So, he directed the tanks and Bradleys to travel on a parallel track nearby and hoped that no other unit, from either division, had the same idea.

For this movement, the squadron was organized into four parts. The advance party, led by CSM Cobb, had the mission to prepare the AA Allen for the arrival of the squadron. The advance party was followed by the main body of the squadron consisting of the ground troops, selected vehicles from the air troops, and CPT Morrison's Headquarters Troop. MAJ Wimbish and the squadron's tactical operations center accompanied the main body and maintained contact with each troop and the brigade headquarters. The third part consisted of the squadron aircraft who moved under the control of their troop commanders. Finally, the fourth part consisted of CPT Philbrick, his flight operations detachment, and some of the aviation troops' vehicles that remained behind to control the movement of the helicopters. CPT Philbrick's goal was to have the helicopters arrive at AA Allen about forty-five minutes after the squadron's ground units. LTC Wilson traveled in an OH-58C helicopter to observe the march and maintain contact with all parts of the extended column, while MAJ Burdan brought up the rear of the main body.[3]

The squadron's movement to AA Allen began on March 19. Just getting on to the designated route proved difficult. There was little "deconfliction," in military terms, as the route was, as feared, also occupied by the traveling elements of both divisions. Once on the trail, other vehicles darted in and around the squadron's column, making it difficult to keep the convoy serials together. Other than this confusion, the road march was generally uneventful. The route of march took them past Phase Line Lime and the region where the 1st Armored Division had demolished the Iraqi Medina Armored Division less than a month earlier. Wrecks of armored vehicles, most still in their shoddy battle positions, were spread across the landscape to the north and south. It was visible evidence of the power of the American offensive.

Arriving at AA Allen in the middle of the afternoon, they found the squadron's helicopters on the ground waiting for them ahead of schedule; so much for detailed planning. Now located behind the other VII Corps units, the squadron adopted more of an administrative formation. The command post took position in the center of a large wagon wheel with each unit (A Troop, B Troop, aviation troops, and HHT) located one and a half kilometers from the center at the four cardinal directions of the compass. Once set up, each troop strung communication wire to the command post.

Now the enemy was boredom. Although the OH-58C helicopters were in great demand to ferry commanders around the vast landscape, the AH-1F Cobra pilots flew few patrols. Tanks and Bradleys remained parked in the assembly area. The officers and noncommissioned officers organized baseball teams, volleyball teams, weight training, and even scorpion fights to keep the soldiers occupied. Occasionally the command received a quota to send troopers down to the recreation boat, a converted cruise ship nicknamed the "Love Boat," anchored off Bahrain. The leaders awarded these trips to soldiers who had done especially good jobs. For a few days, the selected troopers could take showers, eat, and enjoy living in a clean environment. The longer they were in AA Allen, the more the comforts of home began to appear, especially television sets and video cassette players. In the evening you could find soldiers under camouflage nets sitting in makeshift chairs, watching movies or family tapes from home.

One aspect of boredom was the constant thinking of home. Mail began arriving with some frequency, including large amounts of "Any Soldier Mail" that tended to clog the distribution system. Much of this mail was from school children and was designed to cheer up the soldiers. Some was a little more interesting and questioned the need for the army to be in Southwest Asia at all. Everyone was encouraged to spend time replying to these usually thoughtful letters, as a way to keep them occupied as well as maintain some contact with America. In general, it was a great morale booster.[4]

One day scouts from A Troop managed to find a Mobile Army Surgical Hospital (MASH) in the area and conned them into inviting troopers over to play basketball with the guys on their makeshift court and volleyball with the nurses. After 1800 hours that day, many of the troops put on their gray army physical training uniforms, climbed on the back of one of the supply trucks and headed over. The medical soldiers were not especially busy, and they enjoyed the company. Of course, a big attraction for the cavalrymen was the nurses. Even in an era that found many women in the army, it was the first time most of these young combat-arms soldiers had seen ladies in a social setting for almost three months. It was a bright spot in a rather dreary existence.[5]

The division was now in place long enough to set up a "Wolf Burger" stand. Named after CW4 Wesley Wolf, the CENT-COM's chief of food service, these stands, run by the units themselves, dispensed hamburgers, chips, and cokes to soldiers worn out by MREs and other army rations. Near the hamburger stand in the middle of the desert, American telephone companies set up a bank of telephones for the soldiers to call home. There was always a line of soldiers from many units but in most cases, little complaining as each waited his turn for a few moments of private conversation with loved ones back in the States.

Religious services now began to occur on a more regular basis. On Palm Sunday, March 23, A Troop's 2LT David Palmieri took out some palm fronds that he had been saving since Safwan and distributed them to those who had gathered for a religious service. Even for those not especially devout, there was something mystical about being in the Holy Land, not far from the home of Abraham and the early Hebrew tribes. The division's chaplains did their best to get around to all the battalions and conduct services for the interested soldiers.[6]

With the combat over, soldiers began to depart and arrive at the squadron. CPT Eric Esplund from division G2 replaced CPT Seelinger, who surrendered his role as S2 and headed over to a company command in the division's military intelligence battalion. 1SG Parkey left A Troop for the S3 Section to replace SGM Ken Shields who was returning to the United States to retire. Before the squadron left for the 2nd Cavalry's Sector, Bob Wilson promoted Parkey to sergeant major.

Much of this activity was accomplished in the presence of the Bedouins who now began returning to the area. It seemed that you could not go too far without running into an encampment. They were sheep and camel herders, and it was strange to see their goatskin or wool-and-cotton tents with a television antenna stuck out the top of one of them and a Mercedes truck parked alongside in the middle of the desert. It was a strange way of life that most of the soldiers could not understand.

The division commander was determined that his command would keep its fighting edge, just in case the peace talks broke down. As a result, he had his G3 training section establish a series of firing ranges throughout the division sector. The individual brigades operated most of these facilities. The major problem with them was that these were in the Iraqi desert without natural backstops or range fans. If a tank round missed its target, it could travel many miles before it lost its momentum or hit some unanticipated target. With the Bedouins returning to the area the probability of hitting one became greater and the squadron's aviators flew throughout the range area to move the natives and their goat herds out of the line of fire and to safer surroundings. CPT Sauer and SFC Garza planned the squadron's range participation. The squadron's ground troops used the 1st Brigade's range from March 26 to 29, firing small arms, machine guns, hand grenades and other explosives. During the firing practice,

some soldiers, including CPT Bills, discovered that their relatively new 9-mm pistols were inoperative. Obviously, this could
have been quite dangerous if they had needed to use them a
month earlier. While firing the weapons on the tanks and
Bradleys, the crews discovered a number of defective TOW missile rounds, caused by moisture that collected in the canister.
Again, it was a potentially dangerous condition.[7]

On March 29 the 4th Brigade warning order arrived notify-
ing the squadron to be prepared to relieve the 2nd Cavalry
along Highway 8 and the Euphrates River. While everyone reacted with professionalism, all were disappointed that they
were not heading south back to Saudi Arabia. It required quite
a great deal of leadership skills to keep everyone focused on the
tasks at hand and not to be thinking about home and redeployment.[8] The brigade's plan was to use the squadron to screen the
critical portion of the MDL. The 1-1 Aviation with its scout and
attack helicopters would be used to patrol the remainder of the
division's portion of the MDL. Planning for the squadron's mission began immediately.

Before they moved to the Euphrates, the squadron celebrated Easter, March 30, in the desert. Chaplain Lou Parker
held a well-attended sunrise service and the squadron stood
down. It was a time for writing letters and relaxing. Leaders
used the time to catch up on their paperwork, especially the
submission of awards and promotion packets for deserving soldiers.[9] That evening, almost as if the ancient gods of Ur were of-
fended by the plethora of crosses in their desert, a huge sand
storm blew in from the east. While the squadron's crews and
vehicles weathered the wall of wind, rain, and sand fairly well,
division headquarters was not so lucky. Perched on a large
mound of earth that possibly contained some of the remains of
a suburb of ancient Ur, the Big Red One's command post took
the full brunt of the storm's hurricane-force winds. In the rub-
ble left behind, under a pile of collapsed tents and computers,
were the waterlogged remains of many of the division's award
recommendations. It would be weeks before the hard-working
personnel staffs, at division, brigade, and squadron, could repair the damage.[10]

On April 2, as part of the squadron's mission planning, Wilson and Burdan jumped into an OH-58C and flew to the 2nd Cavalry's command post to discuss the mission, the refugees, and the fighting still in progress on the other side of the demarcation line. The regiment was manning more checkpoints along the highway than the smaller Quarter Horse would. In conjunction with the regiment, they picked the three most important locations and planned to occupy them when the squadron arrived. Each of these checkpoints required medical supplies and interpreters, in addition to the standard combat vehicles.[11]

The movement plan called for the squadron advance party to depart on April 5 and for B Troop to depart at 0630 on April 6 with A Troop leaving at 1000 followed by the remainder of the squadron. The air troops would fly out with the other helicopters of the Aviation Brigade. The squadron was to be prepared to assume responsibility for its sector at 1200 hours on April 7. When the advance party arrived, it found the 2nd Cavalry conducting tank gunnery at the site where Burdan had planned to place the squadron command post. Burdan moved the squadron, therefore, farther north along a pipeline road not too far south of the Shia's city of An Nasiriyah. Leaders of the 2nd Cavalry told Wilson that things were still pretty dangerous along this demarcation line. While the refugee flow was slowing, fighting in the towns and villages north of the regimental checkpoints appeared to still be pretty intense and quite visible at night. The next day the remainder of the squadron and the Aviation Brigade arrived in the new 120 kilometer-wide sector. At 0630 hours on April 7, the brigade relieved the 2nd Cavalry and occupied three checkpoints.[12] The squadron command post relocated into the center of its area in order to maintain contact between the cavalry troops over the extended sector, nearly fifty kilometers wide. The air troops, along with the squadron's flight operations, co-located with the remainder of the 4th Brigade, which was located ten to fifteen kilometers from the squadron command post.

The squadron was now in one of the world's most ancient lands. On the south side of the Euphrates, within only a few miles, were the ancient cities of Ur and Eridu. In addition, in all directions the landscape was dotted with small hills or tells which were probably "suburbs" of these earlier civilizations. In the evening or morning, when the sun was just right, an observer could just make out the traces of long-vanished irrigation systems and roads. It was also impossible to ignore the effects of the war. Destroyed military vehicles and buildings were everywhere. Before the attack there had been an airplane on a pedestal at the front entrance of Talil Airfield and Air Force jets had destroyed even it. The effect of the bombs on the airfield's thick, reinforced-concrete hangars was awesome as in every case bombs had penetrated the roofs and destroyed what was inside. It was apparent that the Iraqis had tried to protect their aircraft from the coalition jets by locating them away from the airfield. Ten or twelve burnt fuselages littered a nearby road.

As far back as 2,500 BCE, Ur dominated the southern banks of the Euphrates River and the southern trade routes of the famous "Fertile Crescent." Merchants from this region traded with much of the ancient world, from the Red Sea west to the land of Canaan. It was along these routes, if the chroniclers of Genesis are accurate, that Abraham and his followers, called Hebrews, traveled towards modern Israel around 1,500 BCE. Now, in April 1991, Ur was an ancient ruin and the location of a 1-4 Cavalry checkpoint. After a few days in the area, some of the squadron's leaders hired a tour guide, paid for with dollars and MREs, to take them through the ancient town. The guide spoke minimal English so they used their own interpreters to help out. The sense of past history as they walked among the ruins was very impressive. It reminded MAJ Burdan of Percy Shelley's poem *Ozymandias*:

> "My name is Ozymandias, King of Kings,
> Look on my Works, ye Mighty, and despair!"
> Nothing beside remains. Round the decay
> Of that colossal Wreck, boundless and bare
> The lone and level sands stretch far away.

Damage to the site of Ur by the war appeared to be minimal, even though the Iraqis had built a modern airfield quite near the ruins. The major feature of the city's ruins was the Ziggurat, the stepped pyramid to the stars. Hoping that the Americans would stay away from the area in order to avoid damaging this ancient structure, the Iraqis had moved some of their planes from the airfield and parked them near the monument.

It was to no avail, however, as the Air Force destroyed them all. Shrapnel had hit the Ziggurat in a few places, but that was about all. However, just to be on the safe side and to avoid later charges of damaging a historic site, COL Mowery sent an archeologist and some military Civil Affairs specialists to the site to document the damage.[13]

The squadron manned three checkpoints. Their purpose was to observe the military demarcation line, regulate the movement of Iraqi civilian and military vehicles across that line, and provide humanitarian support for those refugees fleeing the fighting in the north.[14] In addition to the combat vehicles, each checkpoint had a medical team, intelligence collection teams, and Arabic-speaking interpreters. A Troop's Check Point (CP) India was on a small ridge near the Ur ruins that dominated Highway 8 and the roads emerging from An Nasiriyah. They also manned another (CP #1) that blocked a road that ran along an oil pipeline from the west. To the east, B Troop operated Check Point #2, which controlled traffic moving on the south side of the Euphrates, on Highway 8, from the east. B Troop also provided the security for the brigade water point which was located fifteen kilometers northeast of the squadron TOC. The last two checkpoints operated around the clock while CP India only functioned during hours of daylight, partially because there was simply too much activity in the city, not far from the checkpoint, after dark for the small command to handle. At each location, platoons repaired and reinforced the defensive works they inherited from the 2nd Cavalry. They placed barriers across the road so that an approaching vehicle had to slow and pass an inspection point. A tank and a Bradley overwatched the inspection point. The medics were standing by to assist injured refugees. Working out of the Aviation Brigade's assembly area, the squadron's aviation troops backed up and supported the reconnaissance and security effort with scout-weapons teams as required.[15]

Most of the refugee traffic that the Americans encountered fit into five general categories. The first were the local Bedouins and people who lived out in the desert. They drove large, multi-colored trucks loaded with their sheep, which they sold in the small towns. Others simply wandered with their camels as if nothing had changed since the days of Abraham.[16] The second category included refugees from the north who were fleeing south to escape Saddam Hussein. Most of these people had heard that the Americans had set up checkpoints in the south and they came looking for protection from Hussein.[17] A third small group included people who claimed American citizenship and wanted to return to America. In some cases, they had passports or some other means of identification. In other instances, they had nothing other than a command of the English language.

The fourth group consisted of Iraqi soldiers, often deserters, who still wanted to surrender despite the cease-fire. Initially, they were quite a mistrustful group, refusing to drink from the water buffaloes and demanding only bottled water. In the growing heat, this normally lasted only a few hours. Front-line units processed these Iraqis according to the standard procedures and sent them back to prisoner of war holding camps farther to the rear.[18]

The final group consisted of local citizens who availed themselves of the medical support Americans provided. Each day people brought in sick or injured children, husbands, wives, and relatives and asked for help. The situation with the children was quite troubling. Many were sick and dehydrated as a result of starvation or contaminated food and water. Others were badly injured, often by the innumerable unexploded bomblets that lay strewn across the area. The children parents brought in sometimes had hands and feet blown off and were in incredible pain. Often the wounds were festering and infected. Mothers and fathers desperately sought help from the squadron's medics. In a typical case a family brought into a squadron checkpoint one of their sons who had been injured playing soccer near their home. He had stepped on or kicked a mine and had been badly wounded. American soldiers medically evacuated him and one of his parents for treatment. The squadron surgeon, MAJ Roger Hansen, and the physician's assistant, Chief Warrant Officer Richard Harston, bore the brunt of this painful work.[19]

Sometimes the wounds were only tangentially related to the conflict. In one case two children, a girl and a boy, between five and eight years old, approached a squadron position. Both children were burnt over seventy percent of their bodies and, as the soldier who rendered this report noted: "if there was a (burn) worse than 3rd degree, these kids had it," and the injuries were obviously not fresh. Through their interpreter, the Americans learned that the children had been burnt when a cooking stove exploded six days earlier. Both were extremely dehydrated and the wounds themselves were so old and untreated that insect larva infected the sores and blisters. The girl had the worse injuries and, as is American practice, the medics began working on her first, cleaning the wounds and administering liquid though intravenous feeding. The child's father protested and wanted the medics to work on the less-injured boy first, as though his life were more valuable. The soldiers were incensed and when it came time to evacuate the children, they allowed the mother to accompany them, but not the father. Years later the soldier who spoke about this incident was still angry at the father for waiting so long to help his children and then insisting that the less-injured lad was more important than his seriously injured daughter.[20]

In some cases, the medics arranged for the evacuation of badly injured children. When possible, they also sent along one of the parents to keep the child from getting lost somewhere to the rear. Sometimes, especially in the early days of the occupation, sending parents along was not possible. Almost immediately, front-line soldiers began to run into problems with locating the children they had dispatched to the rear. These kids were quickly lost in the medical system. Two or three days later the parents would return asking for their children and the soldiers were almost helpless. There was no tracking system at that time for these children. Each day Iraqi parents visited the checkpoint with a note given them by the 2nd Cavalry before they departed. The notes usually read:

> On this date, we medically evacuated Ismail, the son of Mohammed. The child needed to be operated on for feet and leg injuries.
>
> Signed;
> Sgt Jones.

At CP India the squadron set up a modified medical clearing station to help treat people. In some cases they arranged for the evacuation of badly injured children, always with one of the parents to ensure that the child was not lost in the system.

In cases where the child was evacuated without a parent, the parents wanted to know when their child was coming back and the squadron referred their questions back up the medical channel. Unfortunately, in many cases, the medics received no answers back. Wilson, Burdan and the other officers still wonder how many of those parents ever saw their children again. After the squadron departed later in the month, it could only have gotten worse as there was no one left in the area for the families to talk to. Certainly treatment of refugee and civilian casualties was something the army could have done better in this conflict.[21]

Of course, the plight of the families sickened the squadron, as it did all the Americans strung out along the demarcation line. Seeing a small boy with a terrible leg wound caused by stepping on or kicking a mine while playing soccer or the small children badly burned because their gas stove had been hit by some kind of weapons fire and exploded were sights that most of these veterans were unprepared for.[22]

On most nights soldiers could hear rifle and machine-gun fire coming out of the local towns. Refugees and local citizens recounted stories of Hussein's police force establishing control in the towns at night by arresting known and suspected dissidents and shooting them in the streets of their neighborhoods. Corps-level situation reports are full of blood-curdling tales of terror, destruction, revenge, and murder. In general, there was nothing the squadron could do except report the information up the chain. On occasion, however, things would spill across the MDL. On the last night of CP India's nightly operation, a car with a family inside drove into the checkpoint. They were frantic as they described the Iraqi Secret Police who were right behind and probably going to execute them when caught. Then the family saw a car approaching and screamed (in Arabic) and pointed, "That's them!" Other refugees joined in, confirming that the occupants of the approaching car were some kind of execution squad. Figuring that they were in the wrong place, the

Iraqi agents tried to avoid the roadblock and get away. However, Pope's troopers caught them and sent them back to a prisoner of war camp.[23]

Sometimes the cause of the problem was simple starvation, a typical problem for civilians caught in a war zone. In one instance, a family approached a military checkpoint. The soldiers went through the normal procedures to verify that they did not have weapons. All of the women were wearing their typical black robes and one was obviously hiding something. As a soldier approached and began to question her, she moved away and began acting extremely strangely. The young troops took their weapons off safe and began to react to what could be a hostile incident. Finally, the women disclosed that she was hiding a very sick baby about one year old. She told the soldiers that the child had not eaten for about four or five days because she had run out of breast milk. The infant was in bad shape and the troopers took them both to the medic vehicle and attempted to get the child to suck some milk from a gauze. Nothing seemed to work. At the same time, they gave the woman some of their rations and protected her while she ate, since the men normally tried to take the food and eat it first.[24] The baby would not eat and looked more like a few months old rather than almost twelve months. Six years later, the officer who witnessed the whole scene was still grieving over what he had observed that spring day in Iraq.[25]

The treatment of women and children by the Iraqi males grated on some of the soldiers. In one case CPT Pope noticed a sixteen-year-old girl sitting apart from the family as if she had some kind of strange disease. When he asked her younger brother, who spoke English, he discovered that she had been gang-raped by Iraqi soldiers and was no longer considered to be part of her own family.[26] In another instance a young child came to the checkpoint everyday to talk to the soldiers and get food. He told them that Iraqi soldiers had raped his sister many times and asked for help. It made the soldiers angry, but there was nothing they could do.[27]

One other thing stuck in squadron members' minds during this period: the dogs. Packs of wild, and recently wild, dogs ran throughout the area. Having attacked wounded soldiers and civilians over the preceding weeks, they had little fear of humans. In the days immediately after the end of the war, soldiers would often catch dogs in the process of ripping apart and devouring human remains. It was a sight that sickened anyone who saw it and sometimes resulted in a few rifle rounds being fired to scare the pack off so the body could be recovered. If soldiers left a tent unoccupied, the dogs would sneak in and steal any food they could. The soldiers in the squadron's FM radio retransmission station were grateful that they had barbed wire surrounding their position. At night the dogs often closed in on the station and tried to get to them.

On the other hand, A Troop's 3rd Platoon, who had the responsibility for Check Point #1, found that the dogs in their area were a benefit. They provided an early warning especially at night, since they were territorial and immediately started to bark when someone approached. Lieutenant Palmieri also noticed that the dogs liked the Americans but barked and snarled if Iraqi soldiers came near the checkpoint. Perhaps the dogs had been amongst them just a little too long.[28]

On April 10 the word finally arrived from division to begin preparing to pull out of Iraq. The troopers eagerly began to prepare for the movement. At the same time the squadron conducted M3 ranges to get new crew combinations qualified. On April 13, MG Rhame flew out to the troops still watching the border to reward those soldiers who had earned awards for their performance in Desert Storm. That morning the squadron had CPT VJ Tedesco conduct a recon of the squadron's route from An Nasiriyah to AA Huebner located near King Khalid Military City in Saudi Arabia. The recon allowed the S3 shop to complete the movement order that would be issued once the order to pull out of Iraq arrived. On April 14, the formal order was received directing the squadron's return to Saudi Arabia at 0800 hours the next day.

16   Coming Home

Then it was time to go. After six weeks of negotiations, Iraq formally agreed to the
terms established by the coalition and hostilities officially ended on April 12. As United Nations observers began moving into the buffer zone established along
the Kuwait-Iraq border, the VII Corps began pulling out of occupied Iraq. Almost as quickly as they had attacked into Iraq,
the 1st Infantry Division and its cavalry squadron pulled out.
Like other units, the 1-4 Cavalry experienced four distinct
phases in its redeployment: withdrawal from Iraq, distribution
of personnel and equipment in the staging area called Assembly Area Huebner, moving to the port and preparing equipment for shipment to the United States, and the flight home.[1]

The first phase was to pull the 4th Brigade back from the
checkpoints along Highway 8 and return to the 1st Infantry Division's Assembly Area Allen. The squadron was divided into
five elements: The first element consisted of the air troops'
wheeled vehicles, followed by most of the squadron's helicopters. Then the ground troops departed, followed by a detachment of helicopters and ground vehicles controlled by CPT
Philbrick who was supporting the 4th Brigade's mission to
identify any American equipment that might still be left on
Iraqi soil. The fifth and final element, an advance party, had already been sent to AA Huebner to prepare for the reception of
the remainder of the squadron.

The squadron's air troop wheeled vehicles left early in the
morning on April 15. They had an uneventful journey and arrived at AA Huebner that afternoon where they set up to receive the squadron's helicopters. The squadron's helicopters,

minus those supporting CPT Philbrick, departed later that morning and arrived at AA Huebner that afternoon without any incidents.

The squadron main body consisting of the ground troops began moving at 0800 on April 15. The troopers, veterans of many a tactical road march, were quite efficient. They found themselves actually ahead of the two aviation battalions that had missed their start times. The brigade staff accused Wilson's command of jumping to the head of the line to be the first out of Iraq. After several hours the truth emerged, and at the first rest stop two hours down the road, the squadron pulled over to refuel and let the aviators pass. By late afternoon the entire command had joined back up with the division in AA Allen.[2]

The squadron's officers were in a good mood as they arrived at their temporary assembly area. Wilson and Burdan drove out to the nearby 1st Brigade command post to check in on the division's progress and to say hello. When speaking to the S3, MAJ Kevin Huddy, about the next day's activities it became immediately apparent that the division had given both the 1st Brigade and the squadron the same routes and movement times. Rather than send it up the chain of command for a decision, the two operations officers did some quick adjusting to the squadron's schedule so it would clear the area prior to the 1st Brigade's start time. The new start was at 0515 hours and the brigade S3 said he would forward the change to division headquarters.

That night the command group and Burdan's TOC staff celebrated their imminent departure from Iraq. Specialist Adam Fuller pulled out his music box and they sang to the country music tapes that they had brought from home. They broke out all the candy, canned fruits, and sodas that they had each been hoarding and passed them around. They would need them no more as they were on the way home.

While the ground troops were closing in on their assembly area, the squadron air element under CPT Philbrick supported the 4th Brigade that had a division-directed mission of checking the routes back to Saudi Arabia. The brigade was to locate any friendly or serviceable Iraqi equipment left behind along the route, and locate any obstacles that would hinder the ground vehicles' movement. The brigade assigned the squadron a portion of the routes to reconnoiter. CPT Philbrick and his flight operations section controlled the squadron's reconnaissance effort. Working from his operations van, with a small service support team consisting of fuel and maintenance support, he managed the aviators' activities in the sky. At the end of the first day he pulled off the supply route he was following, moved to higher ground, and called in his scout-weapons teams. Establishing a perimeter with trucks and helicopters they settled down for the night.[3]

The next morning the squadron made its start time, but the 4-1 Aviation Battalion showed up on the same march route and again delayed its departure. Apparently, the battalion had not been able to make it all the way to AA Huebner in Saudi Arabia, as was their original plan, so it just stopped for the night at an intermediate location. In the morning, they began moving when they wanted to, without any obvious control. Wilson had the squadron pull over to allow the aviation unit's fast-moving wheeled vehicles to pass. Of course, that in turn put his unit behind, and the S3 had to contact the 1st Brigade and ask them to slow down. However, that was a minor headache as the weather was wonderful and the route of march took the troopers right through the division's original breach site where they had fought almost two months earlier. While crossing the berm they passed the sign that said: "Welcome to Iraq, Courtesy of the Big Red One."[4]

Continuing past the berm and into the area it had been responsible for screening earlier, the troops noticed that the area now was relatively deserted, so different from those days just before the attack. Most of the equipment was gone and rain had turned the arid desert floor green. Now Bedouins and their flocks of sheep and camels occupied the squadron's old screen line and AA Junction City.

The squadron stopped just before noon on the north side of the Tapline Road at the scheduled stopping point for the night. Of course, the troopers were anxious to continue south to the final destination, AA Huebner, only an hour or so to the south. It was a hot spring day and Burdan spoke with LTC Mike Ryan, the division's provost marshal. Ryan thought it was possible to

continue the move and get there before the end of the day. Un-
beknownst to Burdan, his request to division headquarters to
press on was the third or fourth call from various units that MG
Rhame, who was trying to orchestrate a controlled move and
not a mad dash, had received that morning. Danger 6, as he was
called, chewed out Burdan and told the squadron to "stay
where they were and do what they were told."[5] So most of the
squadron spent the night in column with the soldiers camped
by the side of their vehicles.

CPT Philbrick and the aviators had spent the day continuing their mission of ensuring that the division did not leave any
equipment inside Iraq. They had found a few scattered pieces
and reported them to LTC Cook, at the 4th Brigade command
post, who ran the operation for COL Mowery. At the end of the
day, once again, CPT Philbrick picked out an assembly area and
gathered in the air elements for the night.

The next day, April 17, the wind was blowing hard and the
visibility was down to about a quarter of a mile. With the assistance of the military police, the squadron crossed Tapline Road
in two places without a problem. Crossing this road was always
dangerous, as there was still a large amount of traffic and the local drivers were not expecting any cross-traffic. As the visibility
worsened, the squadron slowed its speed to prevent any break
in the column. Moving close to the assembly area, the vehicles
approached the pre-positioned HEMTT fuel tankers for one last
squadron top-off. At 1326 hours, the squadron sent in its closing report to the 4th Brigade headquarters, indicating that it
was now in Assembly Area Huebner.[6] CPT Philbrick and the air
troops completed the mission a couple of hours later and rejoined the squadron at AA Huebner.

The squadron's new home was part of a desert area designed to hold the entire division. Unlike the previous TAAs
and FAAs, this assembly area was purely administrative and
intended as the location to disassemble the Big Red One and
ship it back to the United States. Units lined their vehicles up as
if in a motor pool and the troops headed for large sleeping tents
with showers close by. In the middle of AA Huebner were several large "fest tents," of the kind found in Germany during October Fest and other celebrations. These contained a pizza

point, small theater, post exchange, post office, telephones, and of course, a burger bar. AA Huebner was also set up near King Khalid Military City (KKMC), a beautiful "city" in the middle of the desert. Referred to by many as the "Emerald City," it was, in reality, a large Saudi military base complete with family housing, mosques, and aviation runways. Other than the food, the most popular facility was the phone bank where there were lines waiting almost twenty-four hours a day.

The purpose of this second phase of the redeployment was to prepare and move the squadron to port. In practical terms, this meant that not only was the squadron going to lose some of its equipment, but it was also going to lose some of its troopers. The first items to go were the M3A2 Cavalry Fighting Vehicles that the squadron had drawn when it arrived at the port back in December. All of the various radios, special mountings, and items brought from the United States had to be removed and loaded into milvans pre-positioned in the squadron area. The troops were a little concerned because this turn-in meant that they would be reissued their old M3s that they had left at the port. A hint of the problems awaiting them emerged when the squadron had to reassume control of five of the old vehicles that had been used by other units in the division. These were in terrible mechanical condition and were missing a great deal of equipment. So, it was a sad day when logistics representatives arrived to take the trusty M3A2 Bradleys. These were superb vehicles and the soldiers could not have asked for anything better.

The squadron would also not be allowed to retain the M1A1 Tanks. In this case, the tanks as well as crews were simply reassigned to the 2nd Brigade. CSM Cobb took charge of ensuring that this was a well-orchestrated transfer. First were troop-level ceremonies to say goodbye to the soldiers. They had been with the squadron from the beginning, and it was a bit emotional to make the change while still in the desert. Then Cobb took the soldiers over to meet their new chain of command. Meanwhile, commanders ensured that the vehicle and unit property paperwork was correct and forwarded it over to the new unit.

In a similar vein, the squadron had to release the infantry soldiers who had been assigned to help fill out the reactivated

A Troop. CPT Pope had a farewell ceremony for these soldiers, who were heading to infantry battalions in the division. During the ceremony Pope awarded each soldier an Expert Infantry Badge to recognize their level of achievement. Across the squadron, others such as tank mechanics, helicopter pilots and crew, National Guard soldiers, and individual replacements said their goodbyes and moved on to other units or back to the United States.

It is amazing how much trash a combat crew in the field for three months can accumulate. CSM Cobb had the engineers dig a large garbage pit just outside the squadron area. It became a magnet for local Bedouins who hovered around the area looking for discarded wood, equipment, and clothing. The fact that Cobb was having the trash burnt each day did not discourage the persistent locals, although the occasional live machine-gun or rifle round exploding did drive them away from the fire for a short while. The squadron had turned most of the ammunition over to corps logistics representatives, and only officers and senior noncommissioned officers retained any ammunition for their units' protection.

Packing of the milvans was quite a process. First, there was some confusion over what the division authorized the soldiers to pack. Could the soldiers ship personal gear, such as radios and stoves, that their families had sent them, or were they only for authorized military equipment? What about captured Iraqi equipment? Could the soldiers bring home war trophies? While it was policy from the beginning that they could not bring home weapons, they had hoped to keep some of the night-vision sights and binoculars that they had acquired. Unfortunately, the new squadron S2, CPT Eric Esplund, had the unenviable task of telling the troop commanders that none of the optics could go with the soldiers. Probably the most valuable souvenir that soldiers could take with them, and they had to be packed in the milvans, were the Soviet-made bayonets that were designed for the AK-47 Rifle.[7]

Each passing day the troopers got closer to their departure from the desert and they could not wait. Each afternoon the winds began to blow and a few hours later transformed into a full-scale sandstorm. The heat and blowing sand were becoming unbearable. Finally, in accordance with the division's redeployment schedule, they packed their equipment, pulled down their tents, and began heading to the port. The squadron departed over three days in six main groups: an advance party under CPT Harmon, a wheeled convoy under CPT Morrison, the air troops under CPT Philbrick, a tracked convoy under CPT Bills, and the rear party under CPT Pope. Finally, the squadron trail party, under MAJ Wimbish, would ensure that any last minute division requirements were accomplished.

On April 21, the squadron advance party departed and checked in with the division's redeployment operations center in Khobar Towers, where much of the squadron had stayed back in January. On the way down to the port, Captains VJ Tedesco and Steve Harmon came across an accident involving two Saudi civilian automobiles. One car had only a young man in it while the other vehicle contained a badly injured husband and wife. A small crowd of people had gathered at the wreck but, amazingly, no one tried to get the occupants out. The Americans pulled the family out of the car and free of the wreckage, began to administer first aid and called for help. The military police arrived and called for an ambulance. Meanwhile the wife had stopped breathing. The MP looked at Tedesco and asked if it was OK to begin mouth-to-mouth resuscitation. This was something we normally wouldn't have thought much about in the United States, but in Saudi Arabia one could not be sure which cultural norm would be violated by having an American male "kiss" a Saudi woman, even if it was to save her life. Tedesco did not agonize and told the MP to do it. The woman soon began breathing again and was loaded onto an ambulance en route to a hospital. Tedesco was not sure if she ultimately survived. Nevertheless, the Americans continued down the road to link up with the rest of the column, feeling pretty good about their act of kindness.[8]

On April 23, at 1700 hours, the wheeled vehicle convoy, under the control of CPT Morrison, departed AA Huebner. First stop for the wheels was KKMC where the soldiers spent the night cleaning their vehicles on the large wash racks. The wash points were set up in a similar manner to those found in major training areas such as Grafenwöhr or Hohenfels, Germany.

With over sixty wash points, each with a high-pressure hose that stretched almost fifty feet, the crews had no problem blasting away over three months of packed mud and dirt. A few hours before dawn almost one hundred vehicles were clean and ready to go. The hard work paid off as the division asked Wilson to have this group on the road at 0400 hours rather than mid-morning as planned. While the troops were exhausted, they were excited to be heading to the port.

The convoy departed before sun-up on April 24, heading from KKMC north to Tapline Road at Hafar al Batin, and then east to the coast and south to the port. At regular intervals, CPT Morrison stopped at the designated relay stations and notified division of the convoy's progress. Upon arrival, BG Bill Carter talked to Burdan, who had accompanied the wheeled convoy to port, and asked him if his soldiers were ready for the final washing and preparation of the vehicles and equipment. While anxious to keep moving, Burdan realized that the troops had not only been up all night but had just finished an eight-hour road march. So, he asked Carter to let his troops have a night's sleep. The general, not wanting to incur any accidents this close to coming home, agreed that the squadron could wait until morning.

The air troops departed Huebner at 0630 on April 24. They flew from the desert heading for the West Heliport outside of Ad Dammam. They rested and refueled at AA Bastogne near the intersection of the Kuwait City and Tapline Roads at 1030 hours and then completed the flight. After landing at Ad Dammam airport, the crews tied down the aircraft and headed for rest at Khobar.

Early that morning, the tracked vehicles under CPT Bills moved to the division pick-up point where they would be loaded onto HETs for the trip back to port. The rear detachment, under CPT Pope, struck the remaining tents, did a final police of the squadron area, and packed all of their personal equipment. For whatever reason the rear detachment CH-47 flight back to port was delayed, and the soldiers spent their last night in the desert sleeping outside and staring, for one last time, at the amazing array of stars that dominate the desert night. The next morning the helicopters arrived, and troopers were on the way home.[9] On April 25, the rear detachment completed clearing AA

Huebner and finally departed for Ad Damman via CH-47 and arrived at Khobar Towers later that day. That afternoon the squadron's tracked vehicles began to be loaded up on the HETs for the long trip to port. On April 26, the squadron's tracked vehicles began to arrive in port and by late afternoon all of the tracked vehicles had arrived. The squadron's trail party under MAJ Wimbish was now all that remained at AA Heubner.

The third phase of redeployment, preparation of the vehicles for the return trip, began at the port early in the morning on April 25. The troopers moved their wheeled vehicles from the holding area to the West Heliport. Here the corps engineers ran the vehicle wash racks. There was a long list of what the squadron was supposed to accomplish at this facility, and the troopers went about their business with a determined efficiency. Since this was a twenty-four-hour a day operation, once in line, it was only a matter of time until the vehicles were on the way to the final holding area. The next day the tracked vehicles began arriving, and, under CPT Bills's supervision, they began joining their wheeled brethren in the long lines.[10]

On April 28, at 0730 hours, the last of the squadron elements finally arrived at Khobar Towers. MAJ Wimbish and the squadron trail party had arrived. They immediately moved their equipment into the squadron area and then departed for the wash racks. The washing project at the West Heliport was operating at full capacity. In addition to the wheeled vehicles, the aircraft were hauled to the wash racks. The temperature at the Heliport rose to 120 degrees out on the tarmac, and the mist from the water was one of the few compensating benefits for hard work in the heat. After each aircraft was clean and dry, it was wrapped in plastic and heated by large blow dryers, creating what was known as the shrink-wrap effect. Now protected, the helicopters were moved to their own holding area in preparation for loading on the ships. The squadron's tracked vehicles were now in line at a wash point on the outskirts of Ad Damman. This was the main wash point for all the division's tracked vehicles. The line was quite long and the vehicles had to be manned twenty-four hours a day or the crew risked losing their place in line.

On April 30, after working twenty-four-hour days, with

crews sitting on and sleeping in vehicles so their place in line would not be lost, the squadron's vehicles were ready. Customs and agriculture inspectors examined each of the now spotless combat vehicles in detail with flashlights and screwdrivers. Once ready, they were driven to a secure holding area at the port. In some instances, the process was more difficult than others. For example, 2LT David Palmieri's platoon had to clean up a Soviet BTR reconnaissance vehicle. It had been hit during the war and a fire had burned some of the interior. In order to prepare it, his platoon had to clean off the burned remains of seats and panels so that the vehicle looked clean on the inside. This required them to spend several hours scrubbing the inside of the vehicle with scouring pads and scouring powder until the thing was clean. It was hot and exhausting work.[11]

With all of the equipment in the holding area, the final phase of the redeployment began. The squadron troopers prepared their personal equipment for the trip home, bought gifts, used recreation facilities, and made calls home. A number of army-approved vendors had set up shop in the Khobar Towers area, selling T-shirts, swords, costumes, brass, gold, and watches. The prices were set by contract and you were not supposed to be able to bargain the merchants down; however, as was Saudi custom, one could occasionally get them to do a little adjustment to their prices. It was very convenient and the soldiers did not need to leave the compound to get things to send home. The army post office always had a line of soldiers with packages.

Some soldiers also took taxis to downtown Dhahran to shop and eat. There were a number of places to shop and there was even a small mall. Here the selection was larger than on base and the troopers visited Kentucky Fried Chicken, Pizza Hut, and other American-style restaurants. At the mall they could buy velveteen paintings of tanks and helicopters, T-shirts, gold, and Arabic clothing. Off base it was quite interesting because they were expected to bargain for each of the items they wanted. Those with access to civilian vehicles, and there were a number still assigned to commanders and staff officers, could go to the air base where an American-style mess hall was set up. Wilson and his officers took advantage of this facility on several occasions.

There was also a service station outside of Khobar that provided contract meals. The military had arranged with the contractor to wash and prepare a number of HMMWVs for shipment. Each driver brought the vehicle to the station and stripped it and then helped them wash it. The contractor provided meals there in a fairly civilized way with tablecloths, silverware, glasses, and waiters. At night the contractor ran a disco and provided near beer. All ranks were welcomed at this service station.

About ten minutes from Khobar there was a public beach. One day, Wilson and some of his officers drove their assigned Chevy Suburban out to spend a day of relaxation. Unfortunately, they got the Chevy stuck and were unable to push it out of the sand. All had a good laugh as a local contractor rounded up a bulldozer to pull the squadron's "staff" car out of the sand. Another beach was in operation down the coast at a place called Half-Moon Bay. It had originally been leased by the British and was still open for American use. Soldiers boarded a shuttle bus and found themselves deposited at a very nice resort with, in addition to the beach, pools, a movie theater, bowling alley, and pool tables. As a concession to Saudi customs, men and women, many from the corps and division staff, did not swim together. The soldiers watched the movie *Look Who's Talking 2* and snacked on free food and soft drinks.

As the troops packed their gear and cleaned the billets, they had numerous briefings from the military police and customs authorities. Wilson placed a troop commander in charge of each flight and ensured they understood the rules. Troopers were forbidden to bring home any acquired weapons, optics, Iranian products, and of course, drugs. The word was that if any contraband were found in your unit during the final inspection, it would go to the bottom of the list for the flight home. There were also plenty of stories on how previous commands had tried to smuggle out weapons and equipment. These stories came with accounts of the punishment, in addition to the delay, that each soldier received.

Then the waiting was over. The soldiers looked great as they formed for one last inspection. All seemed lean, tan, and more mature and looked impressive in their pressed desert camouflage uniforms. All had the Big Red One patch sewn on the right shoulder signifying that they were now combat veterans. The first fifty soldiers, primarily from D and E Troops, departed on May 9. The next day the squadron cleared the billets and HHT, B Troop, and the majority of A Troop headed for the buses with C and the remainder of A leaving the next day.

At the runway the troops marched into a hangar for a final customs check as they watched dogs and military police visit their bags without incident. Then they marched into a Quonset-hut holding area where they awaited their final short bus ride to the plane. The division commanding general, chief of staff, and command sergeant major chose to fly home with the HHT, A and B Troop flight. Wilson considered MG Rhame's choice of his plane as a mark of honor, and the squadron's troopers formed the honor guard for the casing of the division colors signifying the transfer of the Big Red One from Southwest Asia back to the United States.

The flight home for HHT, most of A Troop, and B Troop on America West Airlines was quite enjoyable as soldiers watched movies they had not seen and enjoyed the good food and hospitality of the airline staff. The airline gave each soldier a travel certificate for free airfare for two in the United States. The certificate could be used anytime within the year and anywhere from the east coast to Hawaii. Most everyone could not wait to get home. Of course, there were exceptions. More than one soldier had received a "Dear John" letter and more than a few divorces would take place in the months to come. Fortunately, these were in the minority as most looked forward to the challenge of readjustment. The refueling stop at Kennedy Airport was a joy as the soldiers essentially attacked the Dominos Pizza stand and visited the local bars for their first taste of beer after almost five months in one of the most restrictive cultures in the world.

Arriving in Topeka on May 10, around 2200 hours, this first flight, as did others before and after, boarded buses for the trip down Interstate Highway 70 to Fort Riley. The hills and ranges of western Kansas looked positively green to those accustomed to living in an environment where sand brown was the color of almost everything. Everywhere along the highway and on bridge overpasses were signs saying "Great Job" or "Welcome

Home." Once on post, the bus headed to the air field where soldiers from the garrison and rear detachment, including squadron soldiers who had returned early, helped to lighten the returnees' loads by collecting and securing weapons, protective masks, and other sensitive items. Then the troopers formed up one last time.

Those who have not been part of one have no idea what a welcome home ceremony is like. As the troopers marched into the aircraft hangar decorated for the ceremony the crowd went wild. Lee Greenwood's song "Proud to be an American" blared in the background as the troopers lined up. In the bleachers wives, girlfriends, and children clapped and screamed. Flags and color were everywhere. Then the division commander took center stage and asked for the happy, rambunctious crowd to settle down. First he asked for a moment of silence to remember those division soldiers, fortunately none from the 1-4 Cavalry, who had died in the service of their country in Iraq. Then he publicly, in front of their families, thanked the soldiers for their superb performance over the last several months.

The troops could feel the pride and love of their families and friends in the stands as Rhame spoke. Then he called for the color guard. Five Quarter Horse troopers, with flags and rifles, marched forward and stood in front of the division commander. The sergeant in charge barked out commands as the color bearers lowered the encased national and divisional flags. With the help of his command sergeant major, Rhame pulled off the protective canvas casings, and stood back. The guard sergeant ordered the uncased flags elevated. Now, the 1st Infantry Division, one of the proudest and most decorated units in the United States Army, was home. Raising his hand in salute, Rhame barked "Duty-First!" and "dismissed." The crowd went wild as soldiers broke ranks and families jumped from the bleachers. Soldiers and loved ones collided in hugs, tears, and kisses. Little children who had not seen their father for months, if at all, were not quite sure how to react to the whole scene while older ones struggled to get a word in edge wise. It was an experience that became a precious memory for all who were present.

And into the memories of each and every member of the squadron burnt the experiences of each and every day of that winter and spring. Events such as the alert, leaving the family behind, flying to a strange land, the desert, patrolling the border, the breach, the battle at Norfolk, the Basra Road and Safwan were all memories that would stay with these young men as long as they lived. As Oliver Wendell Holmes's 1884 Memorial Day speech given to fellow Civil War veterans, and played again to a new generation of soldiers in the Ken Burns' documentary playing on television during Desert Storm pointed out:

> We have shared the incommunicable experience of war.
> We have felt, we still feel, the passion of life to its top.
> ... In our youths, our hearts were touched with fire.[12]

Conclusion

hose were dramatic days back in 1991. As the 1-4 Cavalry and the remainder of the Big Red One returned to Fort Riley, it was engulfed in a frenzy of parades and celebrations. All summer those soldiers not on leave were sent around the country to march in local parades and display their equipment. Meanwhile, the Soviet Union disintegrated and the United States stood as the world's lone superpower. In effect the 1991 Persian Gulf War, fought in the Iraqi desert with the weapons, equipment, and army designed to defeat the Warsaw Pact in Europe, became the last conflict of the Cold War and the first of the new Post-Cold War.

It was not, however, the beginning of an era of peace. Before the last troops pulled out of the Arabian Peninsula, American soldiers were back on the ground in northern Iraq to rescue the Kurdish people from the retribution of Saddam Hussein's reconstituted military force. In the next decade American soldiers would find themselves in Somalia, Haiti, the Balkans and, after the attack on the World Trade Center in New York, in Afghanistan. In 2003 the United States Armed Forces returned to Iraq and removed Saddam Hussein from power. Following the Iraqi leader's downfall, a coalition built around American and British forces found itself in the middle of a civil war. In this very confusing conflict, various Islamic and political factions fought each other and the coalition, in an attempt to gain control of this strategic and historic region. By the winter of 2004, the 1st Infantry Division was again in Iraq, not conducting a high-intensity operation, but fighting a war with insurgents by different standards than the troopers of the Desert Storm were familiar with in 1991.

However, the achievements of the earlier war should not be diminished by the more recent conflict in the same area of the world. By any measure of evaluation, this squadron, like the remainder of the 1st Infantry Division, was successful in the 1991 war. It accomplished each task assigned, fought with distinction, and brought all of its troopers home without serious injury. Of course there can be no doubt that it fought this campaign against an enemy who was simply not in the same league. The Iraqi Army had two strengths: a lot of solid equipment and many brave soldiers. Other than that, it had no business being on the same battlefield as the United States Army. It had an incompetent chain of command that had no appreciation of military leadership, operational art, or fundamental tactics. Its soldiers were poorly trained in basic combat skills and lacked proficiency in fundamental crew drills such as tank and artillery gunnery. In each and every tactical engagement against the 1-4 Cavalry, they lost. Yet, this was the same army that had inflicted tens of thousands of casualties on the Iranian Army only a few years earlier.

LTC Robert Wilson brought a squadron to the battlefield that represented the epitome of what a combat unit should be. It had a solid, experienced, chain of command that trusted each other from the commander down to each track commander. The individual soldier, even those who had only recently joined the squadron, was extremely proficient in his individual skills and each crew knew how to fight its combat equipment. The two main types of weapons systems, air and ground, complemented each other and worked as a team as they had never before. In addition, adding tanks back into the squadron organization was a smart move and the decisive element when the squadron encountered heavy forces at Objective Norfolk and on the Basra Road. American leaders had learned the hard way the value of armored protection in World War II, Korea, and Vietnam. The army's leaders had learned their lessons from Vietnam, and rebuilt the force from the bottom up with superb training, leadership, and doctrine. It was not the technology that made this squadron successful, but the quality of its officers, noncommissioned officers, and individual soldiers.

In the haste to demobilize after the Desert Storm, the army returned to the position that cavalry did not need armor. As a result, there were no American armored units in Somalia when they were sorely needed to take care of insurgents and rescue American forces in Mogadishu in 1993.[1] Although the administration of President George W. Bush came into office with a strong desire to transform the army and make it more mobile by cutting out many of its heavy elements, tanks were central to the rapid victory over the Iraqi Army in 2003. Tanks were assigned to the 3rd Squadron, 7th Cavalry, the 3rd Infantry Division's cavalry squadron, and demonstrated their continual value at an intense battle on the outskirts of As Samawah on March 21. As Wilson demonstrated at the Battle of Norfolk in 1991 and the 3-7 Cavalry in their more recent battle, cavalry units still need tanks in order to succeed on the modern battlefield.[2]

The story of the 1-4 Cavalry also demonstrates the importance of trust within a community of officers. Often far from the control of their seniors, the squadron's officers made the decisions that they believed their superiors wanted them to make. When a senior commander was unhappy, such as Rhame was with Wilson during the last stages of Combat Command Carter, he would make the correction and send him back to the unit. When a subordinate leader disagreed, he felt comfortable enough to challenge the boss. This climate of command, traditionally so important in military units, resulted in the entire squadron all striving for the same goals, ready to take the initiative and not concerned that one mistake would result in personal failure or chastisement. The squadron's cutting of the Basra Road was an excellent example of why this command climate is so important.

To most Americans, however, Desert Storm had been all about technology. Many of the training programs and systems that had demonstrated their worth were either eliminated, such as the Combined Arms Services Staff School, or severely modified. In their place, the army began investing in complex command and control systems designed to monitor every subordinate's action from afar. Network-centric warfare, Army Battle Command System, the BLUEFOR (Blue Force, i.e. friendly

forces) Tracking System, and an array of sophisticated communication systems ensured that, in theory, the officer of Operation
Iraqi Freedom was never far from his superior's observation
and direction. At the Army's Command and General Staff College this idea of centralized control was reinforced. An emphasis on educating staff officers and future commanders in the theory of war and ideas such as initiative and agility, taught in the
late 1980s, gave way to mind-numbing repetitions of the "military decision making model," a process guaranteed to insure
that creativity and flexibility would not find their way into military operations. In reality, as the United States Army rediscov-
ered in Iraq in 2005, this centralized approach to military operations was impossible. Whether leading small patrols in Baghdad
or negotiating with a village leader in a distant province, competent leaders had to confront unanticipated situations and
make decisions based only on their own judgment, the mission,
and their senior commander's intent. By 2006, sophisticated observers were describing the "imperial corporal and lieutenant"
who had to make far-reaching decisions on the ground without
electronic supervision by leaders many miles away. The command styles of Tom Rhame, Robert Wilson, Mike Bills, and Ken
Pope are those that the United States Army should emulate in its
increasingly active period of decentralized operations.

After his return from Desert Storm, Bob Wilson continued
to rise through the ranks. He was selected as the 1st Infantry Division's G3 and subsequently studied at the Army War College.
He returned to combat arms as commander of the 3rd Armored
Cavalry Regiment at Fort Bliss, Texas, and supervised its move
to Fort Carson, Colorado. He then served as the executive officer to the commander of Training and Doctrine Command at
Fort Monroe, Virginia. Promoted to brigadier general in 1997,
he headed back to Fort Knox and served as the deputy Commanding General and Commandant of the Armor School and
Center, followed by an assignment with Recruiting Command.
In 2000, the army promoted him to major general and assigned
him to the Middle East as Director of the Office of Military Co-
operation-Egypt. Working for the Commander of Central Command and the American Ambassador in Cairo, he coordinated
U.S., coalition, and Egyptian training exercises as well as the ex-

tensive security assistance program the United States operated in Egypt. In 2003, his hard work paid off as he assumed command of the 7th Infantry Division at Fort Carson. In addition to commanding the division, he supervised a massive mobilization and deployment effort in support of operations in Afghanistan and Iraq. Following his division command he was assigned to the Pentagon as the U.S. Army Assistant Deputy Chief of Staff, G-3/5/7. The army promoted him to Lieutenant General in 2006, and as this manuscript nears completion, he is the Assistant Chief of Staff for Installation Management/Commanding General, Installation Management Command, United States Army, Washington, DC.

Bill Wimbish also continued in the service, commanding the 6-6 Cavalry, an attack helicopter battalion and, as a colonel, the 28th Field Training Group. He was later assigned as a member of the faculty at the Army War College in Carlisle Barracks, Pennsylvania. He is now retired and is the project manager for a futures think tank sponsored by the Director for National Intelligence. Michael Cobb retired from the army and lives outside Fort Knox in Elizabethtown, Kentucky. He is a defense contractor and is currently developing Future Combat System web-based training and doctrinal manuals for the army.

Of the troop commanders, Michael Bills went on to become the commander of the 1-1 Cavalry, attended the Army War College and now commands the 3rd Armored Cavalry Regiment at Ft. Hood, Texas, where he is currently preparing the regiment for its return to Iraq. Ken Pope is a foreign area officer and has served with a Russian Airborne Group in Kosovo and recently completed a tour with the American Embassy in Tallinn, Estonia. Ken is currently a START Mission Commander with the Defense Threat Reduction Agency at Fort Belvoir, Virginia. Doug Morrison went on to become the commander of the 3-7 Cavalry, attended the National War College and was selected to command a brigade. After much soul-searching he turned the opportunity down and was assigned as the Director, Lessons Learned Comprehensive Review Group, Homeland Security Council. He recently retired from the army and is working for a consulting firm. Roy Peters left active duty in June 1994, and later finding his desire to fly helicopters too strong, joined a local Army Reserve Aviation Company, D/158th Avn Bn as a Warrant Officer. He returned to Iraq in 2004–2005 as a CW2 flying combat missions. He is currently an Aviation Safety Inspector with the Federal Aviation Administration. The authors have lost track of the two other troop commanders, James Tovson and Peter Smith. Following the completion of his assignment at Fort Riley, Chris Philbrick, a key member of the squadron staff, commanded an aviation battalion, attended the Army War College and, as of this writing, is the Garrison Commander of Ft. Irwin, California.

Although he has lost track of many of the troopers of the squadron, John Burdan has learned that at least two other squadron officers have risen to command battalions. After serving as a battalion executive officer during Operation Iraqi Freedom I, Matthew Vanderfeltz, the former squadron support platoon leader, returned to translate his experience into army communications doctrine. He is the commander of the 29th Signal Battalion, Fort Lewis, Washington, and as of this writing, has just returned from Mosul, Iraq, where he and his unit supported Operation Iraqi Freedom IV. After a variety of assignments, VJ Tedesco, former squadron S-3 Air, found himself back in Kuwait in 2003–2004 planning the rotation of forces in and out of Iraq. He is now commaner of the 1-37 Armor, 1st Armored Division, and his battalion returned after fourteen months fighting the insurgency in Iraq.

After serving as an instructor at the Army's Command and General Staff College, John Burdan retired from the service and is now a defense contractor living in Colorado Springs with his wife Bridget. For these and all the squadron's veterans of this conflict, the memories of this campaign will remain with them forever: security operations, the breach, the night battle at Norfolk, and the long road to Safwan.

Notes

Introduction

1. Robert Wilson, "Note to Author: Some Comments Ref Safwan," 1997.
2. Robert H. Scales, Jr., *Certain Victory: The U.S. Army in the Gulf War* (Fort Leavenworth, KS: U.S. Army Command and General Staff College Press, 1994).
3. Stephen A. Bourque, *Jayhawk! The VII Corps in the Persian Gulf War* (Washington, DC: U.S. Army Center of Military History, 2002).

Chapter 1

1. Hussars, essentially an honorific name identifying light cavalry designed for war of raiding, reconnaissance, and security. Lancers, as the name implies, used a long lance or spear as their primary weapon. These elite troops, usually clad in gaudy outfits, remained in European armies until the Great War of 1914 confirmed their obsolescence. Dragoons have always been mounted infantrymen, who traveled on horseback but fought on foot.
2. Comments made by Colonel Robert Wagner during his tenure as commander, 2nd Armored Cavalry Regiment, in Germany, from 1980–1981.
3. Mary Lee Stubbs and Stanley Russell Conner, *Armor-Cavalry, Part I: Regular Army and Army Reserve, Army Lineage Series* (Washington, DC: U.S. Army Center of Military History, 1969), 128; Robert M. Utley, *Frontiersmen in Blue: The United States Army and the Indian, 1848–1865*, ed. Louis Morton, *Macmillan Wars of the United States* (Lincoln: University of Nebraska Press, 1981), 22-23, 121-26, 39-40. Robert W. Coakley, *The Role of Federal Military Forces in Domestic Disorders, 1789–1878, Army Historical Series* (Washington, DC: U.S. Army Center of Military History, 1988), 143–59, 65–72, 82–88.
4. Douglas Southall Freeman, *R. E. Lee, Vol 1* (New York: Charles Scribner's Sons, 1934), 432–35; Utley, *Frontiersmen in Blue*, 212–13; Richard J. Zimmerman, *Unit Organizations of the American Civil*

War (Cambridge, Ont: Rafm Co. Inc, 1982), 4; Stubbs and Conner, *Armor-Cavalry, Part I: Regular Army and Army Reserve*, 16. See also Stephen W. Sears, *George B. McClellan: The Young Napoleon* (New Haven: Ticknor & Fields, 1988), 44–49. The regiment did not have a squadron organization as was common later.

5. Stephen Z. Starr, *The Union Cavalry in the Civil War, Volume III: The War in the West, 1861–1865* (Baton Rouge: Louisiana State University Press, 1985), 36–38, 117–21, 226, 244-49, 462–65; Peter Cozzens, *This Terrible Sound: The Battle of Chickamauga* (Urbana: University of Illinois Press, 1996), 102–8, 226; James Harrison Wilson, "The Union Cavalry in the Hood Campaign," in *Battles and Leaders of the Civil War*, ed. Buel Johnson (New York: The Century Magazine, 1887), 470; U.S. Department of War, "The War of the Rebellion: A Compilation of the Official Records of the Union and Confederate Armies" (Washington, DC, 1880–), 924.

6. Warner, *Generals in Blue*, 301–2; Robert M. Utley, *Frontier Regulars: The United States Army and the Indian, 1866–1891*, ed. Louis Morton, *Macmillan Wars of the United States* (New York: Macmillan Publishing Co. Inc., 1973), 216–19.

7. John G. Keliher, *The History of the Fourth Cavalry* [Internet] (2006 [cited 12 November 2006]); available from http://www.25thida.com/4thcav.html.

8. Brian McAllister Linn, *The Philippine War: 1899–1902* (Lawrence: University Press of Kansas, 2000), 42–46, 96, 102); Stubbs and Conner, *Armor-Cavalry, Part I*, 129.

9. Christopher R. Gabel, *The U.S. Army GHQ Maneuvers of 1941* (Washington, DC: U.S. Army Center of Military History, 1991), 30, 65, 72, 105, 107; Stubbs and Conner, *Armor-Cavalry, Part I*, 71, 125–30.

10. Gordon A. Harrison, *The European Theater of Operations: Cross-Channel Attack, United States Army in World War II* (Washington, D.C.: U.S. Army Center of Military History, 1951; reprint, U. S. Army Center of Military History, 1993), 304.

11. Harrison, *The European Theater of Operations*, 416–42; Martin Blumenson, *The European Theater of Operations: Breakout and Pursuit, United States Army in World War II* (Washington, DC: U.S. Army Center of Military History, 1961; reprint, U.S. Army Center of Military History, 1993), 682–83; S. B. Mason, ed., *Danger Forward: The Story of the First Division in World War II* (Washington, DC: Society of the First Division, 1947); Charles B. MacDonald, *The European Theater of Operations: The Siegfried Line Campaign, United States Army in World War II* (Washington, D.C.: U. S. Army Center of Mil-

itary History, 1963; reprint, U. S. Army Center of Military History, 1993), 23, 36, 280–320, 590–91, Map III and VIII.

12. Hugh M. Cole, *The European Theater of Operations: The Ardennes: The Battle of the Bulge, United States Army in World War II* (Washington, DC: U.S. Army Center of Military History, 1965; reprint, U. S. Army Center of Military History, 1993), 80–86, 423–27; Charles B. MacDonald, *A Time for Trumpets: The Untold Story of the Battle of the Bulge* (New York: William Morrow and Company, Inc., 1985), 632–33.

13. Charles B. MacDonald, *The European Theater of Operations: The Last Offensive, United States Army in World War II* (Washington, DC: U.S. Army Center of Military History, 1973), 156–66, 401–6, Maps III, VII, IX; Mason, *Danger Forward*, 384–403.

14. Donn A. Starry, *Armored Combat in Vietnam, Vietnam Studies* (New York: Arno Press, 1980), 54–58, 228.

15. Keliher, *The History of the Fourth Cavalry*.

16. Peter S. Kindsvatter, "The Army-of-Excellence Divisional Cavalry Squadron—A Doctrinal Step Backward?"(Monograph, School of Advanced Military Studies, U.S. Army Command and Staff College, 1995); Personal note from Kindsvatter, former 2nd Brigade Executive Officer and Division Plans officer.

17. CPT Douglas Morrison, interview by John Burdan. HHT, 1st Squadron, 4th Cavalry, tape recording, Fort Leavenworth, KS, 31 March 1994.

18. CPT Michael A. Bills, interview by John Burdan. B Troop, 1st Squadron, 4th Cavalry, tape recording, Fort Leavenworth, KS, 26 August 1995. Old unit organizations are from U. S. Army Field Manual 17-36, *Divisional Armored and Air Cavalry Units*, 1968.

Chapter 2

1. LTC Robert Wilson, interview by Thomas A. Popa. 1st Squadron, 4th Cavalry, 1st Infantry Division, Ft. Riley, KS, 28 July 1991. One of the authors accompanied this group to Europe. An army corps is a flexible organization that can have any number of divisions and combat units. For Operation Desert Shield, the XVIII Airborne Corps, based in Fort Bragg, North Carolina, consisted of the 82d Airborne Division, 101st Airborne Division (Airmobile), 24th Infantry Division (Mechanized), 1st Cavalry Division, 12th Aviation Brigade, 18th Aviation Brigade, and the 3rd Armored Cavalry Regiment. For OPERATON DESERT STORM in February, it would lose the 1st Cavalry Division and gain the 6th (French) Light Armored Division. See Charles Lane Toomey, *XVIII Airborne Corps in*

Desert Storm (Central Point, OR: Hellgate Press, 2004) for details of the XVII Corps.

2. The word "troopers" refers to soldiers who are members of a cavalry unit. In this manuscript, it is used interchangeably for squadron members.

3. CPT Michael A. Bills, interview by John Burdan. B Troop, 1st Squadron, 4th Cavalry, Fort Leavenworth, KS, 26 August 1995.

4. Unless otherwise cited, author John Burdan provides the details of training and general squadron activities. Major Burdan maintained these notes while assigned as the squadron S3. Where appropriate, they are also cited as Burdan Notes.

5. Gary Notestine and CW Wayne Grimes, interview by John Burdan. D Troop, 1st Squadron, 4th Cavalry, 1st Infantry Division, tape recording, Ft. Leavenworth, KS, 18 December 1993.

6. Bills interview, 26 August 1995.

7. Robert Wilson, "Tanks in the Division Cavalry Squadron," *Armor* 101 (July–August 1992).

8. CPT Kenneth Pope, interview by John Burdan. A Troop, 1st Squadron, 4th Cavalry, Fort Leavenworth, KS, 5 October 1993.

9. CPT Christopher R. Philbrick, interview by John Burdan. HHT (Aviation), 1st Squadron, 4th Cavalry, Fort Leavenworth, KS, 12 February 1994; CPT Douglas Morrison, interview by John Burdan. HHT, 1st Squadron, 4th Cavalry, Fort Leavenworth, KS, 31 March 1994.

10. Peter S Kindsvatter, "The Army of Excellence Divisional Cavalry Squadron—a Doctrinal Step Backward?" (Monograph, U. S. Army Command and General Staff College, 1985). As mentioned earlier, the 1st Infantry Division usually assigned the squadron a tank company for increased firepower.

11. Morrison interview, 31 March 1994.

12. COL Terry Bullington, interview by Thomas A. Popa. 1st Infantry Division, G3, tape recording, Fort Riley, KS, 24 July 1991.

13. Wilson, "Tanks in the Division Cavalry Squadron," 6.

14. Bullington interview, 24 July 1991.

15. Morrison interview, 31 March 1994.

16. MAJ William Wimbish, interview by John Burdan. 1st Squadron, 4th Cavalry, Fort Leavenworth, KS, 28 September 1993; Fort Riley Kansas, "After Action Report, Phase I, Mobilization and Deployment (Operation Desert Shield/Storm)" (15 May 1991), III 30–31, IV 37–38.

17. Fort Riley, "After Action Report, Phase I," III 29; 1st Infantry Division G3, 1st Infantry Division on Desert Storm, briefing presented to CGSC students 7 August 1991. Unless otherwise cited, issues of the 1st Infantry Division Headquarters come from the notes of then Major Stephen Bourque. Bourque was the G3-Night Operations Officer. Where appropriate, they are referred to as Bourque Notes.

Chapter 3

1. Gen. (Retired) William E. DePuy, Presentation for the Officers of the 1st Infantry Division at Fort Riley, KS, 27 November 1990.

2. Although the division was scheduled to receive new tanks in Saudi Arabia, it deployed with all of its assigned combat equipment, including its old M1 tanks. All were fully combat loaded and ready for battle if required. In Saudi Arabia, the 2nd Brigade arrived too late to receive the new M1A1 tanks and fought with its original equipment. See David W. Marlin, "History of the 4th Battalion, 37th Armored Regiment in Operation Desert Shield/Storm" (U.S. Army War College, 1992).

3. Bills interview, 26 August 1995.

4. SFC William A. Ball, interview by John Burdan. HHT, 1st Squadron, 4th Cavalry, Fort Riley, KS, 12 August 1995. 1st Infantry Division, *4th Brigade, 1st Infantry Division, Desert Storm Highlights (Draft)*, 1991.

5. Fort Riley Kansas, "After Action Report, Phase I," 33.

6. *4th Brigade, 1st Infantry Division, Desert Storm Highlights (Draft)*; Philbrick interview, 12 February 1994; Stephen Greuning, interview by John Burdan. C Troop, 1st Squadron, 4th Cavalry, Fort Riley, KS, 7 January 1994; Notestine and Grimes interview, 18 December 1993.

7. Note: In most cases the authors use the masculine pronoun in this narrative. There were no female soldiers assigned to the 1-4 Cavalry.

8. Morrison interview, 31 March 1994.

9. Ibid.

10. Debra L. Anderson, personal notes. Anderson was a member of the 1st Infantry Division's G1 staff.

11. Memorandum, MAJ Donald A. Osterberg to Chief of Staff, Subject; Operation Desert Shield, 16 November 1990. Bourque Notes.

12. CPT Vincent Tedesco, interview by John Burdan. S3, 1st Squadron, 4th Cavalry, Fort Leavenworth, KS, 29 June 1996.

13. SFC Donald Wehage, interview by John Burdan. A Troop, 1st

Squadron, 4th Cavalry, Tape recording, Fort Leavenworth, KS, 25 January 1994.

14. MAJ William Wimbish, interview by John Burdan. 1st Squadron, 4th Cavalry, 1st Infantry Division, 28 September 1993.

15. Morrison interview, 31 March 1994.

16. Bills interview; Morrison interview, 31 March 1994.

17. SFC William Molitor, interview by John Burdan. A Troop, 1st Squadron, 4th Cavalry, Fort Riley, KS, 5 January 1994.

18. Ball interview, 12 August 1995.

19. Morrison interview, 31 March 1994.

20. Ibid.

Chapter 4

1. Morrison interview, 31 March 1994.

2. Ibid.

3. Ibid.

4. The term "port" in this book refers to Ad Dammam where all of the squadron's equipment arrived. The United States also used the port of Al Jubayl to unload equipment in Saudi Arabia.

5. CW3 Kirk Waymire, interview by John Burdan. C Troop, 1st Squadron, 4th Cavalry, 1st Infantry Division, Ft. Leavenworth, KS, 1 March 1994; Comment made to Burdan by Waymire after interview session.

6. Molitor interview, 5 January 1994; Waymire interview 1 March 1994; Pope interview, 5 October 1993.

7. Pope interview, 5 October 1993.

8. Department of Defense United States, "Conduct of The Persian Gulf War: Final Report to Congress" (Washington, DC: Government Printing Office, 1992), 378–79; Michael R. Gordon and Bernard E. Trainor, *The General's War: The Inside Story of the Conflict in the Gulf* (Boston: Little, Brown and Company, 1995), 58–59; Frank N. Schubert and Theresa L. Kraus, *The Whirlwind War: The United States Army in Operations Desert Shield and Desert Storm* (Washington, DC: U.S. Army Center of Military History, 1995), 80.

9. VII Corps, *1st Infantry Division (Forward) Desert Shield/Desert Storm After Action Review of VII Corps Debarkation and Onward Movement*, 30 May 1991, 24–26; US Army Central Command, *22nd Support Command After Action Report*, 1991, Vol. IVB, Charts A-5-1 and A-7-2.

10. 22nd Support Command, *125th Support Command After Action Report*, 1991, II-2 to II-3.

11. Donald S. Pihl and George E. Dausman, eds., *United States Army: Weapon Systems 1990* (Washington, DC: Government Printing Office, 1990), 17.

12. Wehage interview, 25 January 1994; Bills interview, 26 August 1995.

13. Steven E. Dietrich, "In-Theater Armored Force Modernization," *Military Review* 73 (October 1993): 40–44.

14. Pope interview, 5 October 1993.

15. Robert Wilson, "Tanks in the Division Cavalry Squadron," *Armor* 101, no. (July-August 1992): 7-9.

16. Waymire interview, 1 March 1994.

17. Notestine and Grimes interview, 18 December 1993; Wimbish interview, 28 September 1993.

18. Gruenig interview, 7 January 1994.

19. Philbrick interview, 12 February 1994.

Chapter 5

1. Steve Vogel, "Metal Rain: Old Ironsides and the Iraqis Who Wouldn't Back Down," *Army Times*, 16 September 1991, 12; John Sack, *Company C: The Real War in Iraq* (New York: William Morrow and Company, 1995), 46; VII-Corps, *Daily Staff Journal, VII Corps Main Command Post, G3 Operations (31 December 1990)*; VII-Corps, *Daily Staff Journal, VII Corps Main Command Post, G3 Operations (03 January 1991)*. Aramco was the Arabian-American Oil Company, one of the largest oil producers in the Middle East.

2. Note: Much of this chapter is based on John Burdan's personal notes.

3. 1st Infantry Division Forward (1IDF), *1st Infantry Division (Forward) Desert Shield/Desert Storm after Action Review of VII Corps Debarkation and Onward Movement*, Army, 30 May 1991, Iraq, VII Corps, briefing chart (Heavy Lift Assets.), 41; Anthony H. Cordesman and Abraham R. Wagner, *The Lessons of Modern War, Vol IV: The Gulf War* (Boulder: Westview Press, 1996), 698–99; William G. Pagonis, *Moving Mountains: Lessons in Leadership and Logistics from the Gulf War* (Boston: Harvard Business School Press, 1992), 123.

4. David W. Marlin, "History of the 4th Battalion, 37th Armored Regiment in Operation Desert Shield/Storm" (U.S. Army War College, 1992), 433.

5. Wimbish interview, 28 September 1993.

6. 1st Squadron 4th Cavalry, *Daily Staff Journal, Tactical Operation Center: 1300 10 January to 0200 11 January 1991.*

7. 1st Squadron 4th Cavalry, *Daily Staff Journal, Tactical Operation Center: 1800 13 January to 0618 14 January 1991*; 1st Squadron 4th Cavalry, *Daily Staff Journal, Tactical Operation Center: 0630 14 January to 1700 15 January 1991.*

8. Bourque, *Jayhawk! The VII Corps in the Persian Gulf War*, 124–26; 1st Squadron, 4th Cavalry, *Daily Staff Journal, Tactical Operation Center: 0630 14 January to 1700 15 January 1991.* This incident caused personal problems for CPT Maloney upon the unit's return to Fort Riley. Some equipment shipped to the desert could not be accounted for and was assumed lost during this transaction. Although LTC Wilson recommended that, under the circumstances, no one be held accountable for the lost equipment, COL Mowery decided to charge the S4 with the loss. The matter was finally cleared in Maloney's favor after an appeal to the division commander.

9. 1st Squadron, 4th Cavalry, *Daily Staff Journal, Tactical Operation Center: 0630 14 January to 1700 15 January 1991.*

10. Ball interview, 12 August 1995.

11. Readers should remember that this deployment took place long before American soldiers encountered suicide bombers and aggressive small-scale attacks in large numbers, as they have during their second war against Iraq.

12. *1st Brigade, 1st Infantry Division, Operation Order: Desert Storm-4*, 25 January 1991, TAA Roosevelt, Iraq.

13. Tedesco interview, 29 June 1996; Bills interview, 26 August 1995.

14. 1st Squadron 4th Cavalry, *Daily Staff Journal, Tactical Operation Center: 1900 16 January to 0615 17 January 1991.*

15. 1st Squadron 4th Cavalry, *Daily Staff Journal, Tactical Operation Center: 0630 14 January to 1700 15 January 1991*, entry 24.

16. The History of the Fourth United States Cavalry, prepared by the Squadron Staff, pg E-4.

17. Bourque, *Jayhawk!*, 141–43.

18. Bills interview, 26 August 1995.

19. VII-Corps, *Daily Staff Journal, VII Corps Main Command Post, G3 Operations (19 January 1991)*; 1st Squadron 4th Cavalry, *Daily Staff Journal, Tactical Operation Center: 1856 18 January to 0600 19 January 1991.*

20. 1st Squadron 4th Cavalry (1-4Cav), *Daily Staff Journal, Tactical Operation Center: 0610 19 January to 1815 19 January 1991.*

21. Ibid.

22. Bills interview, 26 August 1995.

23. Bills interview, 26 August 1995; 1st Squadron 4th Cavalry, *Daily Staff Journal, Tactical Operation Center: 0610 19 January to 1815 19 January 1991*, entry 25.

24. 1st Squadron 4th Cavalry (1-4Cav), *Daily Staff Journal, Tactical Operation Center: 0500 22 January to 1700 22 January 1991*.

25. Pope interview, 5 October 1993.

Chapter 6

1. Bills interview; G3 Operations, Department of the Army VII-Corps, *OPORD 1990-2 OPERATION DESERT SABER*, VII Corps After Action Report, 13 January 1991, Abu Qaar, Saudi Arabia.

2. Army, Department of the Army VII-Corps, *FRAGO 85-91 Displacement of CS and CSS Backbone in Support of Phase II Operations*, VII Corps After Action Report, 23 January1991, Saudi Arabia.

3. 1st Squadron 4th Cavalry, *Daily Staff Journal, Tactical Operation Center: 1712 21 January to 2130 21 January 1991*; 1st Squadron 4th Cavalry, *Daily Staff Journal, Tactical Operation Center: 0500 23 January to 1700 23 January 1991*; 1st Squadron 4th Cavalry *Daily Staff Journal, Tactical Operation Center: 0500 23 January to 1700 23 January 1991*; 1st Squadron 4th Cavalry, *Daily Staff Journal, Tactical Operation Center: 1700 23 January to 0430 24 January 1991*. All squadron staff journals were located at the Springfield, Virginia, U.S. Armed Service Center for Research of Unit Records.

4. 1-4 Cavalry, *Daily Staff Journal*, 24 January 1991; Robert Wilson, "Tanks in the Division Cavalry Squadron," *Armor* 101, (July-August 1992): 6-7; VII Corps, *Commander's SITREP #4 (202100Z-212100Z Jan 91)*, Saudi Arabia, VII Corps After Action Report.

5. Bills interview, 26 August 1995.

6. Ibid.

7. Gruenig interview, 7 January 1994.

8. Philbrick interview, 12 February 1993; 1st Squadron 4th Cavalry, *Daily Staff Journal, Tactical Operation Center: 0500 26 January to 1720 27 January 1991*; 1st Squadron 4th Cavalry, 1st Infantry Division, *Squadron Historical Narrative*, (March 1991).

9. Bills interview, 26 August 1995.

10. Pope interview, 5 October 1993; 1st Squadron, 4th Cavalry, *Daily Staff Journal, 27 January 1991*.

11. Wilson, "Tanks in the Division Cavalry Squadron," 7–8.

12. "Trains" is nothing more than a historical term for the collection of supporting services for the combat forces. This usage probably

emerged during the years of French King Louis XIV and is derived from the French verb *traîner*, to draw or pull.

13. 1LT James C. Copenhaver, interview by John Burdan. A Troop, 1st Squadron, 4th Cavalry, Ft. Leavenworth, KS, 15 April 1994.

14. *4th Brigade, 1st Infantry Division, Desert Storm Highlights (Draft)*, Iraq.

15. Squadron Historical Narrative; VII Corps, *FRAGO 104-91 Enemy probing Actions Continue*, VII Corps After Action Report, 31 January 1991.

16. 1st Squadron 4th Cavalry, *Daily Staff Journal, Tactical Operation Center: 1700 31 January to 0500 1 February 1991.*

17. 1st Squadron 4th Cavalry, *Daily Staff Journal, Tactical Operation Center: 0500 1 February to 1700 1 February 1991.*

18. 1st Infantry Division, Daily Staff Journal, Tactical Operations Center, 1 Feb 1991, entry 65; 1st Squadron 4th Cavalry, *Daily Staff Journal, Tactical Operation Center: 1700 1 February to 0500 2 February 1991*, entry 21.

19. 1st Squadron 4th Cavalry, *Daily Staff Journal, Tactical Operation Center: 1700 1 February to 0500 2 February 1991*; Bills interview, 26 August 1995; Wimbish interview, 28 September 1993. Similar incidents over the next few nights caused LTC Wilson to avoid using the Apaches at night except where absolutely necessary. The Apaches were originally designed for missions deep in the enemy rear area. He felt it was too dangerous to employ the Apaches at night in areas where friendly and enemy elements were in close proximity to each other .

20. MG Robert Wilson, note to author, 22 November 2005.

21. 1st Squadron 4th Cavalry, *Daily Staff Journal, Tactical Operation Center: 0500 2 February to 1700 2 February 1991*; Wilson interview, 28 July 1991; Michael Robels, Summary of 1st Infantry Division Commander's Reports, 30 March 1991, author's collection, entry for 2 February 1991; VII Corps SITREP 4 (21 January 1991).

Chapter 7

1. On January 29, the Iraqi Army launched a three-division attack along the coast of Saudi Arabia toward the port of Ras al Mishab. After an extensive pounding by coalition air units, only elements of one division reached the coastal town of Khafji and were soon ejected. See James Titus, "The Battle of Khafji: An Overview and Preliminary Analysis" (Manuscript, Air University, 1996) ; Rebecca Grant, "The Epic Little Battle of Khafji," *Air Force Magazine* February (1998): 28 ff.

2. Army, VII Corps, *Commander's SITREP #17 (022100Z-032100Z Feb 91)*; Department of the Army, VII-Corps, *FRAGO 107-91 Enemy reconnaissance efforts continue in sector*, 2 February 1991.

3. A task force is a grouping of different company-sized units to accomplish a specific mission. In this case, the tank battalion exchanged a tank company for an infantry company from 2-16th Infantry.

4. 1st Squadron 4th Cavalry, *Daily Staff Journal, Tactical Operation Center: 0500 3 February to 1700 3 February 1991*; Department of the Army, 1st Infantry Division, *Command Report*, 19 April 1991. VII Corps Main Command Post, Commander's SITREP 18, (4 February 1991).

5. VII Corps Main Command Post, Commander's SITREP 17, (3 February 1991); Michael Bracket, interview by Thomas A. Popa, Fort Riley, KS, 23 July 1991; VII Corps FRAGO 107-1991, 2 February 1991; VII Corps FRAGO 110-91, TF Carter Conducts Force Protection Mission, 4 February 1991; David Gross, "History of 37th Armor on Operation Desert Storm," unpublished manuscript (1992).

6. Pope interview, 5 October 1993; Burdan notes.

7. 1st Squadron 4th Cavalry, *Daily Staff Journal, Tactical Operation Center: 1700 6 February to 0500 7 February 1991*; 1st Infantry Division, *Daily Staff Journal, Main Command Post, G3 Operations (7 Feb 91)*; Discussion with CSM (ret) Mike Cobb, 2003.

8. 1st Squadron 4th Cavalry, *Daily Staff Journal, Tactical Operation Center: 0500 6 February to 1700 6 February 1991*; Tedesco interview, 29 June 1996.

9. Bills interview, 26 August 1995; 4th Cavalry (1-4Cav) 1st Squadron, 1st Infantry Division, *Squadron Historical Narrative*, Fort Leavenworth, KS.

10. 1st Squadron 4th Cavalry, *Daily Staff Journal, Tactical Operation Center: 0500 4 February to 1700 4 February 1991*.

11. Gross, "History of 37th Armor on Operation Desert Storm."

12. Bills interview, 26 August 1995; 1st Squadron 4th Cavalry, *Daily Staff Journal, Tactical Operation Center: 0500 5 February to 1700 5 February 1991*.

13. 1st Squadron 4th Cavalry, *Daily Staff Journal, Tactical Operation Center: 1700 5 February to 0500 6 February 1991*.

14. Ibid.

15. 1st Squadron 4th Cavalry, *Daily Staff Journal, Tactical Operation Center: 0500 6 February to 1700 06 February 1991*

16. Burdan notes.

17. Wehage interview, 25 January 1994.

18. Gross, "History of 37th Armor on Operation Desert Storm," 54.

19. Ibid.

20. Ibid.

21. Gross, "History of 37th Armor on Operation Desert Storm,"36–39.

22. Squadron Tactical Command Post, *Daily Staff Journal, Tactical Operation Center: 1700 8 February to 0500 9 February 1991*, 8 February 1991, U.S. Armed Service Center for Research of Unit Records; 1st Infantry Division, *Daily Staff Journal, Main Command Post, G3 Operations (9 Feb 91)*, Army, 9 Feb 91; Bracket interview, 23 July 1991; Author's notes; Gross, "History of 3d Battalion, 37th Armor on Operation Desert Storm."

23. Thomas G. Rhame, Letter to Commander VII Corps, Subject: Serious Incident Report, 14 February 1991; VII Corps Tactical Operations Center (TAC), Staff Journal, 15 February 1991, entry 7; Gross, "History of the 37th Armor on Operation Desert Storm," 51–52.)

24. 1st Infantry Division G3, *Command Report*, Department of the Army, 19 April 1991, VII Corps After Action Report.

Chapter 8

1. 1st Infantry Division (1ID) U.S. Department of the Army, "Operation Desert Shield/Storm Briefing" (paper presented at the VII Corps After Action Report, Leavenworth, KS, 7 August 1991).

2. FM 100-5, *Operations* (1986), 65; VII Corps Main CP (Plans), OPLAN 1990-2, 15.

3. Steve Vogel, "Hell Night," *Army Times*, 23 September 1991, 14; VII Corps Main CP (Plans), OPLAN 1990-2, 15.

4. Officially this area was a neutral zone established by treaty in 1937 that allowed for the free traverse of the various Bedouin tribes in the region. In April 1975 Iraq and Saudi Arabia signed an agreement to eventually divide the zone. The Saudi construction of the border berm indicated that this anticipated division was in effect. From the soldiers' perspective, they were heading into Iraq.

5. LTC Stephen Hawkins "Interview: 1st Engineer Battalion," Interview by Thomas A. Popa , Fort Riley, KS, CMH Desert Storm Interview Tape Collection, 26 July 1991; VII Corps Main CP (Plans), Annex D (Fire Support) to OPLAN 1990-2; Tice, "'Coming Through' The Big Red Raid," 18; Vogel, "Hell Night," 14; Pope interview #1.

6. A defile drill is a tactical procedure that allows a unit to negotiate a narrow passage such as a bridge, a pass through rough terrain,

or other regions that favor an ambush or attack by the enemy. While most of the unit has its weapons trained on the far side of the defile, scouts cross to the other side and look for the enemy. Once they report it clear, the following units bound forward one at a time. When done correctly, it takes away the enemy's chance to surprise the crossing unit when it is most vulnerable.

7. Vogel, "Hell Night," 15; Robels, Summary of 1st Infantry Division Commander's Reports; VII Corps TAC, Staff Journal, 15 February 1991, entry 28; Phone interview between the author and Wesley B. Anderson, 1st Infantry Division Engineer, 2 August 1994.

8. 1st Squadron, 4th Cavalry, Historical Narrative.

9. History of the Fourth United States Cavalry.

10. Pope interview, 5 October 1993.

11. Author discussion with CPT (Chaplain) Lou Parker.

12. VII Corps TAC, Staff Journal 15-16 February 1991; Chronology of 1st Brigade, 1st Cavalry Division, B11; Author's notes.

13. Vogel, "Hell Night," 15; Robels, Summary of 1st Infantry Division Commander's Reports; VII Corps TAC, Staff Journal, 15 February 1991, entry 28; Phone interview between the author and Wesley B. Anderson, 1st Infantry Division Engineer, 2 August 1994.

14. Vogel, "Hell Night," 15.

15. James L. Hillman, "Task Force 1-41 Infantry: Fratricide Experience in Southwest Asia" (Personal Experience Monograph, U.S. Army War College, 1993), 8–9; Bills interview. The intent or direction of the Iraqi reconnaissance effort in the VII Corps sector is still unknown. The weakened front-line divisions did not have the capability to conduct any substantial mounted patrolling. The most likely explanation is that it was directed by the Iraqi VII Corps commander using his own reconnaissance assets. While the VII Corps G2's "100 Hour War" says little about the Iraqi tactical reconnaissance effort, it is obvious that there was one. The thermal sight capability of the M1 and M2s allowed the American soldiers on the border the opportunity to positively identify people and vehicles on the other side. The volume of reports in the duty logs indicates that there were numerous patrols between the border and the front line positions. Tab K, of the "100 Hour War" and the 7th Engineer Brigade study also identify wrecked BRDMs, and other recon-type, vehicles near the border.

16. Finding the boundary lines between divisions is an important mission of most reconnaissance operations. Unit boundary lines restrict movement and indirect fires of defenders. As such, they are

potential weak zones in the defense, and an opportunity for attacking forces to exploit.

17. Bourque's notes 16 February 1991 entry for 2230 hours. During this phase Bourque was 1st Infantry Division G3 Operations duty officer, responsible for monitoring the engagement in the tactical operations center.

18. 177th AR S2, *The Iraqi Army*, 112–13; VII Corps TAC, Staff Journal, 17 February 1991; Bourque's Notes; Hillman, "Task Force 1-41 Infantry," 9.

19. Hillman, "Task Force 1-41 Infantry," 9.

20. VII Corps TAC, Staff Journal, 16 February 1991; Author's Notes; Vogel, "Hell Night," 15; Robert Johnson and Caleb Solomon, "Chilling Tapes Show How Soldiers Died in 'Friendly Fire,'" *The Wall Street Journal* (7 November 1991), A1; Wilson interview; Hillman, "Task Force 1-41 Infantry," 9.

21. Chronology of 1st Brigade, 1st Cavalry Division; VII Corps TAC, Staff Journal, 17 February 1991, entry #7; Hillman, "Task Force 1-41 Infantry."

22. Robert Johnson and Caleb Solomon, "Gulf War Casualty: 'Friendly Fire' Downs Career of a Gung-Ho Colonel," *The Wall Street Journal* (10 September 1991), A1; Headquarters, 1st Infantry Division, Chronological Summary of Events, 26 March 1991; Rick Atkinson, *Crusade: The Untold Story of the Persian Gulf War* (Boston: Houghton Mifflin Co, 1993).

23. Vogel, "Hell Night," 15; Atkinson, *Crusade*, 320; VII Corps TAC, Staff Journal 17 February 1991.

24. Burdan notes; Tedesco interview, 29 June 1996.

25. Burdan notes.

26. Tedesco interview, 29 June 1996.

27. Bills, interview, 26 August 1991.

28. Notestine and Grimes interview, 18 December 1993.

29. Pope interview, 5 October 1993.

30. Burdan notes. The SWTs were often made up of a mix of aircraft from both troops. Among other things, this allowed CPT Smith, E Troop Commander, to better control the helicopter maintenance schedules.

Chapter 9
1. Colin Powell and Joseph E. Perisco, *My American Journey* (New York: Ballantine Books, 1996), 500.

2. Squadron Tactical Command Post, *Daily Staff Journal, Tactical Operation Center: 0500 18 February to 1700 18 February 1991*. 18 February 1991, U. S. Armed Service Center for Research of Unit Records.

3. John C. Davidson, *The 100 Hour Ground War: The Failed Iraqi Plan*, G2, 20 April 1991; Anthony H. Cordesman and Abraham R. Wagner, *The Lessons of Modern War, Vol IV: The Gulf War* (Boulder: Westview Press, 1996), 116.

4. Department of Defense United States, "Conduct of the Persian Gulf War: Final Report to Congress," (Washington, DC: Government Printing Office, 1992), 259. Cordesman and Wagner, 116.

5. Operation Desert Shield was the initial military operation that sent American forces to Saudi Arabia in August 1990. Operation Desert Storm was the overall military operation that evicted the Iraqi troops from Kuwait. Desert Saber was the name of the VII Corps's warplan to execute Desert Storm. The 1st Infantry Division's portion of the war plan was called Scorpion Danger.

6. LTG Frederick M. Franks, *OPORD 1990-2 Operation Desert Saber*, G3 Operations, 13 January 1991.

7. *The 100 Hour Ground War: The Failed Iraqi Plan*.

8. 1st Infantry Division G3, *Command Report*, Department of the Army, 19 April 1991, 1 Infantry Division.

9. 1st Squadron, 4th Cavalry, OPORD 3-91 (Scorpion Danger, Change 1), 22 February 1991; Col Lon E. Maggart, *1st Brigade, 1st Infantry Division, Operation Order: Desert Storm-4*, 25 January 1991 Lon E. Maggart and Gregory Fontenot, "Breaching Operations: Implications for Battle Command and Battle Space," *Military Review* 74, no. 2 (February 1994).

10. 1st Squadron, 4th Cavalry, *Opord 3-91, Scorpion Danger*, 22 February 1991.

11. Burdan notes.

12. Bills interview #1.

13. Burdan notes.

14. Gruenig interview, 7 January 1994.

15. CPT Lou Parker, unpublished manuscript on his recollections as a chaplain during the 1991 Persian Gulf War.

16. Tedesco interview, 29 June 1996.

17. CSM Gary Parkey, interview by John Burdan. A Troop, 1st Squadron, 4th Cavalry, Fort Riley, KS, 1 March 1994.

18. SFC William Molitor, interview by John Burdan, A Troop, 1st Squadron, 4th Cavalry, Fort Riley, KS, 17 March 1994.

Chapter 10

1. G2, Department of the Army VII-Corps, *The 100 Hour Ground War: The Failed Iraqi Plan*, After Action Report, 20 April 1991, Iraq; Richard M. Swain, *"Lucky War:" Third Army in Desert Storm* (Fort Leavenworth, KS: U.S. Army Command and General Staff College Press, 1994), 229.

2. Bourque, Jayhawk!, 205; Anthony H. Cordesman and Abraham R. Wagner, *The Lessons of Modern War, Vol IV: The Gulf War* (Boulder: Westview Press, 1996), 116.

3. Army, 1st Infantry Division (1ID) U.S. Department of the Army, 1st Brigade, *Daily Staff Journal, 1st Brigade, 1st Infantry Division, Operations and Intelligence Net (24 Feb 91)*; 1st Squadron 4th Cavalry, *Daily Staff Journal, Tactical Operation Center: 0500 24 February to 1700 24 February 1991.*

4. 1st Infantry Division, 1st Brigade, *Daily Staff Journal(24 Feb 91)*; *1st Brigade, 1st Infantry Division, Operations and Intelligence Net (24 Feb 91).*

5. Tedesco interview, 9 January 2000.

6. *1st Brigade, 1st Infantry Division, Operations and Intelligence Net (24 Feb 91)*; Parkey interview, 1 March 1994.

7. Bills interview, 26 August 1995.

8. Burdan notes.

9. (1ID) U.S. Department of the Army, *Daily Staff Journal, 1st Brigade, 1st Infantry Division, Operations and Intelligence Net (24 Feb 91)*; 1-4 Cav, *Daily Staff Journal 050024 February to 1700 24 February.*

10. *Daily Staff Journal 050024 February to 1700 24 February.*

11. *1st Brigade, 1st Infantry Division, Operations and Intelligence Net (24 Feb 91)*; Lon E. Maggart and Gregory Fontenot, "Breaching Operations: Implications for Battle Command and Battle Space," *Military Review* 74, no. 2 (February 1994): 25, 31.

12. *Daily Staff Journal 050024 February to 1700 24 February.* Phase 2 was originally scheduled for the next day and involved the destruction of the Iraqi 26th IN division.

13. *1st Brigade, 1st Infantry Division, Operations and Intelligence Net (24 Feb 91)*; CPT Douglas Morrison, interview by John Burdan. HHT, 1st Squadron, 4th Cavalry, Fort Leavenworth, KS, 21 April 1994.

14. Stephen Gruenig, interview by John Burdan. C Troop, 1st Squadron, 4th Cavalry, Fort Riley, KS, 15 April 1994; *Daily Staff Journal, 1st Brigade, 1st Infantry Division, Operations and Intelligence Net (24 Feb 91).*

15. Bills interview, 26 August 1995.

16. (1ID) U.S. Department of the Army, *Daily Staff Journal, 1st Brigade, 1st Infantry Division, Operations and Intelligence Net (24 Feb 91)*; See Bourque, *Jayhawk!*, 252–59, for details on chain of command decisions at Army and Central Command headquarters.

17. *1st Brigade, 1st Infantry Division, Operations and Intelligence Net (24 Feb 91)*; United States Army Intelligence and Threat Analysis Center, *How They Fight, DESERT SHIELD, Order of Battle Handbook, September 1990*; *Daily Staff Journal 050024 February to 1700 24 February*; Gruenig interview, 15 April 1994.

18. Because of success on the eastern flank of the coalition's attack, the coalition commander, General H. Norman Schwartzkopf, asked if Lieutenant General Yeosock's two army corps could advance earlier. The answer was yes. The waiting soldiers had little idea that the Commander of Central Command was trying to synchronize a complex combined attack.

19. *1st Brigade, 1st Infantry Division, Operations and Intelligence Net (24 Feb 91)*; Bourque, 214-19; *Daily Staff Journal 050024 February to 1700 24 February*.

20. Gruenig interview, 15 April 1994; *1st Brigade, 1st Infantry Tactical Command Post (24 Feb 91)*.

21. Maggart and Fontenot, 31; Bourque notes.

22. Robert H. Scales, *Certain Victory: The U.S. Army in the Gulf War* (Fort Leavenworth, KS: U.S. Army Command and General Staff College Press, 1994); Maggart and Fontenot, 27–31.

23. *1st Brigade, 1st Infantry Division, Operations and Intelligence Net (24 Feb 91)*; Gregory Fontenot, "The 'Dreadnoughts' Rip the Saddam Line," *Army* 42, no. 1 (January 1992): 34–35; David Gross, "History of 37th Armor on Operation Desert Storm," (1992), 92–202; Jim Tice, "'Coming Through,' The Big Red Raid," *Army Times*, 26 August 1991, 20.

24. Gregory R. Fontenot, interview by Robert Cook. 2nd Battalion, 34th Armor, 1st Brigade, 1st Infantry Division, tape recording, Fort Riley, KS, 29 March 1991; COL Anthony Moreno, interview by Thomas A. Popa. 2nd Brigade, 1st Infantry Division, tape recording, Fort Riley, KS, 26 July 1991; Atkinson, *Crusade*, 397.

25. *Daily Staff Journal 050024 February to 1700 24 February*; SFC William A. Ball, interview by John Burdan. HHT, 1st Squadron, 4th Cavalry, tape recording, Fort Riley, KS, 12 August 1995; Parkey interview, 1 March 1994.

26. Ball interview, 12 August 1995.

27. SFC William Molitor, Interview by John Burdan. A Troop, 1st

Squadron, 4th Cavalry (#4), Tape recording, Fort Leavenworth, KS, 6 April 1994.

28. Bills interview, 26 August 1995.

29. Burdan notes.

30. Burdan notes. Reconstructing such incidents after a battle is difficult. The squadron command post was moving forward at the time, and many orders and transmissions are not recorded.

31. Swain, 236.

32. Department of the Army, VII Corps, *Commander's SITREP #38 (232100Z-242100Z Feb 91)*; LTG Frederick M. Jr. Franks, Interview by Peter Kindsvatter, VII Corps Command (#3); Ground War, Historical Office U.S. Army Training and Doctrine Command, Corps Tac, Iraq 11 April 1991; MG Thomas Rhame, Interview by Thomas A. Popa, 1st Infantry Division Command, Desert Storm Oral History Collection, Fort Riley, KS, 26 July 1991.

33. Maggart and Fontenot: 33; 1LT Matt Vanderfeltz, interview by John Burdan. Support Platoon 1st Squadron, 4th Cavalry, Tape Recording, Ft. Leavenworth, KS, 9 January 2000; Bills interview, 29 August 1995.

34. Parkey interview, 1 March 1994.

35. *1st Brigade, 1st Infantry Division, Operations and Intelligence Net (24 Feb 91)*; Corps Commanders SITREP #38; 1st Infantry Division, *Chronological Summary of Events*, 26 March 1991.

36. Burdan notes; Philbrick interview, 12 February 1994.

37. Molitor interview, 6 April 1994 .

38. Ibid.

39. Bills interview, 29 August 1995.

40. Burdan notes.

41. VII Corps Headquarters, *Daily Staff Journal, VII Corps Tactical Command Post (25 Feb 1991)*, Army, 25 February 1991; Molitor interview, 6 April 1994; Burdan notes.

42. Burdan notes.

43. David Shade, "Tactical Intelligence in the Devil Brigade Attack," in *1st Brigade Desert Shield/Storm History*, ed. James Stockmoe (Fort Riley, KS: 1st Brigade, First Infantry Division, 1992), 49.

44. Parkey interview, 1 March 1994.

45. 1LT Matt Vanderfeltz, Interview by John Burdan. HHT 1st Squadron, 4th Cavalry, tape recording, Fort Leavenworth, KS, 11 December 1999.

46. Maggart and Fontenot, 33; Army, Department of the Army VII-

Corps, *Commander's SITREP (Combat) #39 (242100Z-252100Z Feb 91)*, VII Corps After Action Report, 25 February 1991, Saudi Arabia.

Chapter 11

1. For details of this engagement see Michael Krause, "The Battle of 73 Easting, 26 February 1991: A Historical Introduction to a Simulation" (Washington, DC, 1991). Bourque, *Jayhawk!*, 338–40.

2. Department of the Army, VII-Corps, *FRAGO 140-91 On Order, VII Corps Attacks to Penetrate and envelope Iraqi Defenses*, 25 February 1991; VII-Corps, *FRAGPLAN 7 w/Change 1*, 20 February 1991; 1st Infantry Division *Daily Staff Journal, 1st Infantry Tactical Command Post (26 Feb 91)*, Daily Staff Journal, entries 24, 29, 30.

3. VII-Corps, *FRAGPLAN 7 w/Change 1*; Department of the Army, 7th Engineer Brigade, *VII Corps Iraqi Material Denial Mission (TF Demo)*, 21 April, 1991; G2, Department of the Army VII-Corps, *The 100 Hour Ground War: The Failed Iraqi Plan*, After Action Report, 20 April 1991.

4. Squadron Tactical Command Post, *Daily Staff Journal, Tactical Operation Center: 0500 25 February to 1800 25 February 1991*, 25 February 1991, U.S. Armed Service Center for Research of Unit Records. 1st Infantry Division (1ID)1st Brigade, "S-2 Intelligence Log Summary, 21 February–3 March 1991," in *1st Brigade, 1st Infantry Division: Desert Shield/Storm History*, ed. CPT Jim Stockmoe (Fort Riley, KS: 1st Brigade, 1991), 194; Burdan Notes.

5. Burdan notes.

6. Burdan notes.

7. 1st Brigade, 1st Infantry Division, "S-2 Intelligence Log Summary, 21 February–3 March 1991," 223.

8. Burdan notes.

9. CPT Michael A. Bills, interview by John Burdan. B Troop, 1st Squadron, 4th Cavalry, Fort Leavenworth, KS, 25 May 1996.

10. Wimbish interview, 28 September 1993; Palmieri interview, 25 January 1994; Wilson interview, 28 July 1991.

11. Ball interview, 12 August 1995.

12. (1ID) 1st Brigade, "S-2 Intelligence Log Summary, 21 February - 3 March 1991," 227.

13. Wimbish interview, 28 September 1993; 1st Brigade, "S-2 Intelligence Log Summary, 21 February–3 March 1991," 227.

14. CPT Christopher R. Philbrick, interview by John Burdan, Aviation, 1st Squadron, 4th Cavalry, 12 March 1994; Burdan notes.

15. Throughout the Cold War, the historic 2nd Cavalry Regiment was

referred to as the 2nd Armored Cavalry Regiment, or 2nd ACR, in reference to its complement of tanks, infantry fighting vehicles, and self-propelled artillery. Its honorific name was the 2nd Dragoons, referring to it original configuration in the 1840s. In this account, 2nd Cavalry and 2nd ACR are used interchangeably.

16. 1st Squadron 4th Cavalry, "Riders on the Storm: A narrative history of the 1-4 Cav's campaign in Iraq and Kuwait-24 January-March 1991)," *Armor* 100, no. 100 (May–June 1991): 15; Wilson interview, 28 July 1991; Philbrick interview, 12 March 1994.

17. 2nd ACR Operations Summary; 1st Infantry Division TAC Journal, 26 February 1991, entry 43. Burdan notes. The "casting" was the vertical line on the map that signified east-west movement. The 2nd Cavalry was in the process of fighting a battle along the "73 Easting," so the contact points were about ten kilometers behind.

18. Department of the Army, *Field Manual 71-100, Division Operations* (June 1990), 6-17 to 6-18; Department of the Army, *Field Manual 100-15, Corps Operations* (September 1989), 7-15 to 7-16.

19. VII Corps TAC Journal, 26 February 1991, entry 8; Wilson interview, 28 July 1991; Rhame interview, July 1991.

20. Details of this doctrine are described in Department of the Army, *FM 71-100 Division Operations*, 1990, 6-17.

21. Maggart, "A Leap of Faith," 25.

22. Bills interview, 25 May 1996.

23. Gregory Fontenot, "Fright Night: Task Force 2/34 Armor," *Military Review* (January 1993), 42.

24. Vogel, "Hell Night," 15.

25. Maggart, "A Leap of Faith," 27; Fontenot, "Fright Night," 44.

26. Vogel, "A Swift Kick," 61.

27. Rhame interview, July 1991; Vogel, "Hell Night," 15; Maggart, "A Leap of Faith," 27.

28. See Stephen A. Bourque, "Correcting Myths about the Persian Gulf War: The Last Stand of the Tawakalna," *The Middle East Journal* 51, no. 4 (Autumn 1997), for details on this battle.

29. 1st Infantry Division Commander's Report (26 February 1991); 1st Infantry Division TAC Journal, 26 February 1991, entry 53.

30. VII Corps FRAGO 144-91 (26 February 1991).

31. Each tank and mechanized infantry battalion contained a Bradley-mounted scout platoon.

32. Maggart, "A Leap of Faith," 27; "The Centurions on Operation

Desert Storm," in Jim Stockmoe, ed., *1st Brigade, 1st Infantry Division, Desert Shield/Storm History* (Fort Riley, KS: 1st Brigade, 1st Infantry Division, 1991), 68.

33. Team C had two tank platoons and one mechanized infantry platoon. Team D had two mechanized infantry platoons and one tank platoon.

34. Robert A. Burns and Robert P. Harn Jr., interview by Robert Cook, 28 March 1991, US Army Center for Military History; Fontenot, "Fright Night," 45.

35. Fontenot, "Fright Night," 45.

36. Maggart, "A Leap of Faith," 28.

37. John S. Brown, "Desert Reckoning: Historical Continuities and the Battle for Norfolk, 1991" (paper, Naval War College, 1992), 3.

38. Vogel, "Hell Night," 15.

39. Brown, "Desert Reckoning," 4–5.

40. Ibid, 18–19.

41. Ibid.

42. VII Corps TOC Journal G3-Operations, 26 February 1991, entry 28; Tom Donnley, "The General's War," *Army Times* (2 March 1992), 16. Both Generals Powell and Schwarzkopf suggest in their memoirs that they had little idea of the intensity of the unit fight in the VII Corps sector (Powell, *My American Journey*, 504; Schwarzkopf, *It Doesn't Take a Hero*, 540).

43. Vogel, "Hell Night," 18.

44. VII Corps G3 Operations, Staff Journal, 27 February 1991, entry 3.

45. Maggart, "A Leap of Faith," 28.

46. Scales, *Certain Victory*, 291; Fontenot, "Fright Night," 47.

47. Bills interview, 25 May 1996; Pope interview, 5 October 1993.

48. Stephen A. Bourque, *Jayhawk! The VII Corps in the Persian Gulf War* (Washington, DC: U.S. Army Center of Military History, 2002), 339. It was a confusing melee in which, in addition to Iraqi fire, the squadron's vehicles were hit by friendly vehicles from at least two units. Nine Bradleys were damaged, two soldiers killed, and twelve wounded.

49. The 4-7 Cavalry screening the 3rd Armored Division was using a 1:100,000 map. The 1-4 Cavalry used 1:250,000 maps. See CPT Douglas Morrison, Interview by John Burdan, HHT, 1st Squadron, 4th Cavalry, Fort Leavenworth, KS, 17 May 1994; Wilson interview, 28 July 1991; Wimbish interview, 28 September 1993.

50. Bills interview, 25 May 1996.

51. Bills interview, 25 May 1996; Pope interview, 5 October 1993; Burdan notes.

52. Burdan notes.

53. Burdan notes; Department of the Army, VII-Corps, *FRAGO 129-91 VII Corps conducts Obstacle Crossing*, 20 February 1991.

54. Bills interview, 25 May 1996.

55. Burdan notes.

56. Burdan notes.

57. Wilson interview, 25 July 1991; Burdan notes.

58. Burdan personally directed one of the B Troop tanks to the T-72 they had earlier observed; it was only 50 feet away from the M1 that destroyed it.

59. Bills interview, 25 May 1996; Burdan notes.

60. CPT Douglas Morrison, Interview by John Burdan, HHT, 1st Squadron, 4th Cavalry, tape Recording, Fort Leavenworth, KS, 21 April 1994; Bills interview, 25 May 1996.

61. "Riders on the Storm," 16.

62. Krause, Battle of 73 Easting; 1st Brigade, 1st Infantry Division, *Staff Duty Log*, 27 April 1991.

63. Wilson interview, 28 July 1991; Bills interview, 25 May 1996; Burdan notes.

64. "Riders on the Storm," 16; Wilson interview; Burdan notes.

65. 1st Squadron 4th Cavalry, Daily Staff Journal, Tactical Operation Center: 1400 28 February to 0500 1 March 1991; Pope interview, 5 October 1993.

66. Mitch Osburn, Interview by John Burdan, A Troop, 1st Squadron, 4th Cavalry, Ft. Riley, KS 3 September 1994; Palmieri interview, 25 January 1994.

67. CW2 Gary Notestine and CW3 Wayne Grimes, Interview by John Burdan, D and C Troops, 1st Squadron, 4th Cavalry, 1st Infantry Division, Fort Leavenworth, KS, 18 December 1993; Pope interview, 5 October 1993.

68. Palmieri interview, January 1994; Pope interview, 5 October 1993.

69. Bills interview, 25 May 1996.

70. Bills interview, 25 May 1996; "Riders on the Storm," 16.

71. Burdan notes.

72. Morrison interview, 21 April 1994; 1st Squadron 4th Cavalry, Daily Staff Journal, Tactical Operation Center: 1400 28 February to 0500 1 March 1991; "Riders on the Storm," 16; Wilson interview; VII-

Corps, *FRAGO 129-91 VII Corps conducts Obstacle Crossing*. Wilson believes that the squadron destroyed about 23 tanks, 25 APCs, and captured over 100 POWs.

Chapter 12

1. Portions of this chapter appeared previously as "A Nervous Night on the Basra Road" in *MHQ: The Quarterly Journal of Military History* 12, no. 1(Autumn 1999), 88–101.

2. Williamson Murry, *Air War in the Persian Gulf* (Baltimore: The Nautical & Aviation Publishing Company of America, 1996), 288–89; United States, Department of Defense, *Conduct of the Persian Gulf War: Final Report to Congress* (Washington, D.C: GPO, 1992), 276.

3. U.S. Third Army, Tactical Command Post (TAC), G3 Fires, Staff Journal, 27 February 1991; Michael R. Gordon and Bernard E. Trainor, *The Generals' War: The Inside Story of the Conflict in the Gulf* (Boston: Little, Brown and Company, 1995), 412–13; Frederick M. Franks Jr., Interview by Mace Carpenter, tape recording, 23 March 1994, School of Advanced Airpower Studies, Air University, Maxwell Air Force Base, AL; Note from Richard Swain to author, 4 June 2004. This is an extremely confusing action that is beyond the scope of this narrative.

4. USARCENT, Desert Storm Intelligence Summary, briefing slide: "Basra Box, G+5", Swain Papers, Combined Arms Center Historical Archives, Fort Leavenworth, KS.

5. Stephen A. Bourque, "Correcting Myths about the Persian Gulf War: the Last Stand of the Tawakalna," *Middle East Journal*, 51 (Autumn 1997): 572–76.

6. 1st Infantry Division TAC, Staff Journal, 27 Feb. 91, entries 52, 54, 59, 61.

7. CPT Michael A. Bills, interview by John Burdan, B Troop, 1st Squadron, 4th Cavalry, 3 February 1996.

8. 1-4 Cavalry Operations Staff, "Riders on the Storm," *Armor* 100 (May 1991): 17.

9. Burdan, Personal Notes; 1-4 Cavalry Operations Staff, "Riders on the Storm," 17.

10. Bills interview, 3 February 1996.

11. 1-4 Cavalry Operations Staff, "Riders on the Storm," 17; Burdan, Personal Notes.

12. Rhame interview, 26 July 1991; Lon E. Maggart, "A Leap of Faith," *Armor* 101 (January-February 1992): 30; 1-4 Cavalry Operations Staff, "Riders on the Storm," 17.

13. 1-4 Cavalry Operations Staff, "Riders on the Storm," 17.

14. Franks Interview, 12 April 1991; Wilson interview, 28 July 1991.

15. Maggart, "Leap of Faith," 30; Steve Vogel, "Hell Night," *Army Times* (October 7, 1991): 18, 24.

16. Rhame Interview, 26 July 1991; and, Maggart, Leap of Faith," 30; Stephen A. Bourque, Personal Notes.

17. John Burdan, Personal Notes.

18. Bills interview, 3 February 1996.

19. John Burdan, Personal Notes; Wilson interview, 28 July 1991.

20. 1-4 Cavalry Operations Staff, "Riders on the Storm," 17; Wimbish interview, 28 September 1993.

21. Message from Douglas Morrison to John Burdan, 12 March 1998.

22. Robert Wilson, Note to Stephen Bourque, 3 April 1998.

23. John Burdan, Personal Notes; 1-4 Cavalry Operations Staff, "Riders on the Storm," 17.

24. Bills interview, 3 February 1996; Burdan, Personal Notes; Wilson, "Tanks in the Division Cavalry Squadron," 10.

25. Phone interview between John Burdan and Roy Peters, 7 Oct 2006; Molitor interview, 27 July 1994.

26. Wilson, Note to Author, 3 April 1998; Wilson, "Tanks in the Division Cavalry Squadron," 10.

27. William Molitor, A Troop, 1st Squadron, 4th Cavalry, interview by John Burdan, Fort Leavenworth, KS, 27 July 1994.

28. Wilson, "Tanks in the Division Cavalry Squadron," 10; Osburn interview, 3 September 1994; Pope interview, 5 October 1993.

29. Molitor interview, 27 July 1994.

30. John Burdan, Personal Notes.

31. Osborn interview, 3 September 1994.

32. Wilson, "Tanks in the Division Cavalry Squadron," 10; 1-4 Cavalry Operations Staff, "Riders on the Storm," 18.

33. Wimbish interview, 28 September 1993; John Burdan, Personal Notes.

34. Ibid.

35. The forward support element consisted of fuel, ammunition, food, maintenance, and medical support vehicles. In most cases, these are soft-skinned vehicles devoid of any significant defensive firepower. Obviously, this vehicle convoy is a tempting target.

36. Bills interview, 3 February 1996; Burdan, Personal Notes; Douglas

Morrison, HHT, 1st Squadron, 4th Cavalry, interview with John Burdan, 17 May 1994, Fort Leavenworth, KS.

37. Bills interview, 3 February 1996; Burdan, Personal Notes; Morrison interview, 17 May 1994.

38. Wilson interview, 28 July 1991.

39. Lou Parker, informal interview with John Burdan, Fort Hood TX, 27 August 1997; Burdan, Personal Notes.

40. Pope interview, 5 October 1993.

41. Kindsvatter, "Notes and Observations During Operation Desert Storm."

42. Stanley F. Cherrie, interview by Richard Swain, 12 September 1991, Swain papers; 1st Infantry Division TAC, Staff Journal, 27 February. 1991, entry 9; VII Corps, G-3 Operations, Staff Journal, 27 February 1991, entry 38, 41, 51; Tom Clancy and Frederick Franks, Jr, *Into the Storm: A Study in Command* (New York: G. P. Putnam's Sons, 1997), 429–30. It is important to keep in mind the many tasks this small staff was simultaneously trying to coordinate. These included the passage of lines of the 1st Cavalry Division through the left flank of the 1st Armored Division, movement of the 2nd Cavalry into position where it could support the 1st Infantry Division, and limiting the movement of the 3rd Armored Division. A few hours later, 3rd Army sent VII Corps the initial order for a theater-wide suspension of offensive action against the Iraqi armed forces. It had only recently moved into position and everyone was exhausted. This small command post's capabilities were now stretched to the limit.

43. Wimbish interview, 28 September 1993; Burdan, Personal Notes.

44. Wilson, "Tanks in the Division Cavalry Squadron," 10; 1-4 Cavalry Operations Staff, "Riders on the Storm," 18. Wilson asked for a tank company, an infantry company, and artillery support. The 1st Infantry Division's TAC log does not indicate that they ever received such a request from 2nd Brigade.

45. 1st Infantry Division TAC, Staff Journal, 27 February. 1991, entry 8. There are several separate channels of communication within a modern combat division. One of those is the fire-support channel. Through these radio frequencies, field artillery officers can exchange target information and request field artillery support. Apparently, the squadron's fire support officer did his job and sent an accurate list of his unit's locations. This information then worked its way up the fire-support channel to the VII Corps TAC. There, an operations officer compared notes with a fire-support officer and noted the 1st Infantry Division unit on the Basra Highway.

46. 1st Infantry Division TAC, Staff Journal, 27 February 1991, entry 10.

47. 1st Infantry Division TAC, Staff Journal, 28 February 1991, entry 1, 2; Wimbish interview, 28 September 1993.

48. Anthony Moreno, interview by Thomas A. Popa, Fort Riley, KS, 26 July 1991, Center for Military History.

49. Rhame interview, 26 July 1991.

50. 1-4 Cavalry Operations Staff, "Riders on the Storm," 17–18; Rhame Interview, 26 July 1991; Franks Interview, 12 April 1991. Poor staff work at this stage of the operation reflects the exhaustion of the personnel in each of the command posts. The 1st Infantry Division's TAC, for example, had been controlling the division's operations, with only marginal help from the division's small Jump Tactical Operations Center, for almost four days. Most of the division's main command post was still on the move in the middle of Iraq. It would not be set up and operational until six hours after the cease-fire on 28 February.

51. Molitor interview, 27 July 1994.

52. Bills interview, 3 February 1996.

53. Ball interview, 12 August 1995.

54. Bills interview, 3 February 1996.

55. Parker interview, 27 August 1997.

56. Wilson, Note to Author, 3 April 1998.

57. Wilson, "Tanks in the Division Cavalry Squadron," 10.

58. David Palmieri, A Troop, 1st Squadron, 4th Cavalry, interview by John Burdan, Fort Riley KS, 20 August 1994.

59. Gary Parkey, interview by John Burdan Fort Riley, KS, 30 September 1995.

60. Bills interview, 3 February 1996.

61. Parker interview, 12 August 1997.

62. Don Wehage, interview by John Burdan, Fort Riley KS, 25 January 1994; Molitor interview, 27 July 1994.

63. Molitor interview, 27 July 1994.

64. CPT Lou Parker, unpublished manuscript on his recollections as a chaplain during the 1991 Persian Gulf War.

65. Burdan, Personal Notes; 1st Infantry Division TAC, Staff Journal, 27 February 1991, entries 19, 21,26, 27, 28.

66. Burdan, Personal Notes.

67. Parker manuscript.

68. Bills interview, 3 February 1991.

69. Burdan, Personal Notes.

Chapter 13

1. 1st Squadron 4th Cavalry, "Riders on the Storm," 19; 1st Infantry Division, *Daily Staff Journal, Tactical Command Post (28 Feb 91)*.

2. Vogel, "Hell Night," 69.

3. Bills interview, 25 May 1996.

4. Ball interview, 12 August 1995.

5. Philbrick interview, 16 April 1994.

6. CW3 Kirk Waymire, interview by John Burdan, C Troop, 1st Squadron, 4th Cavalry, 1st Infantry Division(#1), Ft. Leavenworth, KS, 1 March 1994. Tape recording.

7. Parkey interview, 30 September 1995.

8. Bills interview, 25 May 1996.

9. Burdan notes.

10. Nickname for the division's main command post.

11. Bourque notes.

12. H. Norman Schwarzkopf and Peter Petre, *It Doesn't Take a Hero* (New York: Bantam Books, 1992), 549.

13. Richard M. Swain, *"Lucky War:" Third Army in Desert Storm* (Fort Leavenworth, KS: U.S. Army Command and General Staff College Press, 1994), 293; LTG John J. Yeosock, Interview by Richard Swain, Third Army Operations, Tape recording, Ft. McPherson, GA, 29 June 1991.

14. Jason K. Kamiya, ed., *A History of the 24th Mechanized Infantry Division Combat Team During Operation Desert Storm* (Fort Stewart, GA: 24th Infantry Division, 1991), 29.

15. Yeosock interview, 29 June 1991.

16. Schwarzkopf and Petre, 549–50.

17. COL Stanley F. Cherrie, Interview by Richard Swain, VII Corps G3, Tape Recording, Fort Leavenworth: Combined Arms Center, Fort Leavenworth, KS, 12 September 1991.

18. VII Corps, *Daily Staff Journal, VII Corps Tactical Command Post (1 March 1991)*.

19. 1st Infantry Division, *Daily Staff Journal, Tactical Command Post (28 Feb 91)*.

20. Bourque notes, 28 February–1 March 1991. Bourque was the staff officer on duty that night.

21. Rhame interview, 26 July 1991; VII Corps, *Daily Staff Journal, VII Corps Tactical Command Post (1 March 1991)*.

22. VII Corps, *Daily Staff Journal, VII Corps Tactical Command Post (1 March 1991)*.

23. 1st Infantry Division, *Daily Staff Journal, Tactical Command Post (28 Feb 91)*.

24. Burdan notes; 1st Infantry Division, *Daily Staff Journal, Tactical Command Post (28 Feb 91)*.]

25. VII Corps, *Daily Staff Journal, VII Corps Tactical Command Post (1 March 1991)*.

26. BG Bob Wilson, "Some comments ref. Safwan," Memo to author, 8 May 1997, 1.

27. 1st Squadron 4th Cavalry, "Riders on the Storm:" 19.

28. Traveling overwatch is a movement technique used when contact with enemy forces is possible. The trailing element moves at variable speeds and may pause for short periods to cover, or overwatch, the lead element. See Department of the Army (DA), "Fm 101-5-1 Operational Terms and Graphics" (1997), 1-157.

29. Wilson, 8 May 1997, 2.

30. 1st Squadron 4th Cavalry, "Riders on the Storm:" 19.

31. Burdan and Bourque notes.

32. 1st Infantry Division, *Daily Staff Journal, Main Command Post, G3 Operations, 1 Mar 91*; 1st Squadron 4th Cavalry, "Riders on the Storm," 19.

33. Burdan notes.

34. 1st Infantry Division, *Daily Staff Journal, Main Command Post, G3 Operations, 1 Mar 91*; Rhame interview, 26 July 1991.

35. BG Robert Wilson, Note to Author, 10 July 1997.

36. Burdan memo, 19 March 1997.

37. 1st Infantry Division, *Daily Staff Journal, Main Command Post, G3 Operations, 1 Mar 91*.

38. Wilson, 8 May 1997, 2–3.

39. Wilson, 8 May 1997, 3–4.

40. Burdan, 19 March 1997.

41. 1st Infantry Division, *Daily Staff Journal, Main Command Post, G3 Operations, 1 Mar 91*; 1st Squadron 4th Cavalry, "Riders on the Storm," 20; Rhame interview; Burdan notes.

42. 1st Infantry Division, *Daily Staff Journal, Main Command Post, G3 Operations, 1 Mar 91*; Rhame interview, 26 July 1991.

43. 1st Squadron 4th Cavalry, "Riders on the Storm," 20; Swain, 297.

44. SFC Don Wehage, interview by John Burdan. A Troop, 1st Squadron, 4th Cavalry, 1st Infantry Division, Ft. Leavenworth, KS, 25 January 1994.

45. Burdan notes.

46. Bills interview, 25 May 1996; 1st Squadron 4th Cavalry, "Riders on the Storm," 20.

47. Bills interview, 25 May 1996.

48. Ibid.

49. Wilson, 8 May 1997, 4–5; Email message from Douglas Morrison to author, 24 March 2004, SUBJECT: Comments.

50. Email message from Douglas Morrison to author, 24 March 2004, SUBJECT: Comments.

51. 1st Infantry Division, *Daily Staff Journal, Main Command Post, G3 Operations, 1 Mar 91*; Bills interview, 25 May 1996; Pope interview, 5 October 1993; Burdan notes.

52. 1st Infantry Division, *Daily Staff Journal, Main Command Post, G3 Operations, 1 Mar 91*; 1st Squadron 4th Cavalry, *Daily Staff Journal, Tactical Operation Center: 0001 3 March to 0700 3 March 1991*; 1st Squadron 4th Cavalry (1-4Cav), *Daily Staff Journal, Tactical Operation Center: 0700 2 March to 2400 2 March 1991*; Peter S. Kindsvatter, "Notes and Operations: Operation Desert Storm" (VII Corps, 1991).

53. Bills interview, 25 May 1996.

54. Burdan notes; Tom Clancy and Jr. Frederick M. Franks, *Into the Storm: A Study in Command* (New York: G. P. Putnam's Sons, 1997), 463–70; Schwarzkopf and Petre, 559–64.

55. Burdan notes; Clancy and Franks, 463–70.

56. Burdan notes.

Chapter 14

1. Charles Lane Toomey, *XVIII Airborne Corps: From Planning to Victory* (Central Point, OR: Hellgate Press, 2004), 407–11.

2. XVIII Corps, *Daily Situation Report-022200Z Mar 91*; H. Norman Schwarzkopf and Peter Petre, *It Dosen't Take a Hero* (New York: Bantam Books, 1992), 564–65.

3. VII Corps, "VII Corps FRAGPLAN 8: Assumption of XVIII Airborne Corps Sector," 9 March 1991; VII Corps, "FRAGO 160-91 VII Corps relieves XVIII Airborne Corps in sector beginning 9 March,"

7 March 1991; Peter S. Kindsvatter, "VII Corps in the Gulf War: Post-Cease-Fire Operations," *Military Review* 72 (June 1992).

4. Anthony H. Cordesman and Abraham R. Wagner, *The Lessons of Modern War, Vol IV: The Gulf War* (Boulder: Westview Press, 1996), 961–62; Graham E. Fuller and Rend Rahim Francke, *The Arab Shi'a: The Forgotten Muslims* (New York: St. Martin's Press, 1999); Department of Defense, "Defense Department Briefing: March 5, 1991"; Ben Fenton, "The Gulf; Saddam's tanks move to quash Basra rebels," *The Daily Telegraph*, March 6, 1991; Tom Masland, "Danger for Saddam," *Newsweek, March 18, 1991*, 25; Helen Chapin Metz, *Iraq, a Country Study, Area Handbook Series* (Washington, D. C.: U. S. Government Printing Office, 1990), 95-97.

5. Cordesman and Wagner, *The Lessons of Modern War, Vol IV*; Army, Department of the Army VII-Corps, *Daily Staff Journal, VII Corps Tactical Command Post (4 March 1991)*, Daily Staff Journal, 4 March 1991, Fort Leavenworth, KS.

6. George Bush and Brent Scowcroft, *A World Transformed* (New York: Alfred A. Knopf, 1998), 488-492; Colin Powell and Joseph E. Perisco, *My American Journey* (New York: Ballantine Books, 1996), 516–17; H. Norman Schwarzkopf and Peter Petre, *It Doesn't Take a Hero*, 564–65 ; Cordesman, *After the Storm*, 445.

7. Burdan notes.

8. SFC William Molitor, Interview by John Burdan, A Troop, 1st Squadron, 4th Cavalry, Ft. Riley, KS, 28 July 1994.

9. Osburn interview, 3 September 1994.

10. Molitor interview, 28 July 1994. Although stories about Gulf War Syndrome continue, there is little evidence of any one overarching disease. No squadron soldiers have come forward with evidence of having Gulf War Syndrome. There are no credible studies to date that document any specific relation between service in the Persian Gulf and a soldier's health. However, the issue is still in dispute. Certainly no city health department would allow its citizens to work in the smoke and pollution conditions similar to those endured by the soldiers in March 1991. See http://www.gulf link.osd.mil/combined_analysis/index.htm

11. Burdan notes.

12. Bills interview, 25 May 1996.

13. Burdan notes.

14. Ibid.

15. Ball interview, 12 August 1995.

16. Gruenig interview, 15 April 1994.

17. Burdan notes.

18. Waymire interview, 22 December 1994; Marlin, "History of the 4th Battalion, 37th Armored Regiment in Operation Desert Shield/ Storm." 582–84.

19. Ibid.

20. Burdan notes; Ball interview, 12 August 1995; Tedesco interview, 29 June 1996.

21. Wehage interview, 25 January 1994.

Chapter 15

1. U. S Army Central Command (USARCENT) U.S. Department of the Army, *HQ USARCENT G3 Plans, Historical Narrative of Desert Shield, Desert Storm, Defense and Restoration of Kuwait, and Redeployment*, 6 April 1991.

2. 1st Squadron 4th Cavalry, *Daily Staff Journal, Tactical Operation Center: 0700 4 March to 0700 5 March 1991*; VII-Corps, *FRAGO 158-91 Cdr's intent is to begin to posture the corps to move out of Iraq within a period of 72 hours after receipt of execution orders*, 5 March 1991; VII Corps, Operational Orders and Plans, *FRAGO 161-91 Corps continues relief of XVII Airborne Corps*, 8 March 1991.

3. Burdan notes.

4. Ball interview, 12 August 1995.

5. Osburn interview, 3 September 1994.

6. 1LT David J. Palmieri, Interview by John Burdan, A Troop, 1st Squadron, 4th Cavalry, Fort Riley, KS, 20 August 1994.

7. Bills interview, 25 May 1996.

8. 1st Squadron 4th Cavalry, *Daily Staff Journal, Tactical Operation Center: 0001 28 March to 2400 28 March 1991*, 28 March 1991.

9. Gruenig interview, 15 April 1994; Osburn interview, 3 September 1994.

10. Debra L. Anderson, conversation with author, January 2004. Anderson supervised the preparation of the awards at division headquarters.

11. 1st Squadron 4th Cavalry, *Daily Staff Journal, Tactical Operation Center: 0001 To 2400 2 April 1991*.

12. VII Corps, *Commander's SITREP #80 (062100Z-072100Z APR 91)*, 7 April 1991.

13. Pope interview, 5 October 1993.

14. VII Corps, *Commander's SITREP #74 (312100Z MAR-012100Z APR 91)*, 1 April 1991.

15. Osburn interview, 3 September 1994.

16. Osburn interview, 3 September 1994; Bourque notes.

17. Burdan notes.

18. Palmieri interview, 20 August 1994.

19. Ibid.

20. Wehage interview 25 January 1994.

21. Pope interview, 5 October 1993.

22. Pope interview, 5 October 1993; Palmieri interview, 20 August 1994.

23. Pope interview, 5 October 1993.

24. Lt. George Caraballo, interview with John Burdan, B Troop, 1st Squadron, 4th Cavalry, 1 April 1997. According to the soldier who made this report, the Iraqi men had a habit of gathering whatever food was offered and eating it before the women and children. Needless to say, it was not a situation that endeared the men to the American soldiers.

25. Ibid.

26. Pope interview, 5 October 1993; Carabello interview, 1 April 1997.

27. Osburn interview, 3 September 1994; Carabello interview 1 April 1997.

28. Conversation between John Burdan and LT Palmieri, 20 Aug 1994, Ft Riley, KS.

Chapter 16

1. VII Corps Department of the Army, FRAGO 207-91, *Permanent cease-fire agreement*, 12 April 1991.

2. 1st Squadron 4th Cavalry, *Daily Staff Journal, Tactical Operation Center, 0100-2400 15 April 1991*.

3. Philbrick interview, 16 April 1994.

4. Osburn interview, 3 September 1994.

5. 1st Squadron, 4th Cavalry, *Daily Staff Journal, Tactical Operation Center, 0100-2400 16 April 1991*; Burdan notes.

6. 1st Squadron, 4th Cavalry, *Daily Staff Journal, Tactical Operation Center, 0100-2400 17 April 1991*.

7. Eric Esplund, Interview by John Burdan, S2, 1st Squadron, 4th Cavalry, Fort Leavenworth, KS, 23 December 1998.

8. Tedesco interview, 29 June 1996; VJ Tedesco, note to author, 23 March 2004, SUBJECT: Comments.

9. Esplund interview, 23 December 1998; Palmieri interview, 25 January 1994.

10. Bills interview, 25 May 1996.

11. Palmieri interview, 25 January 1994.

12. Ken Burns, *The Civil War* (Public Broadcasting Corporation, 1990); Oliver Wendell Holmes, An address delivered for Memorial Day, May 30, 1884, at Keene, NH, before John Sedgwick Post No. 4, Grand Army of the Republic.

Conclusion

1. Mark Bowden, *Black Hawk Down: A Story of Modern War* (New York: Penguin Books, 1999).

2. Anthony H. Cordesman, *The Iraq War: Strategy, Tactics and Military Lessons* (Washington, DC: Center for Strategic and International Studies, 2003), 351–53; Gregory Fontenot, E. J. Degen, David Tohn, *On Point: The United States Army in Operation Iraqi Freedom* (Fort Leavenworth, Combat Studies Institute Press, 2004), 123–31.

Glossary

1IDF	1st Infantry Division (Forward). Brigade Task Force from the 1st Infantry Division deployed to Göppingen, Germany, in the 1970s.
1LT	First Lieutenant
1SGT	First Sergeant. The senior noncommissioned officer in a company, battery, or troop.
2ACR	2nd Armored Cavalry or 2nd Cavalry. Nicknamed 2d Dragoons.
2LT	Second Lieutenant. Lowest ranking commissioned officer.
AA	Assembly area. An area in which a command is assembled preparatory to further action.
AH-1F Cobra	Vietnam-era attack helicopter.
AH-64A	Apache attack helicopter.
ALO	Air liaison officer. Air Force officer assigned to army units to assist in control of USAF aviation.
ALOC	Administrative-Logistics Center. Command post for the squadron's service support effort.
Aramco	Arab-American Oil Company.
AVIM	Aviation Intermediate Maintenance.

Basra Highway	Main road between Kuwait City and Basra, Iraq.
BDE	Brigade. Organization with several battalions and commanded by a colonel.
BDU	Battle Dress Uniform. Standard uniform of armed forces in Desert Storm. Standard colors were green and brown camouflage.
BG	Brigadier General. Usually an assistant division commander or corps principal staff officer.
Big Red One	Nickname for the 1st Infantry Division.
BMP	Soviet infantry fighting vehicle which was first introduced in the early 1960s.
BRDM	A Soviet armored reconnaissance vehicle.
CC	Combat Command. This is normally a brigade or larger element under the control on one of the assistant division commanders.
CENTCOM	United States Central Command. Commanded by General H. Norman Schwarzkopf during Desert Storm.
CFV	M3 Cavalry Fighting Vehicle. A modified version of the M2 Infantry Fighting Vehicle, carrying fewer troops and more ammunition. Both vehicles were also nicknamed the Bradley.
COL	Colonel. Commander of a brigade or senior staff officer on a division or corps staff.
Corps	Large combat organization consisting of several divisions and supporting units. Commanded by a lieutenant-general. In 1991, the VII Corps had five divisions, an armored cavalry regiment, an aviation brigade, a corps support command and other supporting units. Total strength of approximately 142,000

soldiers. Commanded by LTG Frederick M. Franks, Jr., during Desert Storm.

CP	(1) Command Post (2) Checkpoint. Imaginary location on the ground to help guide moving units. (3) Contact Point. Location where representatives from two or more units meet to coordinate activities.
CPT	Captain. Commander of a troop, company, or artillery battery.
CS	Combat support. Units such as military police and engineers that directly support the combat effort.
CSM	Command Sergeant Major. Senior noncommissioned officer from battalion through army.
CSS	Combat service support. Units that provide personnel, logistical, medical, and maintenance support.
CVC	Combat Vehicle Crew (Helmet). Nickname for helmet worn by tank and Bradley crewmen.
CWO	Chief Warrant Officer. Generally a pilot. May be in grade of WO 2, 3, or 4.
DISCOM	Division Support Command. Brigade-sized unit responsible for a division's supply and maintenance operations.
Division	In the 1990-era United States Army, the largest combined arms organization. Generally consisted of three maneuver brigades, an aviation brigade, an artillery brigade, and other combat support and combat service support troops. Approximately 20,000 soldiers. The 1st

	Infantry Division was commanded by MG Thomas G. Rhame during Desert Storm.
DSA	Division Support Area. Location of most of the division's logistics units, fuel, and ammunition.
DTAC	Division Tactical Command Post. A more mobile CP than the division's Main Command Post.
EPW	Enemy Prisoner of War.
FAA	Forward assembly area. A VII Corps term used to describe locations west of the Wadi al Batin in preparation for the corps attack.
FIST	Fire Support Team. Coordinates artillery fire at the company and troop level.
FIST-V	Fire Support vehicle. It was a modified M3.
FRAGO	Fragmentary order. A change to the standing operation order or plan.
FSE	Fire Support Element. Coordinates artillery and aviation fires for the squadron or battalion.
GP	General Purpose, as in "GP medium tent."
GPS	Global Positioning System.
GSR	Ground Surveillance Radar.
HEAT	High Explosive Antitank. An explosive munition designed to penetrate an armored vehicle by chemical (explosive) energy.
HEMTT	Heavy Expanded Mobility Tactical Truck. Large trucks that could be configured to carry fuel, cargo, or ammunition.
HETS	Heavy Equipment Transporter System. Truck designed to carry tanks and other large vehicles.

HHT	Headquarters and Headquarters Troop. Command for the squadron staff and all assigned supporting organizations.
HMMWV	High-mobility, multipurpose wheeled vehicle, often called a "Humvee."
HQ	Headquarters.
LOGBASE	Logistics Base. A location that contains a number of fuel, maintenance, supply, ammunition, and other supporting units.
LRSD	Long Range Surveillance Detachment. A dismounted information gathering unit.
LRSU	Long Range Surveillance Unit. This is a corps-level unit.
LTC	Lieutenant Colonel. Commander of a battalion or squadron.
LTG	Lieutenant General. Usually a corps commander.
M1A1 Abrams	The tank used by the army during Operations Desert Storm and Shield.
M3A2 Bradley	The cavalry fighting vehicle (CFV) used by 1-4≠ Cav during Operations Desert Storm and Shield.
M577	An enlarged version of the M113 Armored Personnel Carrier, used by mobile command posts.
MAJ	Major. Usually an officer on a staff.
MDL	Military demarcation line.
MG	Major General. Commander of a division.
milvan	Military van. Essentially a large shipping container that fits on the back of a flat-bed truck.
MOPP	Mission Oriented Protective Posture. An alert

	system that specifies what level of protective clothing and equipment soldiers should wear to counter a chemical, biological, or radioactive threat.
MP	Military Police.
MRE	Meals Ready to Eat. Packaged replacement for Vietnam-era C Rations.
MSG	Master Sergeant. Senior sergeant, equivelant in grade to a First Sergeant.
MTOE	Modified Table of Organization and Equipment. Document used to authorize requesting soldiers and equipment.
OBJ	Objective. An area that is the focus of an attack.
OH-58C Kiowa	Scout or reconnaissance helicopter.
OH-58D Kiowa	A specially modified OH-58 that has a greatly increased fire support capability.
OP	Observation Post. A location manned by troops in combat vehicles or dismounted that is designed to observe a specified area for enemy activity.
OPFOR	Slang for opposing force.
OPORD	Operation order. Document prepared by a headquarters to guide all combat, combat support, and combat service support activities.
PL	Phase Line. A line drawn on a map that helps to control unit movement.
POM	Preparation for Overseas Movement. A series of personal and administrative stations a soldier visits before deploying overseas.
Quarter Horse	Nickname for the 1st Squadron, 4th Cavalry.

ROTC	Reserve Officer Training Corps.
RPV	Remotely Piloted Vehicle. Small camera-equipped aircraft, controlled from a remote station, for reconnaissance purposes.
S1/G1	Personnel officer or staff section. Responsible for maintaining and accounting for all unit personnel. G1 at division or corps.
S2/G2	Intelligence officer or staff section. Responsible for supervising the collection and processing of enemy information. G2 at division or corps.
S3/G3	Battalion or brigade operations officer or staff section. Responsible for preparing and supervising the execution of combat operations. G3 at division or corps.
S4/G4	Supply and logistics officer or staff section. Responsible for supervising all supply and maintenance actions. G4 at division or corps.
SCO	Squadron Commanding Officer.
SFC	Sergeant First Class. Rank of most of the Platoon Sergeants.
SGM	Sergeant Major. Senior noncommissioned officer on a staff.
SGT	Sergeant.
SPC	Specialist (E4).
Squadron	Traditional name given to a cavalry unit of battalion size.
SSG	Staff Sergeant. Usually a squad leader or vehicle commander.
SWT	Scout Weapons-Team. An OH-58 Kiowa scout helicopter and one or more AH-1 Cobra Attack helicopters.

T-72	A late-model Soviet tank.
TA-50	Table of Authorization #50. Slang for field gear.
TAA	Tactical assembly area. A VII Corps term used to describe locations east of the Wadi al Batin and also areas south of the Saudi-Iraqi border during redeployment.
TACSOP	Tactical Standard Operating Procedures. Manual designed to standardize routine activities within the unit.
Tapline	Trans-American Pipeline Company. Also the name of the main north-west highway in Saudi Arabia.
TF	Task Force. This is a battalion-size element that normally has a mix of armor and infantry companies. The term was also used to denote a specially organized brigade-size element.
TOC	Tactical Operations Center. Collection of tracked and wheeled vehicles that coordinate operations for the commander.
Troop	Traditional name given to a company-sized cavalry unit.
UH-1	A Vietnam-era utility helicopter. One was organic to the squadron.
WO	Warrant Officer.
XO	Executive officer. Principal assistant to the commander from company through brigade.

Bibliography

For such a short conflict, the 1991 Persian Gulf War generated an amazing array of books and articles. In addition, this was the first war supported by computers, electronic mail, and copy machines, resulting in the production of many briefing charts, after-action reports, and government documents generated from the field. This bibliography represents only a fraction of the information available, but should assist future scholars in refining their own research plans.

Government Documents
Each command that participated on Operation Desert Storm generated a large number of diverse documents. Originally, most of these documents were part of the VII Corps After Action Report archived at Fort Leavenworth, Kansas. Today, many are also found on the Internet and are beginning to arrive for processing at the National Archives. These documents consist of daily staff journals, operation orders, fragmentary orders, after-action reports, and briefing slides. Specific citations are contained in the notes.

The United States Army of 1991 was just completing a revolution in military art that began in the 1970s. The culmination of this thought was *Field Manual 100-5, Operations (May 1986)*. It was probably one of the most staffed, examined, and used doctrinal publications of all time and generally reflects the thinking of the army in the field. Only recently published was *Field Manual 71-100, Division Operations (June 1990)*. In general, the pace of doctrinal development at the tactical level had placed a variety of old manuals and a variety of service-school drafts in the hands of the users. Fortunately, these documents generally reflected common thought and did not cause excessive confusion. Most units were still using draft editions of *FM 17-95 Cavalry*, at the beginning of the war.

Interviews
There is a wide range of interviews available to augment the official unit reports and documents.

John Burdan interviewed a number of squadron members in the years immediately following the 1991 Persian Gulf War. Copies of these interviews will be deposited with the U.S. Cavalry Museum at Fort Riley, Kansas, and the 1st Infantry Division Museum at Catigny, Wheaton, Illinois. Members interviewed include: Major William Wimbish; Captains Michael A. Bills, Eric Esplund, Douglas Morrison, Lou Parker, Christopher R. Philbrick, Kenneth Pope, Vincent Tedesco; Lieutenants James C. Copenhaver, Mitch Osburn, Stephen Gruenig, David J. Palmieri, Matt Vanderfeltz, Jorge Caraballo; Chief Warrant/ Warrant Officers Wayne Grimes, Kirk Waymire, Gary Notestine; Sergeant Major Gary Parkey; Sergeant First Class William Molitor; Staff Sergeants William A. Ball and Don Wehage; and PFC Leslie Robb.

Army historians from the Center of Military History interviewed members of the 1st Infantry Division, VII Corps, and Third Army. These interviews are now held in the Center of Military History's Desert Storm Interview Collection at Fort McNair, DC. Interviews consulted include: MG Thomas Rhame; BG Steven L. Arnold; Colonels Terry Bullington, Michael Dodson, Terry Ford, Lon E. Maggart, Anthony Moreno; Lieutenant Colonels John Andrews, Edwin L. Buffington, Gregory R. Fontenot, John R. Gingrich, David Gross, Stephen Hawkins, Michael L. Mcgee, and Robert Wilson; Majors Michael Bracket, Jack Crumpler, Tom Connors, James O'Donnell, and Laurence M. Steiner; Captains Robert A. Burns and Juan Torro; and First Sergeant Robert P. Harn.

Other interview collections include those used by Colonel Richard Swain in his writing of *"Lucky War:" Third Army in Desert Storm*. This collection, located at Fort Leavenworth's Combined Arms Center, includes interviews with: Lieutenant General Frederick M. Franks, Jr., Colonel Stanley F. Cherrie,

Lieutenant General Calvin H. Waller, and Lieutenant General John J. Yeosock. Another collection, held at the United States Army Training and Doctrine Command at Fort Monroe, include five major interviews with Lieutenant General Frederick M. Franks, Jr., conducted by LTC Peter Kindsvatter immediately after Desert Storm.

Unpublished Manuscripts

Anderson, Wesley B. Letter to Author, 26 August 1994. Subj: Engineer operations.

Burdan, John. "History of the 1st Squadron, 4th Cavalry in the Gulf War—Draft Manuscript." 1998.

Franks, Frederick M. Jr. "Message: Fighting a Five Armored Division Corps." VII Corps After-Action Report, Fort Leavenworth, KS, 31 March 1991.

Gross, David. "History of 37th Armor on Operation Desert Storm." 1992.

Kendall, John M. "The Closed Fist: VII Corps Operational Maneuver in Operation Desert Storm." Personal Experience Monograph, U.S. Army War College, 1994.

Kindsvatter, Peter S. "The Army of Excellence Divisional Cavalry Squadron—a Doctrinal Step Backward?" Monograph, U.S. Army Command and General Staff College, 1985.

———. "Notes and Observations: Operation Desert Storm." 103: VII Corps, 1991.

Parker, Lou. "Chaplain on Operation Desert Storm." Unpublished manuscript, 2000.

Swain, Richard. "Writing a 'Public' History of the Gulf War: A Paper Read at the Conference on Public History and the Gulf War." Montana State University, 1992.

Weingartner, Steven ed. "Senior Allied Commanders Discuss the Gulf War (Draft Proceedings)." Photocopy, Catigny First Division Foundation and the Robert R. McCormick Tribune Foundation, 1998.

Zotti, Steven. "Mailed Fist or Pursuit Operations: An Operational Analysis of VII Corps During the Gulf War." MMAS Thesis, U.S. Army Command and General Staff College, 1997.

Published Secondary Sources

1st Squadron, 4th Cavalry, 1st Infantry Division. "Riders on the Storm: A Narrative History of the 1-4 Cav's Campaign in Iraq and Kuwait—24 January–March 1991." *Armor* 100 (May–June 1991): 13–19.

Atkinson, Rick. *Crusade: The Untold Story of the Persian Gulf War*. Boston: Houghton Mifflin Co, 1993.

Biddle, Stephen. "Victory Misunderstood: What the Gulf War Tells Us About the Future of Conflict." *International Security* 21, no. 2 (Fall 1996): 139–79.

Biddle, Stephen, and Robert Zirkle. "Technology, Civil-Military Relations, and Warfare in the Developing World." *Journal of Strategic Studies* 19 (June 1996): 171–212.

Blair, Arthur H. *At War in the Gulf: A Chronology*. College Station: Texas A&M University Press, 1992.

Bourque, Stephen A. "A Nervous Night on the Basrah Road." *MHQ: The Quarterly Journal of Military History* 12, no. 1: 88–101.

———. "Correcting Myths About the Persian Gulf War: The Last Stand of the Tawakalna." *The Middle East Journal* 51, no. 4 (Autumn 1997): 566–83.

———. "Incident at Safwan." *Armor* 108 (January–February 1999): 30–35.

———. "The Hundred-Hour Thunderbolt: Armor in the Gulf War." In *Camp Colt to Desert Storm: The History of U.S. Armored Forces*, edited by George F. Hofmann and Donn A. Starry, 497–530. Lexington: The University Press of Kentucky, 1999.

———. *Jayhawk! The VII Corps in the Persian Gulf War*. Washington, DC: U.S. Army Center of Military History, 2002.

Bush, George, and Brent Scowcroft. *A World Transformed*. New York: Alfred A. Knopf, 1998.

Clancy, Tom. *Armored Cav: A Guided Tour of an Armored Cavalry Regiment*. New York: Berkley Books, 1994.

Clancy, Tom, and Frederick M. Franks, Jr. *Into the Storm: A Study in Command*. New York: G. P. Putnam's Sons, 1997.

Cordesman, Anthony H., and Abraham R. Wagner. *The Lessons of Modern War, Vol II: The Iran-Iraq War*. Boulder: Westview Press, 1990.

———. *The Lessons of Modern War, Vol IV: The Gulf War*. Boulder: Westview Press, 1996.

Cordingly, Patrick. *In the Eye of the Storm: Commanding the Desert Rats in the Gulf War*. London: Hodder and Stoughton, 1996.

Dietrich, Steven E. "In-Theater Armored Force Modernization." *Military Review* 73 (October 1993): 34–45.

Fontenot, Gregory. "The 'Dreadnoughts' Rip the Saddam Line." *Army* 42, no. 1 (January 1992): 28–37.

———. "Fright Night: Task Force 2/34 Armor." *Military Review* 73 (January 1993): 38–52.

Freedman, Lawrence, and Efraim Karsh. *The Gulf Conflict, 1990–1991: Diplomacy and War in the New World Order*. Princeton: Princeton University Press, 1993.

Friedman, Norman. *Desert Victory: The War for Kuwait*. Annapolis: Naval Institute Press, 1991.

Gehring, Stephen P. *From the Fulda Gap to Kuwait: U.S. Army Europe and the Gulf War*. Washington, DC: U.S. Army Center of Military History, 1998.

Gingrich, John R. *Battle for Safwan, Iraq*. Personal Experience Monograph, U.S. Army War College, 1992.

Gordon, Michael R., and Bernard E. Trainor. *The Generals' War: The Inside Story of the Conflict in the Gulf*. Boston: Little, Brown and Company, 1995.

Jemiola, Richard W. *The 9th Engineer Battalion in Operation Desert Storm*. U.S. Army War College, 1993.

Keaney, Thomas A., and Eliot A. Cohen. *Gulf War Air Power Survey: Summary Report*. Washington, DC, 1993.

Kindsvatter, Peter S. "VII Corps in the Gulf War: Post-Cease-Fire Operations." *Military Review* 72 (June 1992): 2–19.

————. "VII Corps in the Gulf War: Deployment and Preparation for Desert Storm." *Military Review* 72, no.1 (January1992): 2–16.

————. "VII Corps in the Gulf War: Ground Offensive." *Military Review* 72 (February 1992): 16–37.

Kitfield, James. *Prodigal Soldiers.* New York: Simon & Schuster, 1995.

Langenus, Peter C. "Moving an Army: Movement Control for Desert Storm." *Military Review* 71 (September 1991): 40–51.

Maggart, Lon E. "A Leap of Faith." *Armor* 101 (January–February 1992): 24–32.

Maggart, Lon E., and Gregory Fontenot. "Breaching Operations: Implications for Battle Command and Battle Space." *Military Review* 74, no. 2 (February 1994): 19–36.

Marlin, David W. *History of the 4th Battalion, 37th Armored Regiment in Operation Desert Shield/Storm.* U.S. Army War College, 1992.

McKiernan, David D. *Command, Control, and Communications at the VII Corps Tactical Command Post: Operation Desert Shield/Desert Storm.* Personal Experience Monograph, U.S. Army War College, 1992.

Menarchik, Douglas. *Powerlift—Getting to Desert Storm: Strategic Transportation and Strategy in the New World Order.* Westport: Praeger, 1993.

Metz, Helen Chapin. *Iraq, a Country Study, Area Handbook Series.* Washington, DC: U. S. Government Printing Office, 1990.

Muir, Jum, and Robert Fox. "Basra Rebellion 'Quelled with Mustard Gas'." *The Daily Telegraph*, March 7, 1991, 1.

Murray, Williamson. *Air War in the Persian Gulf.* Baltimore: The Nautical & Aviation Company of America, 1994.

————. "The Gulf War as History." *MHQ: The Quarterly Journal of Military History* 10 (Autumn 1997): 6–19.

————. "Air War in the Gulf: The Limits of Air Power." *Strategic Review* (Winter 1998): 28–38.

Nagl, John P. "A Tale of Two Battles." *Armor* 101 (May–June 1992): 6–10.

Nilsen, David, and Greg Novak. "The 1991 Persian Gulf War: On the Brink of a New World Order (Part 2)." *Command Post Quarterly* 5 (1994): 26-44.

Norton, David. "Cecil's Ride: A Tank Platoon Leader in Desert Storm." *Armor* 108 (November-December 1999): 30–35.

Obenhaus, Stacy R. "Highway to Basra and the Ethics of Pursuit." *Military Review* 80 (March–April 2000): 51–59.

Otis, Glenn K., and Dewy A. Browder. "Tailoring Deterrent to Threat." *Army* (October 1984): 132–41.

Pagonis, William G. *Moving Mountains: Lessons in Leadership and Logistics from the Gulf War*. Boston: Harvard Business School Press, 1992.

Pardew, James W. Jr. "The Iraqi Army's Defeat in Kuwait." *Parameters*, Winter 1991–92, 17–23.

Powell, Colin, and Joseph E. Perisco. *My American Journey*. New York: Ballantine Books, 1996.

Record, Jeffrey. *Hollow Victory: A Contrary View of the Gulf War*. Washington: Brassey's, 1993.

Romjue, John L. *A History of Army 86, Vol. I, Division 86: The Development of the Heavy Division, September 1978–October 1979*. Fort Monroe, VA: U.S. Army Training and Doctrine Command, 1982.

———. *From Active Defense to Airland Battle: The Development of Army Doctrine 1973–1982*. Fort Monroe, VA: U.S. Army Training and Doctrine Command, 1984.

———. *The Army of Excellence: The Development of the 1980s Army*. Fort Monroe, VA: U.S. Army Training and Doctrine Command, 1997.

Romjue, John L., Susan Canedy, and Ann W. Chapman. *Prepare the Army for War: A Historical Overview of the Army Training and Doctrine Command, 1973–1993*. Fort Monroe, VA: U.S. Army Training and Doctrine Command, 1993.

Sawicki, James A. *Cavalry Regiments of the U.S. Army*. Dumfries, VA: Wyvern Publications, 1985.

Scales, Robert H. *Certain Victory: The U.S. Army in the Gulf*

War. Fort Leavenworth, KS: U.S. Army Command and General Staff College Press, 1994.

Schubert, Frank N., and Theresa L. Kraus. *The Whirlwind War: The United States Army in Operations Desert Shield and Desert Storm*. Washington, DC: U.S. Army Center of Military History, 1995.

Schwarzkopf, H. Norman, and Peter Petre. *It Doesn't Take a Hero*. New York: Bantam Books, 1992.

Staff, *Army Magazine*. "Command and Staff Directory." *Army* 40, no. 11 (October 1990):217–42.

———. "The Army Commanders." *Army* 41, no. 3 (March 1991): 49–53.

Staff, *U.S. News and World Report*. *Triumph without Victory: The History of the Persian Gulf War*. New York: Random House, 1992.

Stockmoe, Jim, ed. *1st Brigade, 1st Infantry Division: Desert Shield/Storm History*. Fort Riley, KS: 1st Brigade, 1st Infantry Division, 1991.

Sultan, Khaled bin. *Desert Warrior*. New York: Harper-Collins, 1995.

Summers, Harry G. *On Strategy II: A Critical Analysis of the Gulf War*. New York: Dell, 1992.

Swain, Richard M. "Compounding the Error." *Proceedings* (August): 61–62.

———. "Ground Operations in the Gulf War: Reflections on the Revisionist Critique." *Army* 48 (August 1992): 24–31.

———. *"Lucky War:" Third Army in Desert Storm*. Fort Leavenworth, KS: U.S. Army Command and General Staff College Press, 1994.

Tice, Jim. "'Coming through,' the Big Red Raid." *Army Times*, 26 August 1991, 12, 13, 16, 18, 20.

Toomey, Charles Lane. *XVIII Airborne Corps: From Planning to Victory*. Central Point, OR: Hellgate Press, 2004.

United States Department of Defense. *Conduct of the Persian Gulf War: Final Report to Congress*. Washington, DC: Government Printing Office, 1992.

Van Creveld, Martin, Kenneth S. Brower, and Steven L. Canby. *Airpower and Maneuver Warfare*. Maxwell AFB, AL: Air University Press, 1998.

Vernon, Alex, Jr., Neal Creighton, Greg Downey, Rob Holmes, and Dave Trybula. *Eyes of Orion: Five Lieutenants in the Persian Gulf War*. Kent, OH: Kent State University Press, 1999.

Vogel, Steve. "Hell Night." *Army Times*, 7 October 1991, 8ff.

Willis, Clifford G. "2d Battalion, 3d Air Defense Artillery." Personal Experience Monograph, U.S. Army War College, 1992.

Wilson, George C. *Mud Soldiers: Life inside the New American Army*. New York: Charles Scribner's Sons, 1989.

Wilson, John B. *Armies, Corps, Divisions and Separate Brigades*. Washington, DC: U.S. Army Center of Military History, 1987.

Wilson, Robert. "Tanks in the Division Cavalry Squadron." *Armor* 101 (July–August 1992): 6–11.

Yeosock, John J. "Army Operations in the Gulf Theater." *Military Review* 71, no. 9 (September 1991): 2–15.

———. "H+100: An Army Comes of Age in the Persian Gulf." *Army* 42 (October 1991): 44–58.

Other Sources
Directorate of Intelligence, Central Intelligence Agency. "Operation Desert Storm: A Snapshot of the Battlefield." Springfield, VA: National Technical Information Service, 1996.

Ministry of Defense, UK. "Operation Desert Sabre: The Liberation of Kuwait 1990–91; the Tactics Employed by 1st Armoured Division." 1991.

———. "Operation Granby: An Account of the Gulf Crisis 1990–91, and the British Army's Contribution to the Liberation of Kuwait." United Kingdom, 1993.

John G. Keliher, *The History of the Fourth Cavalry* [Internet] (2006 [accessed 12 November 2006]); available from http://www.25thida.com/4thcav.html

United States Army Threat Analysis Center. "Iraq Battlefield Development Plan." Washington, D.C. 1994.

Index

Humanitarian operations:
211, 221–226
Hunter, CW2, Daniel: 108
Hussein, Saddam: 2, 62, 112,
118, 166, 202, 204, 222, 241

Infante, Ernesto, SGT: 125
Infantry Division (Forward),
1st: 20
Infantry Division,
1st:
  1st Brigade: 19, 60, 82,
  103–105, 107–109, 119,
  120, 122–24, 127, 128,
  135, 137, 139, 143, 146,
  164, 165, 189, 203, 228,
  229
  2d Brigade: 11, 48, 107,
  115, 122, 125, 127, 135,
  164–67, 171, 172, 176,
  177, 183, 186, 197, 201,
  211, 231
  3d Brigade: 60, 93–95, 107,
  127,128, 135, 143, 147,
  164
  4th Brigade: 11, 18, 48, 74,
  104, 109, 189, 218, 219,
  227, 228, 230
  And breaching
  operations: 113–30
  Coordination with 2nd
  cavalry: 140–49
  Coordination with 1st
  U.K. Armoured
  Division: 135
  DISCOM, 1st Infantry
  Division: 67, 282
  Deployment to Southwest
  Asia: 27–30, 34, 35

Equipment: 45–47
Friendly fire incidents: 99,
100
In Germany: 15
Homecoming ceremonies:
238–40
And passage of British
troops: 135
Passage through 2nd
Cavalry lines: 140–49
And plan for assault on
the RGFC: 142–43
And postwar activities:
214–15
And preparations for the
cease-fire: 199
And protection of forces
during buildup: 58–59
Staff problems: 176
Tactical command post:
80, 82, 88, 99, 150, 199,
283
Training exercises: 19–20
24th: 34, 191, 203
Infantry fighting vehicles
American: 17, 110, 259
Iraqi: 46, 151, 153, 156, 157,
168, 179, 194, 209
Infantry Regiments:
16th: 93, 122, 123, 147
41st: 95
Intelligence operations: 76,
78, 84, 118, 221
Intelligence Preparation of
the Battlefield: 112, 193,
211
Iraq Petroleum-Saudi Arabia
Pipeline (IPSA): 134, 153,
158